**Crowood Travel Guides** are the essential starting point for a holiday to remember – and they'll be the signpost to enjoyment every step of the way. Easy-to-follow, practical advice, combined with a warmth and enthusiasm for the peoples and cultures of the world, mean that they'll be turned to again and again for direction and inspiration.

# Madrid and Castile

First published in 1991 by
The Crowood Press Ltd
Gipsy Lane, Swindon
Wiltshire SN2 6DQ
© The Crowood Press Ltd. 1991

**British Library Cataloguing in Publication Data**
Clancy, Catherine
    Madrid and Castile. – (Crowood travel guides)
    1. Spain. Castile. Visitors' guides 2. Spain. Castile, history
    I. Title
    914.641

    ISBN 1–85223–468–7

**Dedication**
To Hermano Albino Jorge Silvestre and Antonio Sigüenza Molina, Real Monasterio de la Santa Espina, with thanks.

Photographs by the author
Maps by Taurus Graphics
Typesetting and page layouts by Visual Image
Printed and bound by Times Publishing Group, Singapore

# Madrid and Castile
# Crowood Travel Guide

### Catherine Clancy

The Crowood Press

# Madrid and Castile

## Contents

**View of the Royal Palace,
Madrid**

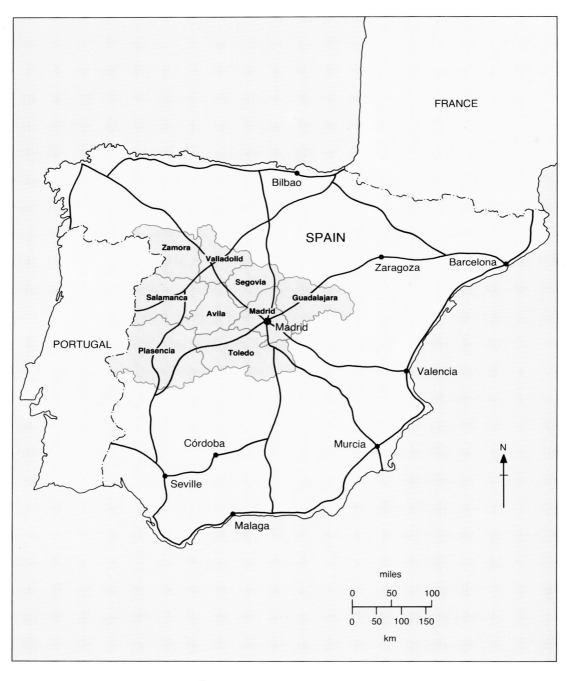

## Introduction

**In praise of central Spain** Madrid, the capital of Spain, lies in the geographical centre of the peninsula. An extraordinary variety of cities surround Madrid, each shaped by its own history, architecture and region. The character of every city is strikingly individual.

The countryside encompasses variety of a different kind. The great mountain chains of the Central Corderilla form a divide between the huge cornfields of the north and the extensive plains of the southern meseta. The rivers are majestic. The turn of the seasons swings from the burning dry heat of the summer to winter frosts. The most beautiful seasons are the spring and autumn.

Compared with coastal Spain, this lovely region is very little visited and the countryside is almost empty of traffic. A visitor will meet the proud Castillian people, uncompromised by the commercialism of tourism. It is a land of tangible history, of spectacular castles, ancient monasteries and great cathedrals. The splendours of old Spain, encompassed in thriving modern bustle, preserved in the tranquillity of their past, are offered to those who venture into this rich, beautiful and unspoiled region.

The great cities of the region are all within a simple half day's drive from the capital, along quiet roads. The area welcomes visitors and offers a rich experience of the cultural heritage of Spain.

**The language** of Castile is the official language of Spain – called *castellano* in Spain and Spanish to the rest of the world. As this is the home of the language, it is spoken here with particular purity.

# Part One: **Pre-Planning**

**The open countryside of the
Zamora-Valladolid region**

## How to Get There

**Plane** Scheduled and charter flights are available from Britain to Madrid. Madrid airport is Barajas. Tel: 205 4372 – information 411 2545, There are several airlines which operate from the UK to Spain. These are as follows:

Iberia, Madrid:   Calle de Velázquez 130. Tel: 261 9100.
　　　　　　　　Calle de la Princesa 2. Tel: 248 6638.
　　　　　　　　Plaza Cánovas del Castillo. Tel: 429 7443.
　　　　　　　　Information (24 hours) Infoiberia Tel: 411 2545.
　　　　　　　　Reservations Tel: 411 1011.
　　　　　　　　UK – 169 Regent Street, London
　　　　　　　　　Tel: 071 437 5622.
　　　　　　　　Birmingham Tel: 021 6433 1953.
　　　　　　　　Manchester Tel: 061 436 6444.

British　　　　　Madrid: Avda Palma de Mallorca 43
Airways:　　　　　Tel: 431 7575.
　　　　　　　　Calle de la Princesa 1, Torre de Madrid
　　　　　　　　Tel: 248 7544.

To travel to the city centre, you can take a bus to Plaza del Descubrimiento 17km (10½ miles). If you decide to take a taxi, make sure the meter shows. To take a taxi from the taxi desk in the airport costs an extra 150pts.

**Ferry** From the UK to Spain by ferry is a good way to travel. Brittany Ferries run a service from Plymouth to Santander, which also carries cars. This leaves Plymouth on Wednesdays and Sundays in the low season, and Mondays and Wednesdays in the high season. The return trip leaves Santander on Mondays and Thursdays in the low season, and Tuesdays and Thursdays in the high season. The trip takes 24 hours. Contact Brittany Ferries at Millbay Docks, Plymouth, PL1 3EW Tel: 0752 221321.

**Train** From Paris trains run daily to Madrid and Chamartin. The 'Madrid Talgo' runs overnight (between 8 p.m. and 9 a.m.) and the 'Puerta del Sol' also runs overnight, carrying cars (between 6 p.m. and 10 a.m.) The trip usually takes approximately 14 hours. Cheap tickets are available for traveller's aged under 26. Other good value ideas include InterRail, which provides a month of unlimited travel throughout Europe, and also Transalpino, which offers a one-way ricket valid for 2 months with stops. More information can be obtained from

Victoria Station (European Information – Tel: 071 834 2345).

**Car** It is, of course, feasible to drive through France to Central Spain. The best crossing point of the Pyrenees would be at Irun. It takes approximately 2 days to drive from London. From Irun there are a number of possible routes. Two suggestions would be: San Sebastián – Vitoria – Burgos – Madrid; and Pamplona – Logroño – Soria – Guadalajara – Madrid. It is also possible to transport your car by train via France, and by ferry direct to Santander.

**Bus** A coach trip from London Victoria to Madrid would take approximately 30 hours with National Express Eurolines. Contact the Coach Travel Centre, 13 Regent Street, London, SW1Y 4LR Tel: 071 730 0202.

**The Spanish Tourist Office** in England is based at 57 St James's Square, London SW1A 1LD. (Tel: 071 499 1169).

**When to Go** Spain is one hour ahead of UK. The general tourist season is April – October. Below are some considerations in choosing holiday dates: Central Spain has cold winters and very hot, dry summers. The temperature is most comfortable during the spring and early autumn. There is plenty of rain in late autumn. If visiting in winter warm clothing is necessary. In the warm seasons it is advisable to take light but substantial clothes – the Spanish tend to dress smartly at all times, particularly in cities. If you intend to undertake substantial walking in the cities, comfortable shoes are advisable.

**Tourist Seasons** Both Spanish and foreign tourists make July and August the heaviest tourist months. Both the city and the countryside change considerably during this time. Madrid is very hot and quiet, with many people holidaying the cool mountain villages. Some museums close for August, and several restaurants take holidays for the month. Salamanca is much visited by students learning Spanish, and its local ambience is compromised for the month. Countryside resorts are lively.

**Wildlife** The countryside looks its best during the spring, with beautiful wild flowers. The cereal-growing areas are pale green during winter and spring, and gold-brown during the summer. The extensive nature parks are recommended particularly in spring, between March and June.

**Fiestas** In general, almost all villages celebrate colourful fiestas in early spring and high summer. Few are celebrated in the colder months.

**The bullfight is a traditional part of the fiesta**

**Sports** The region has many areas suitable for hiking. The best time is spring. January and February are recommended for skiing. For hunting and fishing the main seasons are late autumn and spring.

**Passports and Visas** Visas are not required for EEC nationals for visits of less than three months. Visas are required for paid employment, residence, and for extended holidays and study. These should be acquired before leaving home. Permits for work or residence and extensions of visas must be applied for in Spain within three months of arrival. In January 1993 there will be free movement for workers in Spain.

**Discount Cards** Discounts are available to students, to those younger than 26 years old, and to pensioners, on production of identification. Museums are often free to card holders.

**Driving Licences** British driving licences are valid in Spain. It is advisable to have an authorized translation of the licence, either by carrying a renewable International Driving Licence (from the AA or by carrying a translation obtained from the

**The Spanish Consulate General in the UK is based at:**
20 Draycott Place, London SW3 2RZ. Tel: 071 581 5921.
1 Brooks House, 70 Spring Gardens, Manchester 2. Tel: 061 236 1233.
63 North Castle Street, Edinburgh EH3. Tel: 031 220 1843.

**Visa requirements:**
**US citizens** may stay for 6 months without a visa.
**Canadians** may stay for 90 days without a visa.
**Australians and New Zealanders** need a visa to enter Spain (though requirement may change).

14

Spanish Consulate). With an EEC driving licence (colour pink) extra documentation is not necessary. In general, it is always useful to have more rather than less documentation.

**Customs – Pets** Pets may be taken to Spain on production of two certificates – a health certificate from an authorized vet issued within twenty-five days of travelling and a certificate to state that the animal has been in an area free of disease, issued by the Ministry of Agriculture. On return to England, animals are required to pass a six month quarantine check.

**Duty-Free Allowances** Duty-free allowances into Spain and into the UK are as follows. Travellers from outside the EEC are entitled to double these. (These allowances are not available to travellers under 15 years.)

**Money** Unlimited amount allowed, but should be declared. Personal effects like cameras and sports articles may enter Spain duty-free so long as they also leave the country with the traveller. It is advisable always to carry documents of purchase when going through customs. No fresh meat or plants may pass customs into the UK.

**Insurance** It is advisable to carry travel insurance. Many banks and travel agencies have cover schemes. The Spanish scheme, Spanish Tourist Insurance, may be arranged in Spain or through travel agencies. Cars must carry a Green Card insurance to cover any accident occurring while in Spain (available as a supplement to general car insurance). The facility of a bail bond is worth while. You should note that in most cities cars are highly vulnerable to theft. There are professional thieves everywhere. It is not advisable to take valuables on holiday.

**Health** No vaccinations are necessary for visiting Spain. In order to use the Spanish health service, a form E111 from the UK Department of Health and Social Security is required. Retired people should obtain form E121. Tap water is not harmful and sterilizing tablets are unnecessary. (Bottled drinking water is often preferable as a flavour.) For minor complaints, pharmacists in Spain are highly trained and their stores well stocked. Herbal medicine has always been widely available in Spain. Insect repellents can be purchased easily. Travellers should beware of sunburn, dehydration, and of upsets caused by changes in diet.

**Duty-Free Allowances**

**Tobacco:**

| | |
|---|---|
| Cigarettes | 200 units |
| Small Cigars | 100 units |
| Cigars | 50 units |
| Loose tobacco | 250 grams |

**Alcohol:**

| | |
|---|---|
| above 22% vol | 1 ltr (brandies, liquors) |
| under 22% vol | 2 ltr (aperitives, sparkling wines, wine) |
| beer | 50 ltr |

**Perfume:**

75g/2.6oz.

**Eau de Toilette:**

369ml/13fl.oz.

**Visitors from outside the EEC** may bring in double the quantity of tobacco that is allowed for EEC members:

| | |
|---|---|
| Cigarettes | 400 units |
| Small Cigars | 200 units |
| Cigars | 100 units |
| Loose tobacco | 500 grams |

**Alcohol and perfume –** equivalent to UK visitor allowances.

**For the Spanish emergency services call 091 or The Red Cross.**

## Getting About

**Car Hire**  Relative to other European countries, car hire in Spain is not expensive. There are car-hire companies in most major towns. The main companies are Hertz, Avis and Europcar, all of whom offer a similar package payable by kilometre or number of days. Atesa is the main Spanish car-hire network. There are many smaller companies including Budget and Travanco. It is advisable to check the availability of cars early on. Costs often include vehicle insurance, comprehensive cover, and bail bond (advisable to check). Most companies offer a one-way hire.

**Petrol**  When driving away from major centres, for instance in the far reaches of Zamora or Extremadura, it is advisable to start with plenty of petrol, and to fill when below half a tank. Some areas are poorly equipped with filing stations. Generally, there will be a filling station close to most sizeable towns. Lead-free petrol is not yet widely available. Tourist offices and the AA issue maps which show the main stations.

**Roads**  The network of major roads is excellent. In the countryside of central Spain there is very little traffic, particularly away from the cities. Motorways are good but require payment of substantial tolls. In general, the larger service cafés are not recommended. The network of minor roads are sometimes in poor condition. Secondary mountain roads are better driven by day. In quiet regions there may well be interruptions for sheep or goat flocks crossing the road.

**Parking**  In towns there is usually parking available by the Plaza Mayor, in the centre of the town, particularly during the after-lunch quiet time. Bigger towns have underground parking, and street parking is often available near by. Street parking is well signed and discs surrounded in light blue show the times allowed. It is advisable, whether parking in an underground park or on the street, to put goods out of sight. Many car-parks charge similar prices by night as by day. To park near the centre of the major cities, it is advisable to arrive early (particularly for Toledo). For small villages it is recommended to leave cars outside and walk – many are extremely awkward to navigate. In general, city parking is tight and neat and manoeuvring in and out of awkward spaces is frequently made easier by touching bumpers gently.

---

**Major car hire offices:**

**Avis:** Gran Via 60, Madrid. Tel: 457 9706.

**Europcar:** G Yague 6 bis, Madrid. Tel: 597 1500.

**Hertz:** Calle San Leonardo (by Plaza Espana). Tel: 248 5803.

**Atesa:** Tel: 450 2062.

**Budget:** Juan Hurtado de Mendoza 7, Madrid. Tel: 457 5968.

**Travenco:** Avda de los Toreros 12, Madrid. Tel: 255 7500.

Motorcycles and bicycles are not widely available for hire.

**Rules and Regulations** Passport and insurance documentation should always be carried. Speeding regulations are well signed. Parking signs should always be checked before parking in the street. On-the-spot fines will be issued for speeding or disregarding road signs. Police speed checks will often be hidden just outside towns.

**Taxi** These are excellent, relatively very cheap, and are available in most towns. All taxis in a town are the same colour and carry a green light on the roof and a sign inside, above the passenger seat, reading *libre* when the taxi may be hired. It is important always to be able to see the metre. In Madrid, tourists are particularly susceptible to overcharging. A small charge is supplemented for lifts late at night and for lifts to the airport.

**Bus** For long-distance travel these are an excellent mode of transport. The coach companies in Spain are multiple and very popular, often being faster than trains over the same journey. They usually leave and arrive punctually. The bus stations are often on the outskirts of town. Video films of an unremarkable quality will usually be shown on long journeys – it is advisable to ask for a seat at the back if peace is wanted. Tickets are offered for smoking and non-smoking, both at bus terminals and at many travel agents. Most terminals have a left-luggage department – *Consigna* (normal hours: 8 a.m.–10 p.m.).

In Madrid tickets are sold which combine 10 journeys at once for a cheaper price than single journeys. These can be bought at the metro stations or at "libreria" newsagents.

If catching a bus from a minor town without a terminal, it is advisable to check carefully where the departure point is and the local method of buying tickets – some are bought on the bus; some from particular cafes; some from particular newsagents. The small towns and villages are connected to their provincial capitals by bus. These often run several times a day, including an early journey which collects people in time to arrive for the beginning of the working day.

**Train** The train network is extensive. There are two classes, and several methods of gaining a discount. When buying a ticket, plenty of time should be left to allow for the queues. Tickets may also be purchased in travel agents which carry the 'RENFE' sign. In big stations, booths will be marked with *Cercanas* (local trains) or *Largo recorrido* (long-distance trains) and with *Anticipada* (advance tickets) or *Immediata* (imminent departure). It is vital to queue in the right line. For long distances, it is advisable to book a seat.

**Rail Discounts** *Dias Azules* (blue days): days which do not coincide with fiestas or heavy travelling days. *Tarjeta Joven*: for travellers 12–25 years, discounts tickets by 50 per cent on Dias Azules. *Chequetren*: a discount card of 15 per cent for an individual or named group. *Eurorailpass*: 15-, 25-, 30-, 60-, or 90-day ticket of unlimited travel in Europe and Spain. *Tarjeta Turistica*: unlimited travel for 8, 15, or 22 days in Spain, with supplements only for sleepers and seat reservation. Available in Victoria Station, London, Thomas Cook outlets and in Spain.

There are various types of train, from the very slow to the very fast – *Correo, Semi-directo, Expreso, Rapido, Electrotren,* TER, *Talgo.*

There are a number of tourist train routes which last a number of days and where the ticket includes visits to cities, meals and accommodation. The most famous of these visits Andalucía (*Expreso Al-Andalus*) and the north of Spain (*Transcantabrico*) but there are other shorter trips through Salamanca, Zamora and Guadalajara. For information on these trips, and on steam trains (e.g. the *Tren de la Fresa* to Aranjuez) Tel: Madrid 733 0000/733 2200.

If there are important fiestas, extra trains are often laid on. For long journeys it is best to take water and provisions – frequently there is no buffet car, and if open, it is expensive. Most stations will have a left-luggage department (*Consigna*) or lockers. (Normal hours 8 a.m.–10 p.m.).

**Plane** Apart from Barajas airport, Madrid, Valladolid has an airport for internal flights.

**Accommodation** During spring and summer it is always worth while to reserve hotel rooms in advance. Beware of assuming that less-frequented places will have free rooms – these may fill with itinerant road and building workers. Paid accommodation usually lasts from late afternoon until 12 noon. The best time to reserve a room is just after midday. If possible, inspect the room before taking it.

**Hotels** There are five official categories of hotel, Starred accordingly. Those carrying 5 stars (super-luxury) are taxed (IVA) at 12 per cent, the rest at 6 per cent. Stars are allocated according to facilities, and prices should be displayed in reception. There are few single rooms and a single person should only pay 80 per cent of the price of a double room. An extra bed should be charged at 35 per cent of the double room price, or 60 per cent of the single room price. Hotels will have restaurants and will serve breakfast (the latter is seldom included in the price). If staying more than two days, a traveller is entitled to full-board rates for meals. Information on prices should be found on the back of each bedroom door.

The star value of a hotel can generally be taken as a guide to its cost. All provide a laundry service. Best value hotels are those of medium comfort (3 stars).

**Paradors** For reliable, affordable excellence, the state-run chain of *Parador* hotels is highly recommended. Prices are generally lower out of the tourist season. The Paradors can be found throughout Spain; some are modern, some in historic ancient shells. All are distinguished by the beauty of the surroundings, or the splendour of their buildings. The service is always impeccable and the restaurants good. In central Spain there are a number of these notable hotels. In Avila and Zamora, a couple of old palaces have been converted, and in Sigüenza, Jarandilla and Oropesa, castles have been turned into luxury hotels. For modern accommodation with pools and superb views, the Paradors in Toledo and Salamanca are excellent. (For information contact Central de Reservas de Paradores, Calle Velázquez 25, Tel: Madrid 435 9700. Complete information may be found in the yearly book *Guia de Hotels*.)

**Hostels and Pensions** Hostels are labelled with an 'Hs' and do not offer food. 'HsR' establishments offer breakfast and sometimes a light meal. They are classified from 1 – 3 stars according to the number of rooms with showers, and facilities available. Pensions, with a 'p' over the door, are usually family–run establishments where the traveller can take a simple meal. These are very inexpensive. The least expensive places to stay are *Fondas* (blue plaque with 'F' in white) and *Casas de Huespedes* ('CH'). These are usually family run, often with only the basic facilities. The centre of town, around the Plaza Mayor/main church, is the best area to look for cheap accommodation. Often it is worth while asking the local baker, grocer, or café owner for the whereabouts of rooms.

**Youth Hostels** A list of these may be obtained from the Institute of Young People, Calle de José Ortega y Gasset. Tel: Madrid 401 1300.

**Camping** There are many campsites, categorized according to facilities offered. It is advisable to ring first as they tend to fill in high season. Campsites are seldom closer than 3km (2 miles), to a major town. A full guide may be purchased, called *Guia Oficial de Campings*. Camping is allowed away from campsites if over 115m (165yds) from a national monument or water supply, and 1km (¹/₂ mile) away from a town. Camping is not allowed on mountains, beaches or river banks. Always beware of lighting fires when camping as pine forest fires are notoriously quick to spread.

**Apartments and Villas** These are categorized by 1–4 keys and may be located through UK travel agencies. It is usually necessary to pay a deposit and down-payment in advance.

**Refuges** In mountain regions popular for walking and climbing there is a network of refuges in varying states of repair. It is advisable to check on facilities before relying on them. Information may be found at tourist offices and local sports shops.

**Monasteries and Convents** Some orders offer accommodation, either for a fee or a donation. The number of rooms is limited, and the way of life varying in strictness, but it is always peaceful and contemplative. Information is obtainable from Tourist Offices. There are a small number in central Spain, including Santuario de Peña de Francia (women and men), Tel: Salamanca 215000 in summer; Monasterio de Santa María de El Parral (men only), Tel: Segovia 431298; Convento de Carmelitas Descalzos, Las Bateucas valley, Tel: Salamanca 437133 (men only) – this is one of the most beautiful; and Monasterio de El Paular, Rascafria, Tel: Madrid 869 1425 (men only).

**Money**

**Currency** Coins include 1, 2, 5, 10, 25, 50, 100, 200 pesetas (pts). Notes include 100, 200, 500, 1,000, 2,000, 5,000, 10,000pts. The most useful notes are 1,000 and 2,000pts as it is sometimes difficult to change a 5,000pts note for smaller currency. Telephones take most coinage except 1, 2 and 200pts pieces.

**Banks** Most banks will change currency, traveller cheques or Eurocheques. A sign will indicate 'Cambio, Exchange'. It is always necessary to show a passport. (Eurocheque cards from some British banks will allow direct withdrawal of cash in selected banks in Spain.) The rate of commission should not be above 1 per cent. The system is often cumbersome, involving a wait both at a counter desk and a second at the cash dispensing queue. Normal banking Hours are Monday–Friday 9 a.m.–2 p.m.

Saturday 9 a.m.–1 p.m. In summer. and in the smaller towns, banks tend to shut on Saturday mornings. Transfer of money from the UK to Spain is likely to take ten days. Banks will usually be found near the Plaza Mayor of each town.

**Travellers Cheques** The most widely known are those of American Express, whose Madrid office is efficient in replacing lost or stolen cheques. (They also offer the service of *post restante* to travellers.) These can be changed in banks, good hotels and small change booths called *caja de cambio*. The latter are open long hours, and will be found in Madrid.

**Credit Cards** Cards are widely used by clothes shops, hotels and the more expensive restaurants. They are also accepted for motorway tariffs and petrol. In general, cheques are not used, and cash is frequently preferred to cards even in large quantities. The most recognized card is Visa.

**Tipping for a drink** it is usual to leave 10 pts on the bar, or 15 pts at a table. For a meal 5–10 per cent of the cost should be left.

**Safety** All documents and valuables are vulnerable to theft. It is not advisable to wear valuable jewllery, or to carry all money and documents in the same place. Hotel bedrooms are notoriously vulnerable to theft. A wallet placed beneath clothing is the safest method of carrying valuables. If threatened, particularly in the less salubrious areas of Madrid, it is safer to give money than to refuse, as a thief is more likely to cause actual injury if aggravated. Better hotels have deposit boxes.

**Taxes** There is a general surtax (IVA) on all purchases (including meals, hotel rooms, car rental, clothes and food). At present the rate is 12 per cent, excepting most hotels and restaurants which charge 6 per cent.

**Food** The Spanish mealtimes differ from those in Northern Europe. Breakfast is seldom taken, excepting a coffee. A snack (a croissant, roll or *bocadillo*) is often taken mid-morning. A drink is taken after 1 p.m., before lunch, sometimes accompanied by a *tapa*. Lunch is taken between 2 p.m. and 4 p.m. This is the main meal of the day, and is usually substantial. Tea is sometimes taken later in the afternoon and may include a sweet pastry (*pastel*) and herb or leaf tea (the *merienda*). Bars fill again as the working day closes – after 7.30 p.m. – and evening meals will be taken after 9 p.m. Restaurants serve relatively few people for the evening meal. Groups of friends going out in the city are more likely to take tapas in the evening. In Madrid, local dining will not begin until after 10 p.m.

**Types of Restaurant**
*marisquería* – fish and shellfish
*churrasco* – grills (influenced by South America)
*asador* – specializing in roasts
*horno de lleña* – cooking in wood-fired oven
*tabernal* – informal rustic cooking.

**Restaurants** These tend to close for one night a week – often Sunday, Monday or Tuesday. Holidays are often taken in August or January. There are various classifications in Spain according to facility (1–5 forks). In general, they should provide a *menu del dia* at lunchtime which is a fixed-price daily menu, usually of excellent value and much cheaper than eating a la carte. This consists of a starter (usually pulses, paella, salad or soup) followed by a main course (meat or fish) followed by a *postre* (desert) which is either flan, ice cream or fresh fruit. Wine, beer, water and bread are included. Cover charges are seldom made. Note that IVA of 6 per cent is charged on meals and may or may not be included in prices quoted. For house wine, ask for *vino de la casa* (*blanco* – white, *tinto* – red, *rosado* – rosé).

**Regional Restaurants** In general, there is relatively little variation in regional restaurant menus in Castile. Roasts are superb – try lamb in Valladolid and Segovia provinces, suckling pig in Segovia and Salamanca. These are cooked to such a tenderness that they are cut with a plate rather than a knife. There is no consideration of carving as in the UK. Stews of partridge, popular in Toledo, are similarly short of aesthetic finesse. Most typical food is heavy, cooked with plenty of oil, garlic and spice, and unrefined. Some specialist restaurants (like those of Sepúlveda, Segovia which serve lamb) will have no menu, and serve a set meal instead. Country restaurants tend to fill at weekend lunchtimes, when it is traditional for families to take excursions from the cities.

**Bars** There are many bars, most of which open from 8 a.m. until midnight. Coffee is usually good. It costs a little more to sit at a table than to sit at the bar. Light meals are frequently served in bars and may be *bocadillos* (roll sandwiches with ham, cheese or salami), *tortillas* (potato omelettes) or *tapas* (a variety of dishes placed on the counter from which a customer may choose). Tapas are served in *pinchos* (saucerfuls) or in *raciones* (platefuls), and may consist of shelfish, tripe, sausage, stew, vegetables and other dishes.

A television will nearly always be on, and if football or comedy is being shown, the bar will be lively. There is sometimes an eating room, *comedor*, behind for lunch.

**Wine** Wine is served by the glass. This will usually be the local wine, unless a particular make is asked for. In some areas of the region this is taken with a little sweet soda (trademark: *La Casera*).

**Sherry** In the capital, many bars stock *Fino*, but it must be asked for by the Spanish name, *Jerez* or *Fino de Jerez*.

**Water** Most tap water is not harmful, but is not always very palatable. To order water: *agua con gas* – fizzy water *agua sin gas* – flat water *agua natural/un vaso de agua* – from the tap.

**Picnicking** There are parks in all towns in which to picnic. Fountains of drinking water are to be found in the main squares and near the entrances to parks. In the countryside, a few kilometres from towns, there are often 'Merienda Parks' which are pretty areas with tables, a fountain, trees and occasionally barbecue blocks where picnicking is invited. In general, there are few restrictions on picnicking provided nothing remains behind afterwards. Beware of walking into seemingly empty fields around the province of Salamanca as there is much bull-raising here.

## Shopping and Services

**Shopping for Food** is very much a social occasion. It is necessary to have plenty of time and to be prepared to queue for produce, as friendly chatter while buying food is normal. In markets, long queues usually imply excellent produce, and it is not unusual to wait for 30 minutes to buy. The best places to buy food are the municipal markets. These tend to be placed in the centre of town, and open from 8–9 a.m., until 2 p.m. and sometimes during the afternoon (particularly on Fridays). The choice and freshness here are second to none. In areas which receive many tourists, it is sometimes necessary to watch the server carefully in case bad produce is slipped in. For fruit and vegetables, quality is judged in Spain according to flavour, not necessarily to looks (the best-looking produce is mostly exported), and much that does not look perfect will be extremely good.

**Markets** are laid out according to sections – fruit, fish, fresh meat, pork products. Most stalls will specialize to a degree. Fish stalls in Madrid are superb, with fresh fish flown from the Atlantic. The sellers are happy to prepare fish for a buyer, either filleting or chopping into steaks. The pork stalls sell great varieties of sausage and dried meats. Shoppers frequently spend a long time buying small quantities of a variety of things.

**Coffee (Café)**
*solo* – small cup, strong, black
*con leche* – big cup with plenty of milk (*grande* – bigger)
*americano* – big cup, black, half strength
*cortado* – small glass, strong with a dash of milk
*carajillo* – small cup, strong, black with brandy (cognac), whisky or rum as required

**Beer**
Beer is usually sold draft by glass size, or by bottle
*una caña* – from a draft, about 0.3L/$\frac{1}{2}$pt.
*un chatto* – a small glass (beer or wine)
*una jarra* – 0.5L/almost a pint draft
*un quinto* – bottle beer a fifth of a litre/$\frac{1}{3}$pt.
*una cerveza* – literally a beer, from a bottle

**Street markets add a touch of colour and character to every town**

**Buying ham**
*jamon dulce/york* – cooked ham
*jamon serrano* – dry, cured ham
*jamon jabugo* – the finest quality dry cured ham

Meat stalls will prepare meat as required. It is usual, when buying mince, to buy the meat and then have it ground. Similarly, beefburgers are made immediately. It is better not to try to purchase fresh meat or fish on Mondays.

There are always bars in markets, and outside the markets there are often rural people selling produce beneath the eaves.

**Food Shops** Outside the markets, there are supermarkets and local shops. In neither will the fresh produce be as tempting, but groceries, dairy products and drinks are often cheaper. Hours are from 9 a.m.–2 p.m., 5 p.m.–8 p.m. approx.

Local shops are often a little more expensive, but often characterful and useful. In villages there is often only one small shop, crammed with stock, which sells everything. Street markets are held in all towns at least once a week. The food stalls are usually good and fresh, but other stalls tend to have little of interest to tourists. Always beware of pickpockets and stallholders who short-change.

24

**Bread** will be found in *panaderia* shops, usually baked on the premises. These are usually open from 8 a.m.–2.30 p.m., and 5 p.m.–8.30 p.m. The two main types of bread are *pan de pais* which is heavy and round and will last for several days. Bakers will slice it if asked; and *pan de barra* which is long, thin crusty loaf, that will last only for a few hours. Bread is sold by weight, and prices are constant. It is scarce on Sundays.

**Pharmacists** There is nearly always a pharmacy open throughout the night in towns. A rota card may be found outside the door giving directions to the shops that are open late. Pharmacists are highly trained, know their stock well, and are available to be consulted on minor problems. For everyday products like soap and toothpaste it is better to go to a supermarket.

There is a general chain of small health shops, *santiveri* which sell herbal remedies and teas. A health specialist is usually available for advice.

**Department Stores** There are two main store chains: *El Corte Inglés* (the most prestigious and well-stocked) and *Galerrías Preciados* (less popular). Both offer tax repayment schemes for foreigners.

**Best Buys** The artesan work in central Spain consists mostly of pottery, with varying styles according to region. Particular villages in Toledo and Zamora produce fine lace and embroidery. Jewellery is worked in Salamanca. The most well-known skilled work is found in Toledo which specializes in damascene ware and the forging of swords. When buying damascene, beware of cheap imitation products. Leatherwork is also excellent.

Shoes and accessories are often of superb quality. Fashion is interesting in Madrid and Salamanca, both for women and for men.

**Papers** These are sold in *librería* shops or in street kiosks. European daily papers are found for sale in Madrid and the main cities on the afternoon of their issue. These cost about double their home price, and often lack heavy extra advertising sections. American papers arrive a couple of days after publication (excepting the *Wall Street Journal*, which is printed in France). Various journals, *Newsweek, Economist*, etc., are widely sold. Fashion magazines from several countries are on offer. The local papers, *El Pais* and *Diario 16*, are both fairly liberal. *El Pais* has

**Opening Hours** Shopping hours are variable. In general, shops are open from 9 a.m.–2 p.m. and from 5 p.m.–8 p.m. Exceptions are food shops and patisseries which often open at 8 a.m., and sometimes stay open until 9 p.m.; clothes shops which open at around 10 a.m.; and department stores which open from 10 a.m. and stay open throughout the day.

excellent international coverage and political analysis. *ABC* has a conservative bias, and *Ya* is Catholic-oriented. Sunday papers carry a colour supplement. *Lookout* is a colour magazine for English-speakers living in Spain. *In Spain* is a monthly with comment and general information. The *Iberian Daily Sun* is also available. For a guide of what is on in the major towns read *Guia del Ocio*, which comes out on Thursdays.

News may also be seen on television at 3 p.m., at 8.30 p.m. and later. The radio carries news every hour (British World Service: 12MHz–4MHz).

**Books** There are small numbers of good book shops in central Spain. In general, the Spanish tend not to read a great deal, but the book shops carry a good stock of Iberian classics. There are twice-yearly bookfairs in most cities, where new books and second-hand books are sold at a small discount. *Librería* stands sometimes sell thrillers in English, and there are a couple of excellent English book shops in Madrid.

Tourist guides: These are sold at kiosks in several languages. Town maps are best found at the local Tourist Office. General maps and walking maps may be bought at *librerías*. During August a number of city shops may be closed for holidays.

**Post Offices** It is not necessary to go to a Post Office for stamps (*sellos*). These are also sold at government *tabaconista* shops, where there are also scales for weighing letters. It costs the same to send a card or letter throughout Europe. Post boxes are yellow with red stripes circling their bases. There are usually at least two slots; the box for foreign destinations is marked *extranjero* (foreign). Post Office hours are generally 8 a.m.–1 p.m., and 5 p.m.–7.30 p.m. The bigger ones in Madrid stay open through the day. Poste restante services are offered by all, and letters should be clearly addressed with the surname highlighted, and marked for *Lista de Correos* followed by the town name. Telephones are not available in post offices.

**Telephones** Major towns have public telephone offices (*la telefonica*) where distance calls may be made in comfort and paid by credit card or cash. Normal rates are charged. Telephone booths can also be found in all towns and villages and many bars also have them for public use. Instructions are given in English as well as Spanish. The tone signals are similar to our own. The ringing tone is long steady beeps, and the engaged tone gives short repeated beeps.

To ring anywhere inside Spain, always dial 9, then the provincial exchange, and then the local number. (The Madrid exchange code is 910.) To ring internationally, dial 07 and wait for a high-pitched, continuous signal. When this sounds dial the country code and continue with the area code (without the first 0 if there is one), and local number. Most telephones in Spain will allow international calls. To ask the operator for help, calling from Madrid dial 008 for calls within Europe and 005 for calls outside Europe. If you are calling from outside Madrid call 9198 for European calls, and 9191 for non-European calls.

For calls inside Spain it is necessary to insert at least 10pts. to make a connection. Hotel calls tend to be more expensive.

**Electricity** Most circuits are 220V. The standard plug is 2-pin round-pin. A travel-adaptor plug may be useful.

**Washing Facilities** The 'Superloo' has arrived in Madrid, but otherwise there are plentiful washing rooms in bars and restaurants. In general, cafeterias will have good facilities, as will restaurants and hotels. Some bar, bus or train station facilities are less pleasant. There are launderettes in most towns, and washing services in good hotels.

**Street Crime** Beware of gypsies selling flowers, as one way of gaining money is to demand a price for a bloom, then swiftly to take money directly from a purse as it is opened. Beware of placing cases by the feet at bars; it is easy to be edged up a bar and thus to leave a bag unattended. At airports and train stations, bags may easily be snatched from trolleys.

One ploy adopted by would-be pickpockets is worth being aware of. The thief will spray chocolate at the back of the walker in front. Alerting the person to the state of his jacket, the thief will help remove and clean it, at the same time searching the pockets for valuables. This system is well known in Barcelona and also happens in Madrid.

Part Two: **Local Colour**

**The evening *paseo* in the
Plaza Mayor, Salamanca**

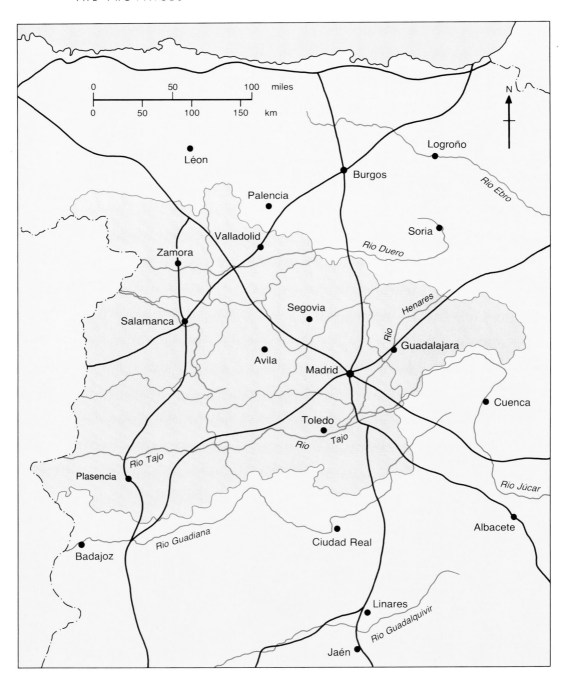

**The Provinces** The central part of the peninsula is divided by a great mountain range, the Cordillera Central, which reaches across from southern Salamanca to Madrid (the Sierra de Gredos) and curves north towards León (the Sierra de Guadarrama). Flanking each side of the mountains is an extensive high plateau called the Meseta (north and south) lying 600m–1,000m (2–3,000ft) above sea level, on which most of the provinces in this guide lie.

**The landscape around Toledo**

To the north of the mountains is Castilla y León, the autonomous community led by the city of Valladolid. Of this vast area, only the southern and western provinces near Madrid are described.

On the curve of the mountain strip is the capital, Madrid which is the political and geographical capital of Spain.

Extremadura spreads south of the range to the west, reaching to Andalucía, conserving a reputation for its economic poverty. This region is barely touched, the guide only introducing the northern tip of the province of Cáceres – Plasencia.

South of the range and to the east, stretch the vast plains of New Castille (Castilla la Mancha), of which only Toledo, the capital of the autonomous community, and Guadalajara are introduced.

31

The population of the central region is very small. The province of Madrid numbers approximately 4 million, but in the whole of the region of Castilla y León, there are only 2.5 million people. The density of population is extremely low compared with the general European average; in this region it is 27 people per $km^2$, while in Castilla la Mancha it is only 21 per $km^2$. Central Spain is highly agricultural, with, excepting Valladolid and Madrid, very little industrial contribution to the country. The climate is continental, with the extremes of hard, cold winters and hot, dry summers.

**Religion** Spain is a Catholic country. Every child is named for a saint, and the Saint's day is as important a celebration as the birthday. Many people attend mass at weekends (Saturday evening/Sunday morning) and the churches are full for the local Saint's day festivals. Many of these festivals are nationally important and involve the whole community.

**Customs** Life is lived out of doors much more than in Northern Europe. Everyone goes out for the *paseo*, a stroll through the centre of town each evening. This is the main social interchange of the community during which everyone, well dressed, may greet acquaintances and catch up on the local news.

Family ties are strong. Three generations often live together,

Courtesy is an essential part of Spanish life. On entering a shop, restaurant, or gathering of any kind, one should greet the assembled company. Similarly, one must bid farewell on leaving.

**The extended family is an important part of the Spanish way of life**

and it is usual for city dwellers to spend their holidays back home in the village from which their family came. Few feel the need to travel to other countries. Young people do not generally leave home until married, and will usually name their children with the traditional family Christian names.

Cafés are the centre of the village for the men, who will be found playing cards through the early afternoon. For the women, the social times are during the shopping rounds at market (where mother and daughter will often be seen together) and in the kitchen later in the day. Families tend to live together far longer than in northern Europe, both sexes often remaining at home until married. These general traits are relaxed in the cities.

**Politics and Economics** The wealth of the region outside Madrid is based on agriculture. The plains of the northern Meseta produce great quantities of grain, and cereal is also extensively grown in La Mancha. Wine is produced in quantity from the banks of the Duero in Valladolid and Zamora, and from pockets throughout the region. (The biggest wine-producing area is just south of the guide region in Castilla la Mancha.) Sugar beet is grown in Valladolid. Olives are produced in Salamanca and Toledo. While Extremadura is a poor agricultural producer, the fertile area of Plasencia grows much market garden produce.

Sheep flocks are grazed for lamb in the eastern half of Castilla y León, and throughout central Spain cheese is produced from their milk. (*Manchego*, from Castilla la Mancha, is a particularly famous artesanal cheese.) Some beef cattle are produced in Avila. Salamanca and, to a much lesser extent, Toledo are major producers of the fighting bulls of the country. In Salamanca and into Extremadura pig farming produces valuable cured ham.

Central Spain is agriculturally prosperous, with little industrial output. After Madrid, Valladolid is the largest city and the only one of industrial importance. Madrid, the financial and political centre of Spain, is thus almost isolated in its modern, industrial and commercial base. The Basque country and Catalonia are the main industrial areas of Spain.

Since the early 1980s there has been huge economic growth in Spain, and foreign investment has soared. Although the rate of unemployment continues to fall, the labour problems of the central region are linked to the lack of industrial base. There is continual depopulation of these provinces to the major industrial areas of Madrid and Catalonia.

Tourism continues to be an important economic factor, but to a far lesser extent in the central region than on the coasts.

**Political Context** There are various political parties, the most powerful being the PSOE (Socialist Workers Party), led since 1982 by Felipe Gonzalez and the Partido Popular (Conservative). The general trade union UGT is becoming increasingly strong. Government is democratic, with a two-house Cortes. The country is governed through regional autonomies under the Prime Minister. Those of Catalonia and the Basque Country are particularly nationalistic.

Spain has been a member iof the European Community since 1986, and a member of NATO since 1982. Politically, it is one of the most stable of the European countries.

The country has been under a constitutional monarchy since the end of the Franco Dictatorship in 1975. The king, Juan Carlos I, grandson of King Alfonso XIII, is married to Queen Sophia (of the Greek royal family) and is highly regarded both in his country and in Europe. His nursing of the state through the changes from dictatorship to democracy has been dramatically successful, facing only one serious crisis in 1981 with the attempted army coup of Colonel Tejero.

**History** Throughout central Spain, the various styles of ecclesiastical, military and secular architecture illustrate much of the historical background of the towns.

The central region was settled by the Romans (219BC Punic Wars), by Vandals and Visigoths (AD400 onwards) and by Muslims (AD711 onwards) before finally being taken over by Christian monarchs from the late eleventh century. Thereafter the region passed through changing Christian dynasties and varying states of political stability and economic prosperity. The legacy of each conquest and each major change in the fortunes of the Castilian countryside are stamped in the architecture of each town.

**219BC (2nd Punic War)** The Romans colonised central Spain, with their main settlements at Salamanca, Segovia and Toledo. Remains can still be seen outside the walls of Toledo, and there is the magnificent Aqueduct in Segovia which stands as a monument to Roman engineering. AD400 (Germanic Invasions). The Vandals and then the Visigoths moved in to replace the Roman colonies. Toledo became the Visigoth capital from AD507, and the influence of the Visigoths can be seen in the simple churches with horseshoe windows and carved friezes. Examples of the Visigoth period can be seen in the Toledo church of San Roman, in the church of Ermita de NS de Melque in Toledo province, and in San Pedro de la Nave in Zamora province.

**AD711 (Muslim Invasions)** Invasions by Muslims who spread across Spain were undeterred until they were defeated at Poitiers by Charles Martel in AD732. The Muslim empire was ruled from the Caliphate of Córdoba which achieved its highest cultural and political power under Abdul Rahman III (912-961). The Caliphate style is evident in horseshoe cusped arches, decorative brickwork, interlacing arches and ornamental calligraphy in brick and stucco. You can see good examples of this in the Toledo mosque, El Christo de la Luz, and in the Moorish defences of that city.

**Eleventh to Thirteenth Centuries** This period saw the reconquest of parts of Spain by Christian kings, yet it was Alfonso VI (1065-1109) who took the present Castilla y León from Moorish rule. (Rodrigo Diaz de Vivar known as El Cid Campeador, fought at this time south to Valencia.) The most potent symbol of reconquest is Santiago of Compostella (St James) whose relics were discovered in 899. Castilla was strengthened by Ferdinand III (El Santo) who united Castile and León. In 1085 Toledo was taken.

Architecturally the style was military, such as the great walls surrounding several cities. Repopulation was begun by Raymond of Burgandy, husband of Alfonso VI's daughter Urraca, using settlers from the north and from France. Fortifications were built to strengthen the line of defences against Moorish armies. This was done usually along hill peaks or rivers. The walls of Avila, Zamora, Ciudad Rodrigo, Segovia and Toledo are good examples of the impressive defences built in this period.

The Romanesque style is usually seen in churches with plain round arches, blind arcading, capitals carved with floral and animal motifs. Belfries were sometimes single-sided, sometimes with a tower. Bigger churches had clusters of round apses, splendid round-arched portals, sculpted with figures. These can be seen in all areas of central Spain except Madrid, where only one Romanesque church exists. Particularly prominent are Segovia, which has a distinctive style of porticoed outside walls, Zamora

Ávila and Toro in Zamora province. The Cistercian monasteries of Zamora and Valladolid, and the old cathedrals of Salamanca, Cuidad Rodrigo, Plasencia and Avila show the movement through to early Gothic style. The quality of Romanesque churches in central Spain indicates the level of stability that followed the sweep of Christian reconquest.

The Clunaic order came into Spain via the Santiago pilgrimage route to the north and spread the Romaneque style of architecture. The Cistercian monastic order and the military orders of knights who owned great tracts of land in Castile, influenced architecture by the churches and castles they built. All religious architecture was united by the crusading nature of the reconquest. Other styles included the Mozarabic (Christian buildings converted to Muslim). Some of the few remaining buildings feature lobed horseshoe arches of brick and stone. This can be seen at the tenth century Wamba and San Cebrian in Valladolid. The Mudéjar style was created by Muslims converted to Christianity. Buildings are usually of brick with decoration reminiscent of the Arabic style - stucco, coffered ceilings and artesanal wood-mosaics. Buildings of this sort are found throughout the region, and were built between the eleventh and fifteenth centuries. Some good examples are the Tordesillas Palace of Santa Clara, the synagogues of Toledo, the Alcazar of Segovia and the castle of Cuellaar, Coca and Medina del Campo in Valladolid province.

**Fourteenth and Fifteenth Centuries** The Christian reconquest continued, with wealth being exacted from existing Moorish states in the form of dues. Economic prosperity grew with the wool trade connections in Flanders. The wool trade gained a huge advantage from the affirmation of the Mesta routes, which gave grazing route privileges throughout the peninsular. New cathedrals were being built as an expression of new prosperity. A high Gothic style was favoured, with lofty high vaults, soaring pillars, elegant, narrow stained-glass windows, decorative motifs, tall delicately carved pinnacles, huge retablos broken by filigree capitals, and side chapels between buttresses. Examples can be seen in Salamanca, Segovia, and much of Toledo (though this was begun earlier).

Universities were thriving at this time with the mixture of Jewish, Muslim and Christian intellects. There were frequent problems between Jewish and Christian quarters, with the black death of 1348 and political jealousy of Jewish influencers of monarchs (often treasurers of the King) leading to pogroms.

Increasingly, palace/fortresses were affirming the strength of landed counts. Military orders were also extremely wealthy.

The marriage of Ferdinand and Isabella in 1479 led to the unity of Aragón and Castile under a single monarchy (although the individual laws and customs of each remained).

The end of Muslim occupation occurred with the taking of Granada in 1492, the same year as the discovery of America by Cristóbal Colón. Religious zeal was encouraged by the expulsion of Jews and later of Muslims, which was then followed by the Inquisition. Almost no synagogues survived. Economic prosperity continued with wealth channelled from the Americas.

The style was high flamboyant Gothic, and Renaissance (Italian influence). Facades were embellished with Isabelline (decorative sculptural style on Gothic), and Plateresque decoration (an extreme form of decoration, on Renaissance or Gothic facades). Examples are Salamanca University, University of Alcalá de Henares, New Cathedral, Salamanca, the Churches of San Pedro and San Gregoria (Valladolid). Renaissance civic architecture can be seen in senorial houses throughout the region.

**Hapsburg Dynasty** Charles I of Spain (Emperor Charles V), inherited the kingdom from his mother Júana 'the mad' (considered unfit to rule), who was married to the son of Emperor Maximilian of Austria. The reign of Ferdinand and Isabella ended without a direct heir (he died young). Their grandson grew up in Austria, tutored as the minor monarch of Castile and Aragón since the age of four, and arrived in Castile to take the crown in 1516. He was elected to the imperial title in 1519, thus inheriting altogether the Netherlands, Flanders, much of Spain, the Americas, Sardinia, Artois and Franche-compte. The capital was in Castile at Toledo. Much wealth brought from the Americas was diverted to funding the four wars against the French (Francis I) and the Italians. Charles abdicated for his son Philip II in 1556 and died in the monastery of Yuste, Plasencia.

Philip II did not inherit the Holy Roman Empire, and lived throughout his reign in Spain. His main architectural legacy was the building of the monastery of El Escorial, whose austere monumentalism was symbolic both of the passionate Catholic zeal of the monarch and the splendour of his extensive Spanish empire. He based his capital in Madrid, changing the geographical centre of the peninsula from insignificance to great importance. The architecture of Madrid, displaying only the styles from the Hapsburgs onwards, illustrates the abrupt birth of the capital.

The navy gained a great victory at Lepanto, led by the monarch's half-brother, Juan of Austria, but suffered severe losses as the Armada pitted against the Protestantism of the English crown, (Mary Tudor was his second wife, although the marriage was never consumated). The wars of Philip II, and his passion for building left the country in debt at his death (1598), even though large quantities of gold were brought in from the Americas.

The style was Renaissance, with severe lines, no ornament and massive, sober design which can be seen in the Ayuntamiento, Toledo.

Philip III IV, and Charles II succeeded, each following the extravagance of Philip II, while lacking his monarchal prudence. While Spain thrived culturally, with the great painters, El Greco (1541–1614), Ribera (1588–1652), Murillo (1617–82), Zurbarán (1598–1664) and Velázquez (1599–1660); and the great literary figures of Cervantes (1547–1616), Calderón and Lope de Vega, it gradually lost many of its prestigious appendages. By the end of the Hapsburg dynasty, much of the great Mudéjar labour base of Spain had been banished as part of the second wave of the Inquisition, the agricultural economy was in decline, suffering the breakdown of relations with the important international Flemish market, and the power of the nobility and church was growing unchecked. Charles II died without heir.

The architectural style remained on the whole quite simple throughout the seventeenth century, though Italian Baroque influence can be seen in several buildings. Examples are Plaza Mayor, Madrid; Jesuit College, Salamanca; and the church of San Isidro el Real, Madrid.

**Bourbons** The new dynasty, founded by Philip of Anjou (Philip V) entered through a war of succession (1701–14). His reign settled the Spanish territories, losing the Netherlands, seizing Sardinia and Sicily, and regaining Menorca (which was lost to the British with Gibraltar in 1704).

Charles III is remembered as 'the enlightened despot', a great reformer and great builder, being responsible for much of the Bourbon architectural splendours that surround Madrid. He supported America in her bid for independence in 1779.

The style was Spanish baroque which was ornate, sometimes flamboyant, with a number of decorative styles overlaying classical forms. The Churriguresque style featured ornate retablos, with gilded twisted columns wound with vines framing paintings, becoming increasingly ornate. Elaborate painting and carving of cherubic figures adorning portals, altarpieces and ceilings can be seen at Toledo Cathedral Transparente (Narcsio Tomé).

The royal palaces surrounding Madrid (e.g. La Granja, Aránjuez) display a style much influenced by French and Italian taste; many artists from Italy were patronized. Examples are the church of San Esteban and the Plaza Mayor, Salamanca.

During the reign of Charles IV, Napoleon declared war on Spain. A subsequent alliance of the two countries led to Charles IV being replaced by Napoleon's brother Joseph. A further invasion by Napoleon (the Peninsular War, known in Spain as the War of Independence) laid waste to many cities of Castile, during which the massacre of *Dos de Mayo* took place on 2 May in the centre of Madrid (captured on canvas by Goya (1746–1828). The invasion was stopped by British forces led by Wellington near the Portugese Border. While Napoleonic troops caused much destruction in the region (many fine architectural buildings still bear scars), the British troops also looted much valuable treasure.

Ferdinand VII regained the Bourbon throne in 1814, although his royal powers were substantially weakened. He left it to his daughter Isabel II rather than to his legal heir, his brother Carlos. Isabel's reign (1833–68) was disturbed by severe republican uprisings, the First Carlist War and strong political factions led by General Baldomero Espartero, General Narvaez, and General Leopoldo O'Donnell. The dissolution of monasteries, ordered by Mendizábal in 1835 (while Isabel was an infant) led to the dispersal of much religious treasure, the establishment of museums, and the acquisition by small parish churches of fine rescued works of art. The monasteries, left empty for some years, did not succeed in regaining their wealth either in land or in treasure.

The fall of the crown allowed the declaration of the First Spanish Republic in 1873, although Alfonso XII regained the throne two years later. Continual political upheaval led to the birth of the general trade union UGT, and to the introduction of universal suffrage in 1890.

Alfonso XIII was the last monarch before the civil war. His reign was marked by political unrest. Spain declared neutrality in the First World War and also in the Second World War. Spain's own Civil War, which lasted from 1936–39, nearly destroyed her. It left the country devastated. Families were divided, great numbers were killed, and the social order was completely disrupted. A whole generation lost its education.

Franco's armies were finally supreme. His dictatorship restored calm and, although harsh, gave the country forty years of stability during which much rebuilding and development took place. Following his death in 1975, the restoration of democracy and of the monarchy, in the person of Don Juan Carlos, took Spain into its present-day position as one of Europe's constitutional monarchies.

## Event Calendar

| | |
|---|---|
| **January to June** | Madrid/Season of Opera |
| **March** | Madrid/International Theatre Festival |
| | Madrid/International Science Fantasy and Fiction Film Festival |
| **April** | Madrid/Alcalá de Henares |
| | Madrid/Cumbra Flamenca |
| | Madrid/Muestra de Danza del Central Cultural de la Villa (contemporary and classical dance) |
| **Easter** | Zamora/Semana de Musica Religiosa |
| **May** | Valladolid/International Theatre Festival |
| | Madrid/Encuentro Internacional de Teatro (meeting of national theatre companies during festival of San Isidora) |
| **Summer** | Madrid/San Lorenzo del Escorial Curso Festival de Musica Barroca. |
| **July** | Ávila/Semana de Polifonica y Organo |
| | Madrid/'Los Verranos de la Villa' (Summer in the City) |
| **August** | Segovia/Festival Internacional (music) |

**September** Madrid/Semana Cultural (music and exhibitions)
Segovia/Semana de Music de Camera
Madrid/Festival de Otoño (dance and theatre)
Madrid/Season of Zarzuela (light opera – runs
    to December)

**October** Toledo/Semana de Musica
Valladolid/International Film Week

**November** Valladolid/Semana Musical 'Santa Cecilia'
Madrid/International Antique Fair
Madrid/Jazz Festival

**Fiestas** The central government allows 14 official days of fiesta holiday (i.e. lost working days) per year. Of these a proportion are nationally observed holidays, and some are locally observed. Every village celebrates its individual fiestas, and cities retain numerous localities which observe their individual days. The quantity of fiestas and celebrations far outnumbers the official number of holidays, and some towns base their celebrations at weekends in order to accommodate the strictures of the law. The vesper of a festival is usually celebrated far into the night.

The fiesta – a party of celebration – is an integral part of community life in Spain, of far greater importance than work. The fiesta demonstrates the strength of a community; those who have left to work in the city return, and the whole community celebrates together several times a year.

The general holiday month is August, during which families join together in their village (*pueblo*) of origin. Those who have migrated to the city for work return even several generations later. It is not the custom to stay in town during August, and holidays are generally taken in two blocks a year; Semana Santa (a week) and August (often at least 3 weeks).

In central Spain, the fiestas are accompanied by flowers and colourful decoration. Local traditional costumes are frequently worn in the villages. In spring and summer, non-religious festivals and Saint's Day town festivals, bulls are usually an integral part of the celebration. Every town has its own patron saint, and also celebrates the patron of the province. In religious processions, apart from the most solemn ones, quantities of sweets (*caramelas*) are thrown from the floats as they travel through the streets.

**Important Regular Markets in the Region**

**Plasencia**
On Tuesday mornings throughout the year there is a spectacular vegetable market.

**Madrid**
On Sunday mornings throughout the year visit the famous Rastro fleamarket.

Information should be available about fiestas and romerías at each provincial tourist office. They are multifold, and a joy to come across.

## Official dates

| | |
|---|---|
| January 1 | New Year's Day |
| January 6 | Los Reyes Magos (Epiphany) |
| March 19 | San José |
| Semana Santa: | Holy Thursday (a holiday in central Spain but not throughout Spain) |
| | |
| Good Friday | |
| Easter Sunday | |
| Easter Monday | |
| May 1 | Corpus Cristi (2nd Thursday after Whitsun) |
| June 24 | King's name saints day |
| July 25 | Santiago (Patron of Spain) |
| August 15 | Assumption of the Virgin |
| October 12 | National Day, Sainta María del Pilar |
| November 1 | All Saints |
| December 6 | Constitution Day |
| December 8 | Immaculate Conception |
| Christmas Day | |

**Whit Sunday**

In Atienza, La Caballada (Guadalajara province), hundreds of horses gallop through the town.

Outside most towns, particularly on any high ground behind, there is usually a hermitage. These have grid windows for pilgrims to see the image within.

**General celebrations** These will be celebrated everywhere to varying degrees. Often the smaller towns will be lesser magnets of spectators.

New Year is welcomed with street dancing. As midnight of the vesper arrives, it is customary to eat a grape at each strike of the clock.

On 6 January is the Feast of Three Kings, in which three processions of kings and mounted retinue pass through the streets on the vesper, throwing sweets to good children and theoretically throwing coal to the bad ones. This is a festival for the family, after which Christmas presents are opened.

For Carnival (early February) disguise is worn. There is dancing and music but little religious content. It is spectacular in Ciudad Rodrigo (Salamanca province) where bulls are run, and Villanueva de la Vera (Plasencia).

On Palm Sunday pale palm leaves woven into ornamental shapes are blessed in church. Boughs grace balconies. A pretty festival for children, who carry the ornaments. Semana Santa, (Easter) is particularly splendid and austere in Valladolid and Zamora. Great artistic treasures and sculptures are processed through the street, carried and accompanied by brotherhoods of penitents in hooded costumes. Slow drum beats follow the processions, which are of the utmost seriousness and many hours long. The floats may be seen at other times of the year in the museums and churches. In Valverde de la Vera (Ávila province) penitents walk with great beams strapped to their backs (Empalaos). It is also spectacular in Barcianos de Aliste (Zamora province). Elsewhere, there is much symbolic and real mortification of the flesh.

Easter Sunday is a day of general fiesta, dancing and music. Spectacular, processions take place in Peñafiel (Valladolid province), known as *Bajada de Angel*. Corpus Cristi is exceptional in Toledo, where the great cathedral monstrance processes through the streets which are decorated with shawls, carpets, pretty cloths, and spread with fragrant herbs. In Camunas (Toledo), two brotherhoods dance in spectacular costume. Ávila and Valladolid also have impressive processions.

In religious processions, excepting the most solemn processions, quantities of sweets (*caramelos*) are thrown from the floats as they travel through the streets.

June 13 is the Summer Solstice (Noche de San Juan) is celebrated by dancing. Summer starts on 24 June with bonfires and fireworks. Every town and village celebrates the summer festival, this is often Saint's day celebrations including days either side. These include dancing, music, sometimes processions but always colour and costume. Bull-running and fights are a spectacle of many. The season of festivity finishes in early October.

December 8 is the Immaculate Conception, which is often celebrated by a candle-lit vigil. Christmas Day is celebrated in family style on the vesper.

**Romerías** These festivals focus on sanctuaries in the countryside between 2 and 20km (1 to 12 miles) from town, and often involve several villages. The days involve processions to the sanctuary and feasting and dancing once there. The occasions are very lively and colourful. Romerías are celebrated throughout the year.

Several romerías are of note, although any are a delight to come across. Some of the best ones are:

Romería de la Caridad, Cuidad Rodrigo (Salamanca province) on 3 February;

Romería de San Pedro de Alcántara, Arenas de San Pedro (Ávila province) on 19 October;

Romería de NS de la Chilla, Candeleda (Ávila province) on the 2nd Sunday in September;
Romería de las Vacas, Ávila town (unusual processions within the town) on the 2nd Sunday in May;
Romería de las Hoce del Duratón, Sepúlveda (Segovia province) on 25 October.
Santa Agueda 5 February In Zamarramala village (Segovia province), a fiesta of the Alcaldesas when women make the decisions of the village for a weekend – lovely costumes.
August 15, 16 La Alberca fiesta (Salamanca province) With rich traditional costumes and dancing, this fiesta is spectacular.

**Fiestas with Bulls** These animals are an integral part of Castilian fiestas. They either run wildly through the streets (*encierros*) – Cuellar has the oldest tradition of this, dating to before 1546, celebrated on 8 September; or meet bullfighters in the ring (*corrida*) or are the spectacular focus of mounted chases through the town or countryside (the Toro de la Vega in Tordesillas, Valadollid province is celebrated on the Tuesday after 8 September). The bullfight itself is a very important component, villages often constructing rings within their Plaza Mayors for the occasion (*see* Chinchón, Madrid province, page 111).

**Bullfighting** This follows a particular ritual; the Suerte de Picar (a mounted picador with short-pointed lance teases the bull to charge his horse and weakens the bull's neck muscles with lance thrusts); Suerte de Banderillas (three sets of darts are placed in the back in an acrobatic display of courage by undefended men); Suerte de Matar (where the matador plays the bull with a cape and finally, achieving a particular position with the bull, kills him with a single sword thrust – this last being a difficult task if attempted with inadequate precision).

A fight will usually consist of three matadors and six bulls. In small towns there are often less, the bullfighters are often still uninitiated into the matador ranks, and the bulls are usually young. In Capellas, the bulls are only played, not killed.
Seats (*gradas*); sun (*sol*); shade (*sombra*); soon shaded (*sol y sombra*).
Starts in general 4.30–7 p.m. Fights last 2 to 3 hours.
Tickets: row (*filo*); gate (*tendido*). It is best to buy tickets at official booths or, for small corridas, at the gate. Do not buy from touts at the gate. Season Easter to October.

The most famous bullfighting fiesta is that of Madrid, surrounding the day of the Patron Saint, San Isidoro, on 15 May. Two weeks of bullfighting take place amid great festivity.

**Bowls is a popular social event and is played almost anywhere**

Part Three: **The Region**

**The Sierras near Torrelaguna**

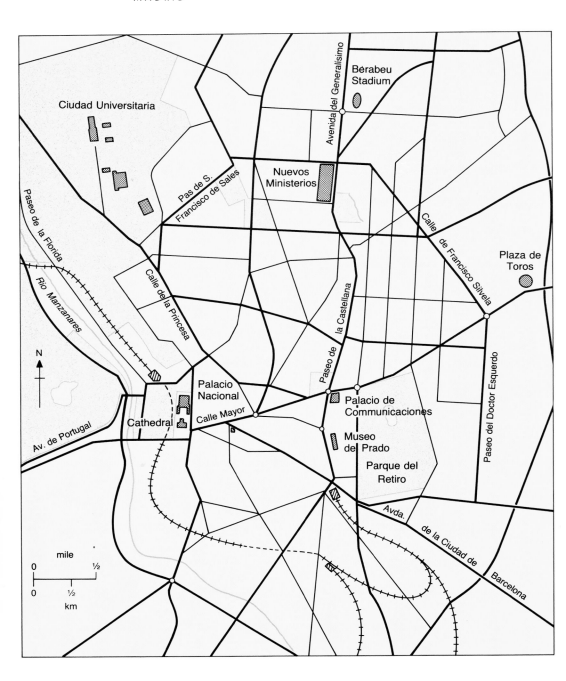

**Madrid,** capital of Spain, lies in the geographical heart of the country with the mountains of Guadarrama and Gredos flanking its north and west boundaries. The historical Castilian cities of Toledo, Segovia, Ávila, Valladolid and Guadalajara are all within a two-hour journey. Within the city are magnificent Hapsburg and Boubon monuments, marvellous collections of fine art, and beautiful parks. The *joie de vivre* of its people is unique.

*The cultural reputation of Madrid is based more upon its museums than its monuments. The jewel is the Museo del Prado, whose world famous collection of paintings, founded by Charles III and added to by the subsequent monarchs, is without parallel.*

**History** Madrid is a young capital city. Until 1561, when the seat of government was moved from Toledo, Madrid maintained the importance of a small provincial centre. It was fortified by the Moors and taken by Christians in 1083 *en route* to capturing Toledo. Even after Philip II's decision to govern from here, the site of the capital oscillated between Valladolid and Madrid until it was stabilized with the decisive building of the Bourbons (Philip V began the Royal Palace). Thus, the cultural context of the city dates from a far later period than that of the provincial capitals of Castile or Extremadura. Influences from Italy, the Netherlands and France are frequent reminders of the international heritage of the dynastic rulers. Renaissance, Baroque and neo-classical are the most common styles among the splendid old buildings of the city, while its modern commercial development has attracted some fine contemporary architecture. Notable ecclesiastical architecture is sparse.

**Contemporary Character** As a modern city, Madrid is noisy and busy day and night. Traffic problems are present even at 3 a.m. At every level of society the bars provide the general meeting-place and, depending on area, these will stay full well into the night. Meal times are late, and evening entertainments later still. Office hours vary between the traditional Spanish pattern (8 a.m.–2 p.m., 5 p.m.–8 p.m.) and that of northern Europe.

**Madrid offers a wide range of Renaissance, baroque and neo-classical architecture**

In climate, the city is at its most pleasant in autumn and early spring. The winter is very cold, and the stifling heat of summertime is notorious. In July and August a significant proportion of Madrileños take refuge in the cool of the nearby hills, leaving the city very quiet. In the warmer months, the outside terraces and superb parks of the city are full of life.

**Layout of the City** As with all cities, Madrid comprises a number of areas whose individual characteristics are distinct. A familiarity with the nature of these districts reduces the apparent complexity of the city, and makes a visit here less formidable.

Cutting through the main city from north to south is the Paseo de la Castellana, becoming Paseo de Recoletos and then Paseo del Prado. The Plaza de la Cibeles – whose fountain is a symbol of the city – is crossed by the important highway of Calle de Alcalá, and forms a central pivot for the areas of the city.

**Old City Puerta del Sol, Opera, La Latina, Lavapies** South-west of Plaza de la Cibeles stretching to the Plaza del Orient and the magnificent Royal Palace – Palacio Real (OPERA) is the oldest part of the city – much of it built by the Hapsburgs in the sixteenth and seventeenth centuries. The hub of the region is the Puerta del Sol, one of the major meeting spots of the city. Nearby are Plaza Mayor and Plaza Santa Ana, the former

**The Puerta del Sol – a major meeting place**

a lively tourist area, the latter a fashionable social area at night. South of these squares are small streets, extending through the old communities of La Latina and Lavapies, both of which are strongly local in character. In the streets between the two, the famous Sunday Rastro fleamarket is held. A number of important museums and monuments are in this area.

**Above Gran Via: Chueca, Plaza de España, Argüeles** West of Plaza de la Cibeles, above the Calle de Alcalá, is a less picturesque area centred around the Plazas of Chueca and Dos de Mayo (known locally as the area of Malasaña). Popular with young Madrileños, for the large number of nightclubs, the area can seem uncouth and unwelcoming to visitors. To the far west, the high-rise surroundings of Plaza de España stand between the Royal Palace and the lovely Parque del Oeste which stretches up to the Ciudad Universidad. Argüelles, at the top of Calle de la Princesa, is a popular meeting area, and shopping centre for the young.

**The famous Rastro coin market**

### East of University City to Paseo de la Castellana

North of the main route running across from Paseo de la Castellana at Plaza de Colon (interrupted by Plaza de Alonso Martínez and Glorietta de Bilbao) is an extensive residential area in which there are a number of government buildings and embassies.

### South of Plaza de la Cibeles: Banco de España, Retiro, Atocha
South east of Cibeles, off the Paseo del Prado, is the famous Prado museum and botanic gardens. Behind lies the most extensive and popular park of the city, the Parque del Retiro.

### North of Plaza de la Cibeles: Serrano, Colón, Goya
The elegant shopping area of Salamanca lies within the grid of the Ensanche, which extends northward and is filled with dignified offices, shops and residences.

### North End of Paseo de la Castellana: Plaza Castilla, Tetuán, Chamartin
The great avenue running north from Cibeles, clothed generously with trees and greenery, is lined with fine cosmopolitan buildings and banks, and at its northern end are gathered the wealthy towering structures of Madrid's modern commercial centre.

### Monuments and Museums
There is a wide variety of museums and monuments to be visited in Madrid, apart from those buildings whose facades are notable. (*Note*: many close on Sunday afternoons and Mondays, and some also close in August.)

In the first category are those recommended as high priority for a visitor with limited time. In the second category are museums of great attraction but a lesser intensity. In the third are a multitude of different museums and monuments whose individuality and specialization recommends them (*Note*: Metro stations appear in CAPITALS.)

### Atocha Station
The iron and glass building was designed by Eiffel of Eiffel tower fame. A station of remarkable contemporary design (Rafael Moreo, 1985) is behind. Paseo de la Delicias (ATOCHA).

### Basílica de San Francisco
This is a very beautiful circular church, built in the eighteenth-century at immense cost, with six chapels and a magnificent dome, 29m (95ft) in diameter. Sabatini completed the edifice, which was started by Fray Francisco de las Cabazas on the site of an old thirteenth-century monastery. The interior is splendid, with frescoes by Goya and

**Madrid Museums**
Outstanding:
- Museo del Prado • Palacio Real
- Basílica de San Francisco

Bayeu, and an inner gallery museum with a valuable collection of paintings by Spanish artists including Zurbarán, Pacheco and Ribalta. The choir stalls were originally in the monastery of El Paular, beneath the Guadarrama mountains north of the capital.

**Ermita de San Antonio de la Florida** This small building requires a special effort, being near no other monument. It is worth while: Francisco de Goya decorated the ceiling of the eighteenth-century temple with courtly frescoes in 1798. (He was subsequently elevated to first painter to the court.) The paintings are marvellous, although badly lit. Goya's headless body rests here, having been brought back from France early this century. Glorietta de San Antonio de la Florida, below the Parque del Oueste by the east bank of the River Manzanares (NORTE, or bus 41, 46, 75, C Open: Winter Tuesday to Friday 10 a.m.–1 p.m. and 4–8/9 p.m., Saturday and Sunday morning only. Shut Mondays and all afternoons in December.

**Museo Arqueológico Nacional** The famous treasures of this museum include the two ancient Iberian busts – the third /fourth-century Dama de Elche, and the Dama de Baza. In the garden the vivid prehistoric cave paintings of Altamira, Santander, can be seen in replica. As well as an important coin collection, and a thorough display of ceramic history, there is an extensive range of items of Egyptian, Greek, Etruscan and Eastern origin, dating from prehistoric times onwards. Antique furniture and medieval and modern art works are also shown.

At the back of the Biblioteca Nacional, Calle de Serrano 13 (COLON/SERRANO) Open: 9.15 a.m.–2.45 p.m. Shut Mondays.

**Casa de Lope de Vega** A pretty tribute to the nineteenth-century playwright whose house is shown furnished with period pieces and has a well-tended patio garden. Manuscripts and editions of his work are treasured.
Calle de Cervantes 11, near Plaza Santa Ana (ANTON MARTÍN) Open: Tuesday and Thursday 11 a.m.–2 p.m. Shut mid-July to mid-September.

**Museo del Prado** One of the great art galleries of the world, gathered by the Hapsburg and Bourbon monarchs. On the first floor are the Spanish masters (Velázquez, El Greco, Murillo, Goya, Ribera, Zurbarán); the Italian masters (Fra Angélico, Raphael); the Venetian school, (Titian); early Dutch (Hieronymous

It is best to arrive at the gallery early as it becomes crowded, particularly at the weekend. A visit is likely to take at least half a day. There is a small restaurant/café on the ground floor for refreshment during a visit, and comfortable seats in several rooms.

Bosch); the German School (Dürer); and Flemish (Rubens, Anton van Dyke, Jan Brueghel, Rembrandt). The French school is also displayed, while the English works are on the ground floor. By the entrance there are excellent guidebooks in several languages. Further explanatory leaflets are offered with the gallery.

The two annexes are entered with the main ticket, and it is not necessary to visit these on the same day. The Casón del Buen Retiro has a number of important modern works, e.g. Picasso's 'Guernica'; The Palacio de Villahermosa houses major temporary exhibitions. Paseo del Prado (BANCO DE ESPAÑA/ATOCHA) Open: Tuesday to Saturday 9 a.m.–7 p.m., Sunday 9 a.m.–2 p.m. Shut Sunday afternoons and Mondays.

**Centro de Arte Reina Sofía** Recently opened with small transitory exhibitions, a cafe and a threatre.

**Museo de Cerralbo** The personal collection of the seventeenth Marquis of Cerralbo includes porcelain, weaponry, tapestries, furniture and paintings. It is genteelly displayed in his late nineteenth-century palace (gifted by him to the state). The porcelain is quite beautiful, and amongst the fine selection of paintings are works by El Greco, Ribera, Tintoretto and Zurbarán. Calle Ventura Rodríguez 17 (PLAZA DE ESPAÑA) Open: 9 a.m.–2 p.m. Shut Tuesdays and during August.

**Palacio Real** Bourbon royal residence of great splendour. Also known as Palacio del Oriente, the palace was built to replace the burnt Alcázar. It was begun in 1737 under Philip V and was completed in Charles III's reign. The architects, Sachetti, Sabatini and Ventura Rodríguez, produced a magnificent neo-classical building of granite and limestone. The interior is lavishly decorated in French and Italian style, with superb ceiling paintings (Spanish and Italian masters) and fine furniture. Charles III's state rooms are sumptuous, with wonderful stucco decoration by Gasparini and walls hung with satin and sixteenth-century tapestry. The Fábrica del Buen Retiro produced the remarkable porcelain in the Sala de Porcelana, and the magnificent chandeliers came from the glass works in La Granja, Segovia. The collections of ceramics and French and Flemish tapestry are magnificent.

The substantial art collection is now exhibited in the New Museums (Goya, Velázquez, El Greco, Watteau). Adjoining exhibitions are in the Royal Library, the Farmacia Real (Pharmacy – left in its original state), Armería Real (Armoury) and the Caballerizas (Coach Museum – in the gardens of Campo de Moro). Tickets can include all the collections, or selected parts. The palace entrance is opposite the centre of the Plaza del Oriente gardens.

A guide is obligatory. A tour of the state rooms takes about an hour. It is best to visit early to avoid crowded tours. A guidebook (on sale at the ticket office) is useful; the guides offer several languages but tend to sweep through the palace splendours quite rapidly.

Plaza de Oriente (OPERA) Open: winter Monday to Saturday 9.30 a.m.–12.30 p.m. and 3.30–5.15 p.m., summer 9.30 a.m.–12.45 p.m. and 4–6 p.m., Sunday 9.30 a.m.–1.30 p.m.

**Convento de la Encarnación** Founded half a century after Las Descalzas, by the wife of Philip III, this Augustine convent is again wealthy in frescos and paintings. The church, built by Ventura Rodríguez, is particularly ornate.

Plaza de la Encarnación, near Plaza de Oriente (OPERA). Open: Tuesday to Thursday 10.30 a.m.–12.45 p.m. and 4–5.15 p.m., Friday to Sunday 10.30 a.m.–1.30 p.m. Shut Mondays. Run by the Patrimonio Naciónal.

**Museum de Lazaro Galdiano** This magnificent private collection (donated in 1948 to the state) is housed in the many rooms of the merchant's splendid mansion. The *objets d'art* are of numerous types – sculpture, porcelain, ceramics, clocks, coins, weaponry, scientific artefacts, tapestry and jewellery. Amongst the most highly prized small collections are the ivory carvings and enamel treasures. The extensive, valuable collection of paintings is superbly hung, with important representatives of the English School (Gainsborough, Reynolds, Lawrence); Flemish School (Hieronymus Bosch, Issenbrandt); Spanish School (El Greco, Velázquez, Zurbarán, Murillo, Goya); and the Dutch and Italian schools.

Calle de Serrano 122 (N.DE BALBOA) Open: 10 a.m.–2 p.m. Shut Mondays and during August.

**Palacio de Liria** The georgous residence of the Duchess of Alba, designed by Sabatini and Ventura Rodríguez, contains a wonderful art collection which is reputedly the richest still to be privately owned in Spain. Italian, Spanish and Dutch paintings are displayed. The artists include Fra Angélico, Perugino, Titian, Velázquez, Rembrandt and Goya.

Calle de la Princesa 20 (PLAZA DE ESPAÑA/ARGÜELLES). Open; Saturday morning by appointment only. Shut during August. Tel: 247 5302.

### Real Academia de Bellas Artes de San Fernando

Designed by José Churriguera, this building houses a great collection of Spanish art including Goya, Zurbarán, Murillo, Velázquez, El Greco, Ribera, Cano and Coello. Italian and Dutch works are also exhibited as well as religious sculpture. An excellent place to consider the work of these artists in tranquility.

Calle de Alcalá 13, (SOL). Open: Tuesday to Friday 9 a.m.–7 p.m., Saturday to Monday 9 a.m.–2 p.m.

**Museo de Cera** This museum displays an amusing series of wax figures – a match for Madame Tussaud's.

Paseo de Recoletos 41, off Plaza de Colón (COLON).

**Museo de Ciencias Naturales** For special interest far up Paseo de la Castellana, off the Plaza San Juan de la Cruz (best reached by bus). Open: winter 1 p.m.–2 p.m. and 3 p.m.–6 p.m., summer 9 a.m.–2 p.m.

**Real Monasterio de las Descalzas Reales** This convent displays a rich collection of art including El Greco, Titian and Velázquez; religious artefacts; Flemish tapestries; and sculptures. A magnificent staircase frescoed by Spanish and Italian masters leads up to the galleries beyond the cloister. The convent was founded in 1559 by Doña Juana de Austria, daughter of Charles V, for Franciscan nuns of Santa Clara, and it is still partly occupied by a closed order. A visit here is rewarding, and the display is excellent (winner of 1988 European Museum of the Year).

Plaza de las Descalzas Reales (SOL). Open: Monday to Thursday 10.30 a.m.–12.45 p.m. and 4–5.15 p.m., Friday to Sunday 10.30 a.m.–1.30 p.m. Run by the Patrimonio Nacional and shown with a guide.

**Museo del Ejercito** An exhaustive collection of army trophies and weaponry both in Europe and America.

Calle de Méndez Nuñez 1 (BANCO). Open: Tuesday to Saturday 10 a.m.–5 p.m., Sunday 10.45 a.m.–1.45 p.m. Shut Mondays.

**Museo Español de Arte Contemporaneo** This is an extensive collection of modern art and sculpture, some of which is exhibited in the surrounding gardens. Peaceful and well organized.

Avda Juan de Herrera 2 (CIUDAD UNIVERSIDAD). Open: Tuesday to Saturday 10 a.m.–6 p.m. Sunday 10 a.m.–3 p.m. Shut Mondays.

**Museo Municipal** The Churrtigueresque façade of this brick building is surprising in this architecturally impoverished area. There is an interesting exhibition of the growth of the capital using models and architects' drawings. Otherwise a relatively minor museum.

Calle de Fuencarral 78, near Glorietta de Bilbao (TRIBUNAL). Open: Tuesday to Saturday 10 a.m.–2 p.m. and 5–9 p.m., Sunday 10 a.m.–2.30 p.m. Shut Mondays.

**Museo Nacional de Artes Decorativas** A generous collection of jewellery and metalwork, glass, textile, furniture, ceramics and artesanal techniques from Spain. Well exhibited and fascinating, but with sixty-two rooms.

Calle de Montalbán 12, near Cibeles (BANCO) Open: Tuesday to Friday 10 a.m.–5 p.m., Saturday and Sunday 10 a.m.–2 p.m. Shut Mondays.

**Museo Nacional de Etnológico Antropológico** Artefacts and weaponry of primitive cultures worldwide.

Calle de Alfonso XII 68, by the Jardín Botánico (ATOCHA) Open: 10 a.m.–2 p.m. and 4 p.m.–7 p.m. Shut Sundays and Mondays.

**Museo Naval** A celebration of Lepanto, and of the discovery of America, among an exhibition of old maps, nautical instruments and model ships. The chart of Juan de la Cosa, by which Columbus sailed on his first voyage to the New World, is exhibited.

Calle de Montalbán 2, near Cibeles (BANCO) Open: Tuesday to Sunday 10.30 a.m.–1.30 p.m. Shut Mondays, rainy days and during August.

**Museo de Reproduciones Artísticas** Reproductions of the classic cast sculptures from antiquity to the Renaissance.

Avda de los Reyes Católicos 6, (CIUDAD UNIVERSIDAD) Open: Tuesday to Saturday 10 a.m.–5 p.m.

Shut Sundays, Mondays and during August.

**Museo Romantico (Romantic Museum)** A palace lushly decorated and furnished with mid-nineteenth-century paintings and furniture, clocks and *objets d'art*.

San Mateo 13, by Museo Municipal (TRIBUNAL). Open: Monday

to Friday 10 a.m.–6 p.m., Saturday and Sunday 10 a.m.–2 p.m. Shut August to mid-September.

**Museo Sorolla** Oil paintings and frescos of the artist displayed in his house. These are supplemented by other works. Paseo General Martínez Campos 37, near Plaza Emilio Castelar off Paseo de la Castellana (R. DARIO). Open: Tuesday to Sunday 10 a.m.–2 p.m. Shut Mondays and during August.

**Museo Taurino** An unusual and interesting museum for anyone with a curiosity about the development of bullfighting. Beside the magnificent bullring, Plaza de Toros de las Ventas (VENTAS). Open: 10 a.m.–2 p.m. Shut Mondays.

**Planitarium** A spectacular building, with superb representations of space. South-east of Atocha, Park Tierno Galván (MENDEZ ALVARO). Showings: Saturday and Sunday 11.30 a.m., 1 p.m., 5 p.m., 6.30 p.m., 8 p.m., Monday and Friday morning and 5.30 p.m., 7 p.m.

**Royal Tapestry Factory** A small museum with a collection of eighteenth and nineteenth-century tapestries and drawings. The factory still works, and the carpet and tapestry production can be watched. Calle de Fuenterrabía 2, (MENÉNDEZ PELAYO). Open: Monday to Friday 9.30 a.m.–12.30 p.m. Shut Saturdays and Sundays and during August.

**Temple of Debod** a gift from the Egyptian president, the 1BC Egyptian temple stands in this lawned park, with a fountain-sprayed pool at each end. It was moved stone by stone from its position in the Nile valley, now flooded by the Aswan dam. It is small inside, with beautiful columns and clear hieroglyphics. Parque de Rosales, the southern tip of Parque del Oueste (PLAZA DE ESPAÑA). Open: Monday to Saturday 10 a.m.–1 p.m. and 5–8 p.m., Sunday 10 a.m.–3 p.m.

**Modern Commercial City Area** A number of highly acclaimed modern buildings have been designed here. Architects of special note are Rafael Moneo, Saenz de Oiza, Garcia de Paredes, de la Sota, J.A.Coderch and E.Torroja.

Along the Paseo de la Castellana, commercial buildings of particular note are Banco de Bilbao (Saenz de Oiza), Bankinter (Moneo), Bankunion (Corrales y Molezun), others include the buildings of Banca Catalana/Occidental (small glass block) and Banco Adriática. A cluster of contemporary buildings around

**Torres Blancas** is extraordinary set of high-rise residential blocks built to a design of curving lines and circles (Saenz de Oiza) Avda América (AMÉRICA); Girasol, built by Coderch in 1986, in Calle de Lagasca, is a building with remarkable angular apartments (SERRANO). The television tower Torre España, built in 1982 for the World Cup, is spectacular (O'DONNELL).

NUEVOS MINISTRIOS is notable. Torre Picasso, by Minoru Yamashki, is the tallest tower in Spain (Plaza Picasso). The Congress and Exhibition Hall, by Pintado Riba, has a facade decorated by a mural of Miró; the huge twenty-hectare commercial complex of Azca was built in 1967 and designed by Antonio Perpino.

**Walking in the Historic City** Madrid is a relatively compact city, and it is most rewarding to explore the old area on foot. Its many parks and cafes give ample refreshment to visitors. The straight elegant streets of the Ensanche and the area west of Plaza de Colón are more tiring to walk, without the delights of variety in ambience and surroundings that the older areas offer.

If time is short, contrasting flavours of the city can be tasted by walking a little around the small streets of SOL in the old city (including the Plaza Santa Ana with its tapas bars, and the Plaza Mayor); or by visiting the great Castellana boulevard near the Plaza de la Cibeles (with its traditional-style cafés) whose fountains and fine buildings illustrate the cosmopolitan splendour of the city, or even simply by taking a little fresh air in one of the beautiful parks.

**Antique shops along Calle del Prado can offer some surprising bargains**

The old part of the city, dotted with fine buildings, attractive squares and museums, is made up of several colourful communities and edged with the magnificent views and gardens of the Royal Palace to its west. To the east around the Prado museum, are the lovely botanic gardens and Retiro park. It is a substantial area, much of which clothes a hillside, and displays the usual characteristics of old cities – distinct districts with streets that are often narrow and cobbled; an abundance of small old-fashioned shops; dominating churches; and much poor housing. The main thoroughfares, Calle Mayor and Calle de Arenal are always full of people, and the streets leading to the popular social areas are lively. The back ways potter without much interruption.

**Puerta de Sol** Puerto del Sol is the centre of the area, always animated and busy, although no longer with many amusing bars. Although the roar of traffic and lack of cafés makes the square rather uncomfortable, it is possible to sit by one of the fountains and see an astonishing variety of people walk by. The old-fashioned Hotel Plaza looks over the square and opposite is the bakery and tearoom of La Mallorquina whose delicious *neopolitanas* (custard pastries) command regular queues in the late afternoon. The 'Kilometre 0' plaque (measurement point for the country's roads), sits on the portal of the massive eighteenth-century government building which was the central Post Office. At the entrance to the pedestrian streets is the delightful symbol of Madrid – the bear eating from a strawberry tree.

Radiating from Puerta del Sol are many of the thoroughfares of the old city, and numerous small streets, e.g.: Carrera de San Jerónimo to the Prado and towards Santa Ana • Calle de Alcalá to Plaza de la Cibeles • Calle de Carmen and Calle Montera to Gran Via (continuing west to Plaza de España or east to Plaza de la Cibeles) • Calle del Arenal to Plaza de Oriente and Royal Palace • Calle Mayor via Plaza Mayor to Cathedral de la Almudena and the royal palace area (also leading near to Basílica de San Francisco).

**East and South from Puerta del Sol** Carrera de San Jerónimo leads to the Prado Museum, and indirectly to Plaza Santa Ana, passing two special delicatessens – a splendid Museo de Jamón, hung with hundreds of dried hams, with a central bar and a shop counter to serve its speciality to the throngs who step in, and the

**Fish is superb in Madrid, flown in daily from the coasts**

rather beautiful old-fashioned delicatessen, Llardy's, next door, where delicate pastries or consommé can be taken (or a sophisticated meal upstairs). The left turn up Calle del Príncipe meets Plaza Santa Ana. At night the area bursts with life; during the day it is quiet.

Walking down towards the Prado, the quiet little streets offer a few old shops, and antiques are sold along Calle del Prado. The imposing nineteenth-century classical Palacio de las Cortes Españolas (the Spanish parliament) sits to the left, guarded by lions cast from the melted iron of Moroccan Canons.

Plaza Santa Ana, home of Madrid's classic Teatre Español and focus of many Madrileños in the evening, is also reached through the knot of thin streets south-east of Puerta del Sol. While the streets around Santa Ana are full of tapas bars and cafés, varying from highly fashionable excellence to lesser-quality goods, the narrow ways leading here from Puerta del Sol are generally rather squalid, with many prostitutes, cheap bars and quantities of pension signs.

**North-East from Puerta del Sol** Calle de Alcalá, leading directly to Plaza de la Cibeles, is interesting for its grandiose views and for the great nineteenth-century cosmopolitan buildings that

**Plaza Mayor on a Sunday morning**

61

line it. The excellent fine art museum of the Academia de San Fernando is found here (*see* page 56).

### North from Puerta del Sol

The pedestrian streets north of Puerta del Sol, full of shoe shops, boutiques, cafés and the big department stores, lead up to Gran Via – a main street for traffic, banks, travel agents and cinemas (also the Grassy jewellery shop). Off Calle de Preciados (whose curved tail, leading to Plaza Santo Domingo, houses a number of good fish restaurants) at Plaza Callao, is Calle de Bordadores which leads to the beautiful convent of the Descalzas Reales (*see* page 56).

From the pedestrian Calle Montera, across the Gran Via, is the splendid Telephone Exchange, and the arterial road Calle de Fuencarral cuts northwards to arrive in the Malasaña district of the city. As the Gran Via runs into Calle de Alcalá, there are impressive views towards the great fountain of Cibeles and the more modern city beyond.

### West from Puerta del Sol

Calle de Arenal, full of shops, bars and people, joins directly from Puerta del Sol, passing the quiet church of San Ginés on the left. (Its Capilla del Cristo has a small collection of paintings by El Greco). Plaza Isabel II, by the theatre, where the OPERA metro disgorges, is a popular meeting area. Bars and restaurants surround the square. Café del Oriente is particularly graceful, overlooking the Plaza del Oriente (open late into the night and with a sophisticated restaurant), and there are fashionable Tascas along the northern side of the theatre.

The Plaza de Oriente is a lovely garden of grass and trees interspersed with the statues of kings.

The Teatre del Ópera (being converted for opera performance rather than concerts) sits behind. In front is the magnificent royal palace, and to the north is the Convento de la Encarnación.

West from Sol along Calle Mayor is the Plaza Mayor near which are a number of interesting monuments, picturesque streets and lively eating places.

### Plaza Mayor

The Plaza is a splendid arcaded renaissance square. Very popular with tourists, it attracts relatively few Madrileños except when live band concerts are given here in the spring, and when the stamp fair is held here on Sunday mornings.

Tapas bars, little restaurants, souvenir shops, the famous little hat shops and a tourist office line the arcades. In the steep curve

**Amongst the statues** of the gardens is reputedly the finest in Madrid – that of the equestrian Philip IV, designed from a painting of Velázquez.

The symmetrical square of Plaza Mayor was originally built for the Hapsburg Philip III, and remodelled in the eighteenth-century by Juan de Villanueva. It was the scene of coronations, royal weddings, canonizations, an *auto-da-fé* and bullfights until the end of last century.

beneath the far south-west side of the Plaza (diagonally across from Puerta del Sol), are the tourist attractions of the 'Cuevas' (traditional bars under the arcades), and the favourite restaurants of Botín, Cuchi and Casa Paco (*see* pages 83–84).

Plaza Mayor is a second centre point for thoroughfares: Calle de Atocha to the tip of the Botanic Gardens (by the Prado) and Atocha Station • Calle de Toledo, leading towards Plaza de Cascorro and the Rastro area • Calle Cava Baja, leading by curves to the Basílica of San Francisco • Calle Mayor, continuing towards the cathedral of the Royal Palace area.

### South-East from Plaza Mayor

Calle Atocha leads south-east from Plaza Mayor directly to the splendid railway station of Atocha (on the corner of the Botanic Gardens), passing the area of Santa Ana. It is an amusing busy street of bars, food markets and junk shops. The triangle between Calle Atocha and Calle de Toledo (south from the Plaza) includes the Plaza Tirso de Molina and a sprinkling of delightful well-known little bars.

### South from Plaza Mayor

The streets of Rastro market are directly south of the Plaza, reached via Calle de Toledo. The seventeenth-century cathedral of San Isidro, in which rests the body of the city's patron saint, is on Calle de Toledo near the Plaza. It is a heavy, dark building with an imposing façade, built originally as a Jesuit church.

Straight on from the cathedral is the Plaza de Cascorro which is the head of the extensive Sunday morning Rastro market whose stalls fill the length and surroundings of Calle Ribera de Curtidores (*see* page 95).

Meanwhile, Calle de Toledo curves down from the cathedral to the Glorietta Puerta de Toledo – a triumphal arch built in 1827 to commemorate victory over Napoleon – forming a definite border to the community of La Latina to its west. A tremendous two-levelled food market opens by this thoroughfare, and the community is penetrated by several little streets which lead easily to the magnificent circular Basílica de San Francisco (*see* page 52).

### South-West of Plaza Mayor

The curve of Calle Cava Baja leads to the Basílica de San Francisco through the area of La Latina. Within the small triangle of the Plaza Mayor, San Francisco and the Cathedral de la Almudena by the Royal Palace, is the pretty Plaza de la Paja. The triangle is packed with curving

**The Sunday coin market**

**Market stall, Rastro**

streets and old churches. Here, in the oldest part of Madrid, are the old Mudéjar Torre de Lujanes, the Plateresque façade of Casa Cisneros and the Ayuntamiento building (off the Calle Mayor towards Plaza Cordón); the church of San Andrés (off the Plaza de la Paja) with an old baroque chapel to San Isidro; San Pedro el Viejo (Calle del Nuncio), originally fourteenth-century, built on Mosque foundations graced with a Mudéjar tower; across from which is the ornate Capella del Obispo (Bishop's chapel) with its superb sixteenth-century reredos.

**West from Plaza Mayor** The busy Calle de Bailén crosses the end of Calle Mayor and leads from the Basílica of San Francisco, above the children's playground of Vistillas park, to the great buildings of the Royal Palace, (which take up practically the entire length of the road). At the beginning of its viaduct passage over Calle de Segovia is a delightful spot for refreshment – overlooking the unending dustry green-spotted Casa de Campo park (*see* page 68) across the Manzanares. The view, supplemented by the lush greenery of the palace gardens, gives a glorious impression of the closeness of countryside to the capital.

Just by the end of the Calle Mayor, overlooking the palace gardens, is the skeletal Cathedral de la Almudena, an almost luminously white gothic and neo-classical structure, still without a roof, which was begun over a century ago and will probably never be finished.

**North of Gran Via** The streets north of Gran Via, again with distinct areas, have less charm for the visitor on foot. Several roads cut through from Gran Via to the parallel road from Plaza de Colón to the Parque del Oeste: Calle de Fuencarral to Paseo de Recoletos • Calle de San Bernardo to Calle de Fuencarral • Calle de la Princesa to the Parque del Oeste.

**West of Paseo de Recoletos** Behind the Wax Museum (*see* page 56) is a small attractive area of justice courts and the splendid baroque church of Santa Bárbara (also known as Las Salesas Reales). Its façade is decorated with sculptures and the mighty dome is frescoed by the González Velázquez brothers. The tomb of Ferdinand VI, designed by Sabatini and worked by Gutiérrez, rests within. West of the green Plaza de Alonso Martínez (around which are two good *cervecerías* (beer bars), is the Romantic Museum and the Municipal Museum (*see* page 57). The

**Modern architecture**

local centre of this little area is the Plaza de Chueca, surrounded by narrow streets supporting a number of restaurants. Good bars are also found, particularly in Calle de Augusto Figueros. Around Plaza de Alonso Martínez and near the museums are many night clubs around which people throng at night.

**West of Calle de Fuencarral** Plaza Dos de Mayo is the social centre of the area west of Calle de Fuencarral – an unremarkable quiet and impoverished residential area by day and the heart of the infamous Malasaña at night. Calle de San Vincente, just off the Plaza, is the haunt of hundreds of Madrid's youth, who frequent the quantities of late-night bars along the street. Although very animated at night, the area is notorious for abuse of drugs, and thus for street crimes. On Glorietta de Bilbao, crowning the area, is the attractive and fashionable Café Commercial, and nearby are other good bars.

**North of Palacio Real** Towards the beautiful Parque del Oeste (*see* page 69) from Malasaña the streets become wealthier and less local in ambience. Plaza de España is surrounded by towering buildings (the Tourist Office is located here) and has pleasant fountains and trees. A monument to Cervantes stands in the centre.

Calle de la Princesa, running northwards from Plaza de España, is lined with travel agencies, quality food shops and delicatessens. Calle de Alberto Aguilera, bordering the area to the north, is particularly rich in shops, and on the corner is another branch of the ubiquitous El Corte Inglés department store. In the streets fanning out towards the park are many good restaurants and, close to Plaza de España, the wonderful Cerralbo villa. Paseo del Pinto Rosales, running beside the gardens, is pleasant, with terraces of cafés (although these are very quiet in winter).

**West of Paseo de la Castellana** This large area is not recommended for walking – being repetitive, residential and with very few refreshment places. Government buildings and embassies are hidden amongst the shady quiet roads, and some of the best (and most expensive) cooking in the city is found in the secluded restaurants.

Much of the university was destroyed during the civil war when it provided the headquarters and battle ground for the Nationalists.

The complex of buildings is modern and unspectacular although its Contemporary Art Museum and Museum of the Americas are interesting (*see* page 56). Below is the northern block of the Parque del Oeste which is tranquil and very well tended. At the top of Calle de la Princesa is the popular student gathering area of Argüelles.

**South-East of the Plaza de la Cibeles** It is delightful to walk here. This is one of the most pleasant areas of Madrid – with the Prado, the Botanic Gardens and the Parque del Retiro (*see* page 53). It is tranquil, quiet, unmolested by much traffic and bathed in greenery of the promenades and parks.

The fountain of Cibeles has magnificent surroundings. To the north-west is the gardened Palacio de Buenavista (built for the Duke of Alba in 1769 and now Ministry of the Army); to the north-east is a second palace (that of Linares – probably to become a museum); to the south-west is the Banco de España (under which rest the tangible gold reserves of Spain); and to the south-east is the well-named Palacio de Comunicacións, built to immense domed proportions in 1918 and well worth visiting.

Just along the noisy Calle de Alcalá at the Plaza de la Independencia is the Puerta de Alcalá, built by Sabatini for Charles III, standing at an entrance to the Parque del Retiro. The few road running south of these two plazas are quiet, elegantly clad, and rich with mueums. The leafy central part of the Paseo del Prado, running south from Cibeles, is filled with welcoming terraced cafés.

The church of San Jerónimo el Real stands proudly, high behind the Prado museum in a spacious setting although its interior is somewhat disapointing, much restored since its foundation in 1505 by the Catholic monarchs.

At the foot of the Botanic Gardens (*see* page 68) is Calle Cuesta Claudio Moyano with numerous stalls offering second-hand books of all sorts. The stalls are always here, but they are most busy on Sunday mornings. Past the splendid Ministry of Agriculture, at the base of Calle Atocha (running straight down from Plaza Mayor) is the iron railway station built by Eiffel. Opposite is the Centro de Arte Reina Sofía (*see* page 54). Here, on the Ronda de Atocha, are bars and hotels catering for tired backpacking tourists.

**North-East of Plaza de la Cibeles** This is a huge gridded area mostly built in the second half of last century. Walking here is tiring, but the district of Salamanca is renowned for the quantity, sophistication and style of its boutiques.

The Paseo north of Cibeles, called Recoletos, is here. It has famous old cafés like Café Gijón and Café León on its west side. These are worth visiting in mid-afternoon for a quiet drink in a traditional atmosphere, or early evening to be among fashionable madrileños. On the opposite side is the great National Library. Behind is the excellent archaeological museum and next door is one of the fine old palaces that used to line the street (once owned by the Marquis of Salamanca but now owned by Banco Hipotecario). Continuing north, the great road is lined with presigious office buildings and embassies – easier to look at from a bus than by foot.

The Plaza del Descubrimiento is beside Plaza de Colón. There is an eye-catching monument in honour of Columbus underneath which is the main bus terminal to the airport and Madrid's new cultural centre. Modern theatre and art exhibitions are presented here. Walking underneath is made an experience by the unusual design of the fountain. Above the Plaza are the high Torres de Jerez. The unusual bottle museum of Chicote, historic mixer of cocktails, is here.

The elegant shopping area of Salamanca is bordered by Calle de Goya (running eastwards) and Calle de Serrano (running northwards). Both are lined with shops – Serrano being particularly famous for its fashion boutiques (although suffering from traffic noise). The inner crossing roads reaching north to Calle de Juan Bravo and east to Calle del Conde del Peñalver are spotted with boutiques, good restaurants, offices and hotels. Beneath the overpass, as Juan Bravo crosses the Paseo de la Castellana, is an area where several contemporary sculptures are exhibited permanently, representing the works of the open-air sculpture museum (works by Chilida, Serrano, Sempeere, Martí). At the top of Calle Serrano is the important and beautifully laid-out museum of Lázaro Galdiano and, further up the Paseo Castellana, is the Science Museum (*see* page 55).

**North end of Paseo de la Castellana** This is a comfortable area to walk. Away from the busy traffic lanes of the Castellana it is quiet, but the scale of the crisp office blocks and huge luxurious hotels is really too large for an explorer on foot.

**Parks** The gardens of Madrid are marvellous. There are six of particular note: the extensive Parque del Retiro, the Jardín

Botánico nearby, the Campo del Moro beneath the Royal Palace, the Parque del Oeste stretching from Plaza de España right up to the University, the park of La Fuente del Berro, and finally the vast scrub and wooded area of the Casa del Campo in which is the Zoo and an amusement park.

**Campo del Moro** Campo del Moro is a most graceful park of exotic trees and lawns, laid out in front of the magnificent façade of the Royal Palace. It is often closed to the public. Beside is the formal pattern of box hedges in the garden of Sabatini, entered off Calle de Bailén between the palace and Plaza de Éspaña. It was designed in 1933 and is peaceful, with few people and wonderful views.

**Jardín Botánico** The Botanic Gardin, by the Prado museum, was laid out by order of Charles III in 1781 specifically for scientific study. The range of plants, shrubs and trees is extensive, and each individual is labelled. Open every day until 8 p.m. or dusk, the garden is pretty, refreshing and fascinating to any who are interested in plants.

**Parque del Casa de Campo** Casa de Campo park is unlike the city parks. Originaly a royal hunting area, it was reforested in 1559 by Philip II, and is now a huge dusty park dotted with trees. If approached by cable car, superb views of the royal palace and the hill-city can be caught. This is a favourite family excursion on weekends, when many take picnics to enjoy in the extensive privacy of the rolling banks. The park is wilder, drier and less cultivated than the others, with little greenery apart from the oak and pine trees.

The metro (EL LAGO, BATAN) and a city bus (33) from Plaza Isabel II (by OPERA) will also arrive in the park. A swimming-

**Parque del Retiro**

pool, a lake with boats for hire, and tennis courts are also provided here. The Zoo and an Amusement park are here, the Zoo (BATAN) opening from 10 a.m.–dusk, and the Amusement park (BATAN) opening Monday to Wednesday 6 p.m.–1 a.m., Thursday to Saturday 6 p.m.–4 a.m., Sunday 12 p.m.–1 a.m.

**Parque de la Fuente del Berro** Parque de la Fuente del Berro lies south of the bullring, Ventas de Toros. Cool, tranquil and beautifully laid out, it is little known, being away from the centre. It has delightful paths, and lovely fountains.

**Parque del Oeste** Just beyond Plaza de España is the Parque del Oeste, the first part of which is called La Rosaleda. Within stands the Eqyptian Temple of Debod. This long stretch of green curves down the steep bank that reaches almost to the Manzanares River, with chestnut and elm trees, a lovely rose garden (a rose show is held in the park in the spring) and, in the northern part, a series of delightful winding paths which transport the wanderer far from the city. The views across the river are unimpaired. Just below is the Hermitage of San Antonio, in which the frescos of Goya are treasured. From half-way along this park, near the childrens' playground opposite the corner of Calle Marqués de Urquijo, is a teleferique link with the park on the opposite bank of the river, the Parque del Casa de Campo.

The monument to Alfonso XII

**Parque del Retiro** Parque del Retiro is a huge green area of trees, statues, winding paths, formal grounds (including a most beautiful rose garden to the south), lawns and small lakes. The gardens surrounded a monastery in the time of Philip II and formed the surrounding of a palace of Philip IV (burnt in the mid-eighteenth-century). The park is enclosed by a high iron balustrade with magnificent entrances. The gate from Calle Alfonso XII leads into an avenue of flowers and trees in which are placed statues of Spanish kings from the same original set as those in the Plaza de Oriente. The park is popular from early afternoon until dark, and throughout the weekends when families and friends wander through, enjoying the rowing boats on the lake (presided over by the monumental 1922 tribute to King Alfonso XII) or just strolling. Two buildings, the Crystal Palace (a beautiful iron and glass structure) and the Palacio de Velázquez (whose decorative brickwork was designed by Daniel Zuologa), are within the park boundaries – both housing exhibitions.

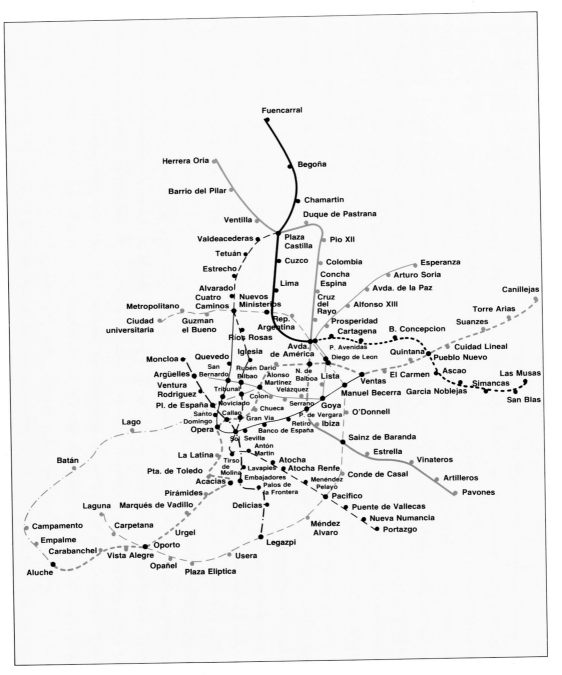

## Tourist Office

| | |
|---|---|
| Calle Duque de Medinaceli 2 | 429 4951 |
| Torre de Madrid, Plaza de España | 241 2325 |
| Plaza Mayor 3 | 266 5477 |
| Aeropuerto Barajas | 205 8656 |
| Estación Chamartin | 315 9976 |
| Institute of Young People (exchange, tourism, youth hostel network), José Ortega y Gasset, 71 | 401 1300 |
| Student Card Information, as above; | |

## Embassy

| | |
|---|---|
| USA, Calle de Serrano 75 | 577 4000 |
| UK, Calle Fernando el Santo 16 | 419 1528 |
| Ireland, Calle de Claudio Coello 73 | 276 3500 |
| Australia, (and New Zealand) PSO Castellana 143 | 279 8501 |
| Canada, Calle Nuñez de Bilboa 35 | 431 4300 |

**Madrid Exchange code** is: 91

## Transport - Urban:

| | |
|---|---|
| Metro – runs 6–1.30 a.m. | 435 2266 |
| Bus – runs 6–12 p.m. | 401 9900 |

Information: Puerta del Sol; Plaza del Callao; Plaza de la Cibeles
Metro and bus tickets: *Bono* – 10 journeys saver
Metro exclusive: *Metrotur* – 3- or 5-day ticket
Taxis – 1,600 in the city – 40pts per km.
100pts standard supplement, 150pts airport,
50pts late night · · · · · · · · · · · 247 8200/445 9008

## Transport - Distance:

| | |
|---|---|
| Left luggage (*Consigna*): | Airport bus terminal, Plaza de Colón |
| | Estación Sur de Autobuses, Canarias 17 |
| | RENFE stations |
| Lost Property (*Objetos Perdidos*), Plaza de Legazpi 7 | 588 4346 |
| RENFE (national train network) Information | 733 300/429 0202 |
| Reservation | 501 3333 |
| Renfe Stations: | Chamartin, for north and east Spain |
| | Atocha, for Andalucía and Portugal |
| | Príncipe Pio, for Galicia and Salamanca |
| Tickets for tourists: | *Tarjeta Turística* (general savings) |
| | *Tarjeta Joven* (young savings) |
| | *Tarjeta Dorado* (elderly savings) |
| | *Días Azules*: cheap days |

Tourist trains to various major cities (including guide in cities)

Excursions including lodging and food:

> *Doncel de Sigüenza* (through Guadalajara):
> Sundays
> *Al Andalus* (to the south): 4–5 day trips
> *Ciudad de Cáceres* (through Extremadura):
> September, October, November
> *Plaza Mayor de Salamanca*

Many different companies run coaches to the nearby cities and towns. Information from Tourist Office.

| | |
|---|---|
| Bus: | Estación Sur, Calle de Canarias 17 |
| | (PALOS DE LA FRONTERA)  468 4220 |
| | Estación Norte, Paseo de la Florida 11 (NORTE) |
| General routes: | Toledo: Estación Sur – every hour at least |
| | Aranjuez: Estacíon Sur – hourly |
| | Guadalajara/Alcalá: from Avda de America 18 – every 15 mins |
| | Ávila: Estación Norte – twice daily |
| | La Granja: Calle Monteleón 31 |
| | (SAN BERNARDO) – once daily |
| | Salamanca: Plaza Conde de Casal 6 – every 2 hours |
| | Cuenca: Plaza Conde de Casal 6 – every 2 hours |
| | Segovia: Estacíon Norte – every 3 hours |
| | El Escorail, Isaac Peral 10 (MONCLOA) – hourly  243 3645 |

## Air

| | |
|---|---|
| Airport: | Aeropuerto Barajas  205 4372 |
| | Information  411 2545 |
| | (from Colón 401 9900) |
| Airport by Bus: | from Plaza del Descubrimiento every 30 minutes. |
| Airport information: | 231 4436/205 4372 |
| Iberia Office: | Calle de Velázquez 130  261 9100 |
| | Information (24 hours)  411 2545 |
| | Reservations  411 2011 |
| British Airways: | Calle de Serrano 60  431 7575 |
| AER Lingus: | Edificio España, Grupo |
| | Ascensures 3,10  241 4216 |

| TWA: | Planta 2 | 410 6012 |
| Pan American: | Gran Via 88 | 241 4200/248 8535 |

### Amusements

| Zoo de la Casa del Campo (BATAN) | |
| Open: 10 a.m.–dusk | 711 9950 |
| Amusement Park, Casa del Campo (BATAN) | 463 2900 |

Open: Monday to Wednesday 6 p.m.–1 a.m., Thursday to Saturday 6 p.m.–4 a.m., Sunday 12 p.m.–1 a.m.

| Aquarium, Maestro Vitorio | 8 231 8172 |

Open: 12–2 p.m. and 5–8.30 p.m.

| Municipal Sports Institute | 463 5498 |
| Swimming pools: Bravo Murillo 133 | 233 5924 |
| Toledo 1 (LA LATINA) | 265 7619 |
| Icerink: 'Diamond's', Los Yébenes 38 | 719 2895 |

Open: Tuesday to Friday 8.30–10.30 p.m., Saturday and Sunday 5.30–10.30 p.m.

Cuidad Deportiva del Real Madrid, Paseo de la Castellana 259

215 0046

Open: every day 11 a.m.–1.45 p.m. and 5–11.30 p.m.

Roller skating: Rolling Disco, Estación Chamartin    315 3000

Open: everyday 4.30–10.30 p.m. (Saturday and Sunday until 12 a.m.

### Events

Hipodromo de la Zarzuela, ctra de la Coruña (NIV) 7km    207 0140 (inaugurated 1941 – part of National Heritage) bus from MONCLOA.

| Seasons: | spring: February to June |
| | autumn: September to December |

Meetings: Saturday and Sunday, fiestas. Start 11.30 a.m./3.30 p.m., variable

Most important stakes:

spring 27th day – Grand Premio
autumn 6th day – Memorial Duque de Toledo
Information        207 0141/207 9895

Plaza de Toros de las Ventas, Alcalá 237,(VENTAS)    246 2200 fights Sunday p.m. and some Thursdays (Main season: April–September)

Football: Real Madrid: Estadio Santiago Bernabeu, Paseo de la Castellana 104 (every fortnight)    250 0600 or Estadio Vicente Caldrón,

Vigen del Puerto 67,    266 4707

**The Royal Palace**

73

### Sports

Main Madrid Sports Club: Real Club de la Puerta de Hierro,
Avda Miraflores 28035, 216 1745
Golf: 11 courses in the region Fed: Capitán Haya 9–8,
455 2682/455 2757
Assoc Española: Real Club Puerta de Hierro
Main club of Madrid: Club de Campo Vilkla de Madrid,
Ctra Castilla 28040, 207 0395
Most prestigious club: Herreria Club de Golf, San Lorenzo del
Escorial, 890 5111
Polo: Real Club Hierro (May, June October)
Fed. Assoc. Comandante Zorita 13, 233 7569
Tennis: Cuarta 24 (Cuidad Jardín), 259 0977
Ski: Nearby stations: La Pinilla, Valdesquí, Navacerrada, Fed.
Española de Deportes Invernales, Calle de Claudio Coello 32,
275 8943/275 0397
Hunting: Fed. Española de Caza: Avda Reina Victoria 72–1,
253 9017/253 8867
(also for information about hunting tourism and safari), Licences:
Calle de Jorge Juan 39, 435 5121
Fishing: ICONA ( Fed. of Nature Conservation) Avda Gran Via de
San Francisco 35–41, 266 8200/266 8400.
Licences: Calle de Jorge Juan 39, 435 5121
Pelota: Fe. Española de Pelota, Los Madrazo 11–5, 232 3879
Mounting climbing: Calle de Alberto Aguilera 3, 445 1381
Automobile racing: Fed. Española de Automovilismo,
Avda de Menéndez y Pelayo 67, 273 5600
Flying: Real Aero Club de España, Calle de San Jerónimo 15,
429 8534

Horses: Hipodrome (bus from MONCLOA). Real Sociedad de
Fomento de la Cria Caballar de España 207 0141

### Riding Outside Madrid

*Rutas a Caballo*, Augustina de Aragón 14, 435 5891
(Madrid, Segovia, Cadiz, etc.).
*Al-Mansur*, Glorietta Puente de Segovia 3–8, (Extremadura) 402 1187
*Caminos a Caballo*, Calle Duque de Liria 3, 242 3125
(Gredos, Guadarrama Sierras).
*Caballo Tours*, Calle de Covarrubias 26, (Gredos Sierras and Tietar
Valley). 445 6424

74

## Culture

Ticket Agency: *Localidades Galicia* Plaza del Carmen 1 (near SOL),
531 2732/531 9131.
Information on what's on: monthly leaflet from Tourist Office.
*Guía del Ocio* (out on Thursdays); film, theatre, restaurants.
Consejería de Cultura de la Comnunidad Autónoma de Madrid
457 9882

## Venues

General season for performance of orchestral music: October to
May. Auditorio Nacional de Música, Calle Príncipe de Vergara
136, (CRUZ DE RAYO) concerts: 7.30 and 10.30 p.m. 337 0100
Teatro Monumental de Madrid, Calle de Atocha 65 (ANTON
MARTIN), 429 1281. Fundación Juan March, Calle de Castelló 77
(NUÑEZ DE BALBOA), 435 4240.
Mid-day chamber music concerts: Monday mid-morning
Saturday. Teatro Real, Plaza Isabel II 247 1405: Contemporary
and classical (Contemporary Music Foundation 247 3573).
Exhibitions: Café Libertad 8, (CHUECA) 532 1150. Centro de Arte
Reina Sofia, Calle de Santa Isabel 52 (ATOCHA) 467 5062. Palacio
de Velázquez, Parque de Retiro 273 5245. Palacio de Cristal,
Parque de Retiro.

## Cultural Festivals

January to June:     Opera and Zarzuela season – Teatro Lírico
Nacional de la Zarzuela (Information and tickets Jovellanos
429 8216)
March:     International Theatre Festival of Madrid
(1 month – 16 productions)     221 1734
International Festival of Imaginary and Science Fiction Films
(IMAGFIC)
April:     *Cumbre Flamenca* - Flamenco – (10 days)
April to May:     *Muestra de Danza* - Contemporary dance
448 1000
June to September: *Madrid de Verano* – programme of music, film
theatre, often performed outside in Parque de Retiro and Temple
of Debod, Plaza Felipe II, etc.     247 2233
September:     Festival de Otoño (autumn) – arts, music,
theatre, dance     457 9882
September
to December:     Festival for young people – theatre,
music, film (week)

| November: | Internacional Jazz Festival (20 days) | 232 7190 |

**Fiestas**

| February: | Carnival |
| May: | Fiesta de San Isidro – patron saint of Madrid: town in celebration; superb bullfights and street parties. |
| August: | Fiesta of San Lorenzo; San Cayetano; la Paloma |

**Fairs**

| January: | Iberjoya – National Jewellery and Metalwork |
| February: | Fitur – International Tourism |
| | Arco – International Contemporary Art |
| March: | Ibermoda – Fashion (2 fairs) |
| | Expo-ocio – Leisure Time |
| April: | Expomúsica – instruments, contemporary systems |
| May: | Book Fair, Second-hand Book Fair |
| | Finart – International Crafts Fair |
| June: | Book Fair |
| October: | Ibermoda – Fashion, Iberpiel-Marroquinería – Spanish and Morrocan Leatherwork |
| November: | Feriarte – Antiques |

Guided tours round Madrid and nearby places of interest: *Conozcamos Madrid*: book from Tourist Office. Pullmantur excursions: Plaza de Oriente 8, 241 1805 (booking at most travel agents).

**Hotels** Madrid has a great number of hotels from the most luxurious to the simplest. Only a few have been selected here, and it is necessary to book in advance.

**Outstanding** *The Ritz* Plaza de la Lealtad 5, Tel: 221 2857. Built in 1910, this is one of the most elegant, luxurious hotels in the world, with suites of magnificent splendour dressed with antiques. The dining-room is beautiful, bound in marble and gold, lit by great chandeliers. The gardens are exclusive and delightful. Of the utmost refinement.

159 rooms d&b 59000 (AE DC MC V) restaurant. A fasionable place for a summer cocktail, and of the highest reputation for its Sunday morning brunch.

*Villa Magna* Paseo de la Castellana 22, Tel: 261 4990. An exclusive modern hotel of the highest luxury and elegance.
194 rooms d&b 42000 (AE DC MC V) Restaurant.

**Category 1** *The Palace* Plaza Cortes 7, Tel: 429 7551. A great hotel opposite the Ritz and the Prado, with elegant rooms and an old-fashioned ostentation.
158 rooms d&b 21500 (AE DC MC V).

*The Wellington* Calle de Velázquez 8, Tel: 275 4400. Beloved of. the bullfighting fraternity both historically and today. A diginified hotel, beside the Parque del Retiro. Good flamenco is performed at the Zambra club here, Tel: 435 5164.
231 rooms d&b 19800 (AE DC MC V).

*The Miguel Angel* Calle de Miguel Angel 31, Tel: 442 0200. Very deluxe and elegant while managing to retain a somewhat traditional ambience as well. Just off the central Paseo de la Castellana, by Plaza Emilio Castelar.
304 rooms d&b 23200 (AE DC MC V).

*Tryp Palcio* Paseo de la Castellana 57, Tel: 442 5100. The leading Tryp hotel, northern end of Castellana, regal.
182 rooms d&b 19150 (AE DC MC V).

*Monte Real* Arroyo Fresno 17, Tel: 216 2140. North-west of the city, beyond the university city, 1km from the famous Puerta de Hierro golf club, in tranquil splendour and elegance away from city bustle. Surrounded by beautiful gardens.
77 rooms d&b 22000 (AE DC MC V).

**Category 2** *Alcalá* Calle de Alcalá 66, Tel: 435 1060 . Very comfortable, by the famous shopping area of Salamanca and close to the Parque del Retiro.
153 rooms d&b 11500 (AE DC MC V).

*Plaza* Plaza de España, Tel: 247 1200. In one of the two tall towers on the Plaza, close to the Royal Palace, with views which stretch right across the city and over to the extensive Casa del Campo park westwards. Has a dramatic roof-top pool.
306 rooms d&b 14580 (AE DC MC V).

*Pullman Calatrava* Calle de Tutor 1, Tel: 241 9880. Close to the Parque del Oeste and Plaza de España, quiet and modern.
99 rooms d&b 11650 (AE DC MC V).

**Category 3** *Liabeny* Calle de la Salud 3, Tel: 232 5306. In a quiet area between Puerta del Sol and Gran Via (on Plaza

**Building on the corner of Plaza España, Madrid**

Carmen), comfortable and convenient.

209 rooms d&b 9100 (AE V).

*Regina* Calle de Alcalá 19, Tel: 521 4725. Older elegance near Plaza Sol. 142 rooms d&b 7100 (AE DC MC V).

*Emperador* Gran Via 53, Tel: 247 2800. One of the most elegant of the hotels in the older part of Madrid, with a roof-top pool. The terrace affords good views across the old city and the Ensanche.

232 rooms d&b 11000 (AE DC MC V).

*Tryp Fenix* Calle de Hermosilla 2, Tel: 431 6700. A new hotel with a very traditional decor of gilt mirrors and polished wood doors.

216 rooms d&b 17300 (AE MC DC V).

*Gran Hotel Velázquez* Calle de Velázquez 62, Tel: 275 2800. Very pleasant traditional Spanish hotel, close to the Paseo de la Castellana and to the Salamanca Shopping area. With a fashionable tea-room.

130 rooms d&b 10600 (AE DC MC V).

*Emperatriz* Calle de López de Hoyos 4, Tel: 413 6511. Modern, elegant and refined, just off the Paseo de la Castellana at the north end. Excellently run.

170 rooms d&b 11000 (AE DC MC V).

*Tryp Rex* Gran Via 43, Tel: 247 4800. Old and grandiose.

147 rooms d&b 7150 (AE DC MC V).

*Tryp Victoria* Plaza del Angel 7, Tel: 231 4500. Attractive with old-world charm, in the hub of the social quarter of Santa Ana. (Of Hemingway fame.)

110 rooms d&b 7150 (AE DC MC V).

*Opera* Cuesta Santo Domingo 2, Tel: 241 2800. Rather sombre but convenient for the Royal Palace, by the Teatro del Opera.

81 rooms d&b 5550 (AE DC V).

*Paris* Calle de Alcalá 2, Tel: 521 6496. Overlooking the Plaza de Sol, and old but well-established hotel.

114 rooms d&b 5800 (DC V).

*Zurbano* Calle de Zurbano 81, Tel: 441 5500. Modern and quiet, near the top end of Paseo de la Castellana, amongst the fashionable commercial part of the city.

262 rooms d&b 10900 (AE DC MC V).

*Serrano* Calle Marqués de Villamjor 8, Tel: 435 5200. Small and simple, close to the Salamanca shopping region.

34 rooms d&b 8700 (AE V).

**Category 4** *Tryp Asturias* Calle de Sevilla 2, Tel: 429 6676. Well run without frills, just up San Jerónimo from Sol.
175 rooms d&b 4925 (AE DC MC V).
*Francisco I* Calle del Arenal 15, Tel: 248 0204. Dignified small hotel between Sol and Opera. Good restaurant.
58 rooms d&b 4900 (AE DC MC V).
*Inglés* Calle de Echegaray 10, Tel: 429 6551. Rather shabby and noisy at weekends, but central in Santa Ana.
58 rooms d&b 4900 (AE DC MC V).
*Regente* Calle Mesonero Romanos 9, Tel: 521 2941. Big solid old hotel, just off Gran Via.
124 rooms d&b 4200 (AE MC V).
*Mediodia* Plaza del Emperador Carlos V, 8, Tel: 227 3060. Huge old-fashioned hotel opposite Atocha station, close to the Prado and the Parque del Retiro.
161 rooms d&b 3600.
*Londres* Galdo 2, Tel: 531 4105. Simple, fairly characterless but very central by Puerta del Sol.
57 rooms d&b 5150.

**Youth Hostels:** *Richard Schirrmann*, Parque de Casa del Campo, Tel: 463 5699. Out of the centre, but good communications by bus 33 (LAGO).
*Santa Cruz de Mercenado* Calle Santa Cruz de Marcenado 28, Tel: 247 4532. Central – (SAN BERNARDO).

**Social Madrid** Madrileños tend to eat meals late – lunch from 3 p.m. onwards and the evening meal from 10 p.m. onwards. Frequently they will eat in a far less formal fashion, taking *tapas* instead, accompanied by drinks. Madrid has some spectacular *tapa* bars, serving excellent shellfish and meats. Tapas are generally taken earlier than the sitting meal times. They begin after 1 p.m.

Morning and afternoon snacks are commonplace. Excepting perhaps a coffee on the run, breakfast is rarely taken before work, but a pastry or small *bocadillo* (filled roll) will often be taken mid-morning, accompanied by coffee or beer. The cafés serve pastries during the afternoon *merienda* (5 p.m. until 8 p.m.) after which the pastellerías close (usually 9 p.m.), the paseo (evening stroll) finishes, and the bars fill with *tapas* again.

The hours of the working day vary from the northern European hours to those of the south of Spain. In general, offices will be working from 8 a.m., although public offices may open between 9 and 10 a.m. Food shops open early, fashion shops open late. (Many municipal markets are only open during the morning). Lunch breaks are taken from 2 p.m. onwards, and many offices and shops are closed until 5 p.m. or later. General closing is between 7 and 8 p.m. After closing, it is customary to take a drink with work friends.

**Going Out** The most social meal of the day is lunch, taken leisurely and substantially. A late afternoon rendezvous may involve tapas and drinks, starting between 8 and 9 p.m. (It is not usual to dine out frequently.) An evening out often involves meeting much later (after 11 p.m.) and then eating and drinking. Night bars do not begin to fill until 2 a.m. A siesta ( snooze of varying length) is taken by most people, either after lunch, or early evening.

Particularly good areas for general restaurants are: Puerta del Sol stretching south to Santa Ana and Plaza de la Paja (past Plaza Mayor), Chueca and Malasaña.

**Dress** Women and men always look groomed although often casually dressed; there are very few occasions when formal clothes are worn. Similarly, it is seldom the custom to dress for occasions – black tie is very unusual. However, style and fashion are very important.

### Eating in Madrid
**Restaurants** should have a Menu del Dia at lunchtime which will be quicker and cheaper than eating from the á la carte menu. (Most bars will also serve a menu, often to be taken at the bar or in the *comedor*/dining-room behind.) Evening meals are seldom offered as a set menu.

Visitors often eat much earlier than people living in Madrid, and therefore in many restaurants, the ambience produced by local popularity will not be apparent until very late in the evening.

Although Madrid is far from either the Mediterranean or the Atlantic, its fish and shellfish are of top quality and freshness; the markets are accustomed to flying fish from the coasts at least daily.

**Cafés** The café style is an important and very comfortable part of the social life of the city. There are a relatively small number that are well established, and their success is based on traditional decor, fashion and historical prestige. The cafés are patronized throughout the afternoon, filling particularly from 8 p.m. onwards. Some close relatively early, and the music varies from classical to live jazz.

**Tapa Areas** *Tapas* are found everywhere, as people in every locality take them. Quality and ambience varies greatly. Certain areas have become especially fashionable for their tapa bars, and it is usual to visit a selection rather than stay at a single venue for the evening. In most restaurants there is also a tapa bar for the waiting customers and for those who wish to eat less formally – in fish restaurants these are superb. (These are not listed under Tapas.)

**Snack Bars** Apart from the Spanish variety, fast food is little found here. Burger outlets will be found in Gran Via and around Puerta del Sol. The most amusing string of Spanish snack bars is the Museo de Jamones – which has several branches (particularly Carrera de San Jerónimo, off Sol) – which serves portions (*raciós*) of several varieties of dried ham, pastries and bocadillos. (The expense varies according to the curing of the ham and the original feed of the animal – Jamón Ibérico is expensive partly because the animal is fed only on acorns.)

VIPS is a chain of stores/restaurants that stay open until after 3 a.m.; they are very popullar at all times of day with a variety of clientelle. Food and style are typically American. There are many branches, e.g. in Argüelles, and in the Ensanche, crossing Velázquez and José Ortega y Gasset.

**The Old Town** In the old city there is a profusion of bars and cafés. The whole area around Puerta del Sol reaching south to Plaza Santa Ana and Plaza Mayor is filled with bars and restaurants, often with good window displays. Any visitor is spoilt for choice. Plaza Santa Ana and Plaza Mayor are particularly lively.

**Around Puerta del Sol** No longer very fashionable, but always full of people. Particularly popular during the *paseo* hours.

**Cafés** *Mallorquina* – a tea-room overlooking the square with superb pastries.

**Restaurants** Pasaje Matheu; an alley full of restaurants between Puerta del Sol and Plaza Santa Ana, with tables outside beneath awnings in an alley unmolested by traffic. Attractive setting, and very popular with tourists. (Just off Calle Espoz y Mina up from Puerta del Sol.)

Calle de Preciados; several good restaurants serving fish and good tapas at the bars.

** *Korynto*, No. 56 Tel: 521 5965 – close to Puerta del Sol, outstanding in its area for fish. Has a smart restaurant.

Particular Madrid specialities apart from shellfish and dried hams, are tripe and squid. (Tapas rounds can become surprisingly expensive. The dishes are often quite rich, and it is tempting to order much more than is easily consumed.)

Bars and small restaurants offer *Platos Combinados* which are one-plate meals, usually fried fish or meat, chips and salad/vegetable.

*** Outstanding: International reputation for excellence.

** Highly recomended: Fashionable and sophisticated.

* Notable: Good quaility.

81

*Casa de Aganda*, No. 44 – with great roasting oven penetrating the room, coffered ceiling and good family atmosphere. Roast lamb.

Calle de San Jerónimo

★★ *Lhardy's*, No. 8, Tel: 522 2207 – a sophisticated restaurant. Downstairs, elegant ladies take consommé or patisserie; upstairs, in a beautiful wood-lined turn-of-the-century room, is the elegant dining-room.

*Museo de Jamones* – both a delicatessen and a bar, from which the variety may be sampled with beer or wine. Hanging from the ceiling are hundreds of hams of every sort.

Calle Jovellanos (off San Jerónimo)

★★ *Armstrongs*, No. 5, Tel: 522 4230 – sumptuous post-modern/colonial style, with waiters in white gloves. Palm trees decorate the room. Refined cuisine. Shut Sunday evenings and Mondays (AE DC V).

★ *Irizar*, No. 3, Tel: 231 4569 – intriguing and individual Basque and French cooking.

Shut Saturday noon, Sundays, Easter, Christmas (AE DC V).

**Santa Ana** This is a fashionable area both with tourists and for well-to-do Madrileños. Gently buzzing during the weekday evenings, it is extremely crowded at weekends when the streets are awash with visitors from the nearby towns and tourists until well into the night.

**Tapas:** Expensive here but excellent.

*La Trucha*, Calle Manuel Fernández González 3, closed Sunday nights and during August – good fish *tapas* and crowded.

*La Toscana*, terrific atmosphere around the bar, 'meal of the day' is unspectacular but delicious. Can sit to eat.

*La Chuleta*, – some of the best *tapas* in the area. Excellent shellfish and *pulpitos* (tiny squid/ink fish) and very good display.

### Cafés and Old Music Bars:

*Salón de Prado*, Calle del Prado 4 – often with piano accompaniment. Extremely genteel and attracts the fashionable set.

*Caf' del Círculo de Bellas Artes*, Calle de Alcalá – marble floors and comfortable sofas. Very fashionable amongst the art world.

*Café Central*, Plaza del Ángel 10 – jazz after 10 p.m. lively, traditional and relaxed style.

*La Fidula*, Calle de las Huertas 57 – tiny stage with classical or jazz musicians. Chased glass windows, cosy.

**Bar front, Madrid**

*Cerveceria Alemania*, Plaza de Santa Ana – with grand café style and good tapas. Famed through the writings of Hemingway.

*La Luna*, Calle León – jazz bar, small, dark cosy. Tiled bars; colourful, several rooms deep and fashionable, serving good Fino sherry:

*Viva Madrid*, Calle Manuel Fernández González 7

*Los Gabrieles*, Calle de Echegaray

**Restaurants:** ★★*El Cenador de Prado*, Calle del Prado 4, Tel: 429 1549, shut Sundays and 8–23 August – sophisticated and innovative cuisine, in elegant rooms. Very highly regarded (AE DC MD V).

★ *Platerías*, Plaza Santa Ana II, Tel: 522 6334 – daily changing of menu, delicious food, tasteful setting.

Calle de Echegaray and Calle Ventura de la Vega – several very inexpensive but honest restaurants, particularly;

*El Luarques*, Ventura de la Vega 16, Tel: 429 6174 – Ásturian. Shut Sunday evenings, Mondays and during August.

*Lerranz*, Calle de Echegaray 26, Tel: 429 0634 – good simple dishes.

**Plaza Mayor** More tourists go here than locals, but the bars are always full and there is plenty of choice. Around the Plaza are a number of *tapa* bars and *Mesóns* which specialize in particular categories of *tapas*, e.g. *Mesón de la Tortilla / Boquerón*. Just outside, under the south-west corner (archway Cuchilleros) are the famous *cuevas* in which meals are served in varying traditional decor. Further along are the streets Cava Baja and Cava Alta – extremely picturesque and with plentiful eating places.

**Restaurants:** full and lively, often exclusively tourist for the first evening setting and with plenty of madrileños at the later time.

*La Toja*, Siete de Julio 3, Tel: 266 4664 – popular locally for fish. Full on Sundays (AE DC V).

★ *Botín*, Calle Cuchilleros 17, Tel: 266 4217 – one of Madrid's most famous restaurants, opened in 1725 and still serving excellent traditional Castilian fare of roast suckling pig (*Cócinillo* and lamb. Pituresque rooms are clad with tiles and hung with traditional rustic items (AE DC MC V).

★ *Casa Paco*, Puerta Cerrada 11, Tel: 266 3166 – known for its superb steaks. The bar in front is always lively. Shut Sundays (DC V).

★ *El Cuchi*, Calle Cuchilleros 3, Tel: 266 4424 – good mexican fare, pretty decor, and boisterous atmosphere (AE DC MC V).

★ *Casa Lucio*, Calle Cava Baja 35, Tel: 265 3252 – great fun, with several small rooms, and good Castilian food. Very popular at Sunday lunchtime with Madrileños. Shut Saturday lunch and during August (AE DC V).

**Plaza de la Paja** A quiet square between Plaza Mayor and Basílica San Francisco surrounded by restaurants which is very pleasant in the spring.

★★ *Gure-Etxea*, No. 12, Tel: 265 6149 – Basque restaurant in the pretty quiet square near Basílica San Francisco. Shut Sundays and during August (AE DC V).

★ *La Costanilla*, No. 8, Tel: 265 6125 – elegant roasts from the oven by the dining-room. Lively. Shut Mondays.

**Rastro Area** Behind Tirso de Molina and across to Plaza de Cascorro; popular in the evenings and at weekend lunchtimes when many families are around. For lunches and tapas there is a good choice in Calle del Mesón de Paredes, Jesús y María and La Espalda near Tirso de Molina.

*Taverna de Antonio Sánchez*, Calle del Mesón de Paredes 13 – old-fashioned, bullfighting decor. A long, thin, dark place with reasonable food and barrel wine. Very popular locally.

*Wine Bodega*, Top of Calle de Embajadores – packed on Sundays, empty otherwise, a very attractive tiled old-world *bodega* with no frills and barrel wine. Shellfish tapas on Sunday mornings are delicious.

★ *Asador Frontón II*, Tirso de Molina 7, Tel: 468 1617 – good roasts, excellent fish (AE DC MC).

*Casa Hortensia*, Olivar 6, Tel: 239 0090 near Lavapiés, Asturian popular and simple. Shut Wednesdays and Sundays.

**Opera** An area more refined than most of the old city, although Plaza Isabel II is a popular meeting-place.

**Cafés** *Café Oriente*, Plaza de Oriente, Tel: 241 3974 – a very elegant café, with a terrace on to the gardens of the square. Known for its Irish coffee and pastries. Has a refined restaurant with Basque and French cooking, sophisticated and refined. Shut Saturday lunchtimes, Sundays and during August.

★★ *El Anciano Rey de los Vinos*, Calle de Bailén (by Segovia bridge) old-fashioned bar, tiled, with good tapas. Few stools, so tiring to visit after the Royal Palace. Shuts at 3 p.m. and 11 p.m.

**Restaurants** Several popular, quality *tascas* beside the theatre on Calle Felipe V, with lively small bars in front.

★★ *Café, Oriente*, elegant, French cuisine.

★ *La Taberna del Alabardero*, Calle Felipe V, No. 6, Tel: 247 2577 – good cooking served in small dining-rooms.

*La Bola*, Calle de la Bola 5(just up from Felipe V), Tel: 247 6930 – very cheerful. Walls clothed with dark red wooden coachwork. Shut Sundays.

### Gran Via

**Restaurants** This road, and its surrounding streets are good for lively exotic cooking; fast food (Macdonalds, etc.); and family-style steak restaurants.

*La Barraca*, Calle de la Reina 29, Tel: 232 7154 – Valencian restaurant with a superb paella and rice dishes. Small and lively. In the street just behind Gran Via to the north, (AE DC MC V).

*Himalaya*, Calle Isabel la Católica 13, Tel: 248 9055 – lively Hindu food. A local favourite. Just south of Gran Via near Plaza de España.

**Bars of Special Note** *Chicote* Gran Via 12 – the historic cocktail bar, still mixing superb cocktails in understated dignified style. The room is more like a café. The bottle museum of the master cocktail creator used to be in the basement but is now in the Torre de Jerez, Plaza de Colón. In the Franco era there used to be a secret door through to:

*Cock*, Calle de la Reina 17 – old-fashioned, carpeted, with dark wood panelling and a very sophisticated clientele still favouring the intelligentsia. Open very late. (Entered now from Calle de la Reina, behind Gran Via.) Both shut Sundays.

### Chueca and Malasaña

The area around Chueca is rich in restaurants serving inexpensive good food, and old-fashioned *bodegas* serving barrel sherry or wine. The area is extremely popular with Madrileños, and also has a number of good *cervecerias* and cafés. At night there are hundreds of people here, particularly in the street San Vincente Ferrer (Malasaña) where there are many bars. In this area it is advised not to take valuables.

### Old-Fashioned Bodegas

*Bodega Ángel Sierra*, Plaza Chueca – tiled and attractive.

*Los Pepinillos*, Calle Hortaleza 59 – uncomprised by frills.

*Casa Camacho*, San Andrés 2

**Cafés and Cervecerias** *Café Comercial*, Glorietta de Bilboa – with marble and mirror old-style decor.

*Cerveceria International*, Calle Requeros 8 – brick lined but excellent beer (*tapas*).

*Cerveceria Santa Bárbara*, Plaza de Santa Bárbara 8 – by the gardens, popular and good (*tapas*).

*Café Latino*, Calle de Augusto Figueroa 47 – old-style, with several rooms, off Chueca.

*Café Universal*, Calle de Fernando VI 13 – just off Plaza de Alonso Martínez with genteel atmosphere and classical music. Good cocktails.

**Restaurants** Several around Plaza de Chueca and its local streets, a good area for exotic and international styles of cooking.

*El Inca*, Calle de Gravina 23, Tel: 532 7745 – popular Peruvian restaurant.

★ *La Gastroteca*, Plaza de Chueca 8, Tel: 232 2564 – refined restaurant in an unrefined area. Inventive and sophisticated dishes. Pretty rooms.

★ *Spagetti & Bollecini*, Calle de Prim 15 , Tel: 521 4514 (by Paseo de Recoletos) – cheerful and excellent Italian. Shut Sundays (AE V).

*Café de la Salva*, Calle de Argensola – turn of the century decor and cosy comfort. Shut Sundays.

★★ *El Mente de la Villa*, Calle Santo Tomé, Tel: 419 5506 – small restaurant, refined and tranquil with romantic ambience. Japanese chef. Beautiful. Shut Saturday noon, Sundays and part of August. (AE DC MC V).

*La Carreta*, Calle de Barbieri 10, Tel: 532 7042 – just south of Chueca; Argentinian, always packed, with excellent grills and huge salads.

★★ *Horno de Santa Teresa*, Calle de Santa Teresa 12, Tel: 419 0245 – classical Asturian cooking. Excellent roasts (AE DC MC V).

★ *La Fuencisla*, Calle de San Mateo 4, Tel: 221 6186 – accomplished traditional home cooking. By Plaza de Santa Bárbara (V).

★ *Apriori*, Calle de Argensola 7, Tel: 410 3671 – excellent pizza and steak restaurant. Elegant and comfortable. Shut Saturday lunch and during August.

*Bar del Teatro*, Calle de Prim 5, Tel: 531 1797 – cellar serving ham, eggs and salad. Delicious. Shut Saturday noon and Sundays.

## Around Calle de la Princesa and Parque del Oeste

**Cafés** Many *terrazas* on the Paseo de Pinto Rosales overlooking the park.

**Tapas** in the Argüelles area, at the north of Calle de la Princesa. This area of bars is mostly patronised by the young students of the city. The squid and octopus served here is delicious.

**Restaurants** ★ *Café Viena*, Calle Luisa Fernanda 23, Tel: 248 1591 – plush decor, tranquil meal with piano accompaniment. Shut Saturday noon and Sundays (AE DC MC).

★★ *Juan del Alsade*, Calle de la Princesa, Tel: 247 0010 – a suave, cool restaurant, excellent cooking (AE DC MC V).

★ *Mesón Lluria* – in the gardens of the Duchess of Alba's palace. Cold atmosphere but popular with good food.

★ *La Bilbaina*, Calle del Marqués de Urquijo, Tel: 241 8698 – good, cheerful restaurant, with superb fish cooking.

★ *Currito*, Pabellón de Viscaya, Casa de Campo, Tel: 464 5704 – grill and oven roasts of meat and fish beside the park lake. Very popular in summer. Terrace with trees (AE DC V).

## East of University City to Paseo de la Castellana

**Restaurants** Many of the highest quality. ★★★ *Luculo*, Calle de Génova 19, Tel: 419 4029 – within a patio, with gardens behind. Extremely elegant and refined both in food and decor. Shut Saturday lunch, Sundays, 15 August to 15 September (AE DC V MC).

★★★ *Jockey*, Calle Amador de los Rios 6, Tel: 419 1003 – is unreproachable cuisine, businessman's favourite, opposite the Ministry of the Interior in the north-western ensanche by Paseo de la Castellana. Shut Sundays and during August (AE DC MC V).

★★★ *Fortuny*, Calle de Fortuny 34, Tel: 410 7707 – elegant palace with a beautiful terrace. Splendid cuisine sumptuous surroundings. Shut Saturday lunch and Sundays (AE DC MC V).

★★ *Annapurna*, Calle de Zurbano 5, Tel: 410 7727 – Indian restaurant of great dignity, with elegant decor. Shut Sundays (AE DC MC V).

★ *Asador Tierra Aranda*, Calle de Sandoval 12, Tel: 447 4836 – superb lamb roasts served in the traditional Castilian style, (AE DC MC V).

Pinocchio, Calle de Zurbano 6, Tel: 410 3171 (also Padre Damian 37) – excellent pizzas, lively, simple modern brick decor.

**Panorama of Madrid**

*Ananías*, Calle de Galileo 9, Tel: 448 6801 – old blue-tiled *tasca*, cheerful, always packed.

*La Parra*, Calle Monte Esquinza 34, Tel: 419 5498 – relaxed and highly fashionable – a venue for the atmosphere rather than the food. Shut Saturday noon and Sundays (DC AC V).

**South of Plaza de la Cibeles** An area of sophistication.

**Restaurants** ★★★ *Horcher*, Calle de Alfonso XII 6, Tel: 522 0731 – highly respected, in surroundings of green baize and antique wall hangings. Conservative cuisine, and excellent game in season. Shut Sundays (AE DC).

★★ *Balzac*, Calle de Moreto 7, Tel; 239 1922 – refined Basque cooking. Shut Saturday lunch and Sundays (AE DC MC V).

★★ *La Gamella*, Calle de Alfonso XII 4, Tel: 532 4509 – inventive international cooking by American chef. Shut Saturday lunch and Sundays (AE V).

*Buen Provecho*, Calle de Ibiza 35, Tel: 273 3251 – half delicatessen, half restaurant, with a communal table in the middle. Similar to Gran Colmado in Barcelona. Good *tapas*. (other side of the park). Shut Sunday evenings.

**The Ensanche and Paseo de Recoletos** This area is vast, and contains some very sophisticated restaurants, and some of the most famous old cafés in the Spain, most with terraces outside.

**Cafés** Along Paseo de Recoletos, and further down across Plaza de la Cibeles, are delightful terraces of cafés. The ambience in summertime is particularly restful but also sophisticated.

*Café Gijon*, Paseo de Recoletos 19 – one of the old favourites. Dignified, elegant and intellectural in atmosphere (serves food at lunchtime).

*Café León*, Calle de Alcalá 57, – of similar ilk and fame as Café Gijón, leather armchairs.

*Embassy*, Paseo de la Castellana 12 – with a reputation for producing excellent pastries for the *merienda* (tea). Genteel.

*Café Hispano*, 78, Paseo de la Castellana (up by Plaza Emilio Castelar) – a new café, with a good reputation for its Sunday morning brunch.

*Mallorca*, Calle de Serrano, behind Plaza de la Descubrimiento – charcuterie/patisserie with a bar upstairs; good *bodego* and exquisite chocolates downstairs where champagne and smoked salmon are served. Refreshing and very pleasurable to visit.

**Restaurants** ★★★ *El Amparo*, Callejón de Puigcerdá 8, Tel: 431 6456 – very elegant with refined Basquan and nouvelle cuisine. Shut Saturday noon, Sundays, Easter and during August (AE V).

★★★ *Suntory*, Paseo de la Castellana 36–38, Tel: 577 3733 – Japanese restaurant of superb quality. Shut Sundays (AE DC MC V).

★★ *Nicolasa*, Calle de Velázquez 150, Tel: 261 9985 – Basque and international, complicated menu, sophisticated. Shut Sundays and during August (AE DC MC V).

★★ *Al-Mounia*, Calle de Recoletos 5, Tel: 275 0173 – exceptional North African restaurant, luxuriously decorated in Mudéjar style: the lounge tables are copper trays, and the surroundings are furnished with sculptured wood and oriental fabric. Sophisticated cooking. Shut Sundays, Monday noon and during August (AE DC).

★★ *La Trainera*, Calle de Lagasca 60, Tel: 275 4717 – Cantabrian. Particularly fine reputation for its shellfish. Shut Sundays and during August (V).

★★ *Alkalde*, Calle de Jorge Juan 10, Tel: 276 3359 – superb Basque cooking, in entertaining beamed rooms hung with wrought-iron lamps and copperwork. Always packed and lively. The excellent fish can be taken as *tapas* in front. Shut Saturday evenings and Sundays in July and August (AE DC MC V).

★★ *El Pescador*, Calle de José Ortega y Gasset 75, Tel: 402 1290 – lovely canopy of fish laid out beside the bar, and lively ambience within. Shut Sundays and during August and September.

★ *La Recoleta*, Calle de Recoletos 9 – a high-quality charcuterie *bodega* in front. Delightful restaurant amongst antiques behind. Fashionable meeting-place (V).

★ *L'Entrecote Goya*, Calle de Claudio Coello 41 – a steak restaurant, casual decor and very popular at lunchtime. Shut Sundays.

*El Mesón*, Calle de Velázquez 74 – good *tapas* and lunch menu.

*O'Caldino*, Calle de Lagasca 74, Tel: 431 9967 – lively, with delicious Gallegan fish dishes.

*Monteagudo*, Calle de José Ortega y Gasset 54, Tel: 402 8491 – simple Galican restaurant.

★ *Ox's*, Juan Ramón Jiménez 11, Tel: 250 2258 – modern paintings on salmon-pink walls. Superb roasts. Shut Sundays, Easter and during August (AE DC MC V).

*Casablanca*, Calle Barquillo 29, Tel: 221 1568 – highly fashionable but intimate, with excellent fish and meat often accompanied by soft piano. Run like an exclusive club. Shut Saturday.(AE DC MC V).

*Vips*, Calle de José Ortega y Gassett – snack-bar and café.

**Bars of Special Note** *Balmoral*, Calle de Hermosilla 10 – in an oak-panelled room of distinguished English country decor, the cocktails mixed here are some of the finest in Madrid.

*Palace Hotel Bar* – a fashionable and sophisticated meeting place of great style.

### North End of Paseo de la Castellana

**Restaurants** Many of superb quality.

★★★ *Zalacain*, Calle Alvarez de Baena 4, Tel: 261 4840 – one of the highest-regarded restaurants in Spain and Europe, in an exclusive villa to the north of the Paseo de la Castellana. In luxurious style. Shut Saturday noon, Sundays, Easter and during August (AE DC V).

★★★ *Príncipe de Viana*, Manuel de Falla 5, Tel: 259 1448 – very elegant Basque/Navarese cuisine. Shut Saturday lunch, Sundays, Easter and during August (AE DC MC V).

★★ *La Dorada*, Calle de Orense 64–66, Tel: 270 2004 – sophisticated decor in the style of the ship, with wonderful fish. Reputation extends throughout Europe. Shut Sundays (AE V).

★★ *Combarro*, Calle Reina Mercedes 12, Tel: 254 7784 – a Galician chef, and magnificent display of fish at the entrance. Shut Sunday evenings and during August (AE DC MC V).

★★ *O'Pazo*, Calle Reina Mercedes 20, Tel: 253 2333 – Galician, elegant. A long-held reputation for excellent plain cooking of fish. Shut Sundays and during August.

★★ *El Bodegón*, Calle del Pinar 15, Tel: 262 3137 – exquisite and very careful Basquan cooking.

★★ *Itxaso*, Capitán Haya 58, Tel: 450 6412 – Basque. Quiet and elegant, with superb dishes. Shut Sundays and during August (AE DC MC V).

★★ *Senorio de Bertiz*, Calle del Comandante Zorita 6, Tel: 233 2757 – a beautiful restaurant, serving Basquan and international cuisine. Excellent. Shut Saturday lunch, Sundays and during August (AE DC MC V).

★★ *La Gabarra*, Santo Domingo de Silos 6, Tel: 458 7897 – Basquan chef. Elegant. Shut Saturday lunch, Sundays and during August (AE DC MC V).

**Telephone exchange, Madrid**

★★ *Aldar*, Alberto Alcocer 27, Tel: 259 6875 – young, refined Morrocan restaurant, with lovely summer terrace. Shut Sunday evenings.

★★ *Ganges*, Avda Brazil 3, Tel: 455 7317 – superb Indian restaurant.

★★ *Blanca de Navarra*, Avda de Brazil 13, Tel: 455 5581 – refined and elegant, small rooms, fashionable with excellent service. Shut Sundays (AE DC).

★★ *Cabo Mayor*, Juan Hurtado de Mendoza 11, Tel: 250 8776 – imaginative, with beautiful wood-lined dining-room. Shut Sundays and end of August (AE DC MMC V).

★★ *Castillo de Javier*, Capitán Haya 19, Tel: 593 3501 – splendid roasting oven in view of the *comedor* (dining-room).

★★ *Sacha*, Juan Hurtado de Mendoza 11, Tel: 457 5952 – with a terrace for springtime, and a lovely traditional bistro-style decor within. Shut Sundays, fiestas, Easter and during August (AE DC).

*Paulino*, Calle de Alonso Cano 34, Tel: 441 8738 – superb food from imaginative young chef. Very popular, inexpensive and always full. Shut Sundays.

*Oliveri*, Paseo de la Castellana 196, Tel: 259 7719 – wonderful ice-cream.

**Outside Madrid** ★★ *El Mesón*, 13km (8miles) on the C607 towards Colemar Viejo, Tel: 734 1019 – in a delightful situation, extremely popular for weekends (AE DC MC V).

★★ *Los Remos*, 13km (8miles) along NVI towards Galicia, Tel: 207 7230 – serving excellent fish. Shut Sunday evenings and end of August (AE DC MC V).

**Night-Clubs** All the following are very fashionable, but often particularly so at certain times of the evening.

*Archy*, Calle Marques del Riscal 11 – very fashionable from 1a.m. onwards. A glamorous first stop on the club circuit. Closes 3.30 a.m. (Has a restaurant and bar for selected people downstairs.)

*Zenith*, Conde de Xiquena 12 – an important early club, less refined than Archy. Closes at 4 a.m.

*Joy Eslava*, Calle del Arenal 11, Tel: 266 5440 – in a converted theatre, with a superb laser/light show and excellent music. A great night-club. (Around the corner, along Paseo de San Ginés is the Chocolatería San Ginés, which opens from 1 a.m. through the night serving superb *churros* and chocolate to the night-clubbers.)

*Pacha*, Calle de Barcélo 11, Tel: 446 0137 – one of the loudest disco clubs in the city - popular from 2 a.m. onwards. Highly fashionable after 5 a.m.

*Mau Mau*, Calle del Padre Damían 23, Tel: 457 7800 (the Eurobuilding) – highly sophisticated club, with an exotic setting Glamorous.

*Oh! Madrid*, Ctra de la Coruña, Tel: 207 8697 – a marvellous summer club, with dancing around a large pool in the gardens of a country house. Very fashionable.

*Kitch*, Calle de Galileo 32 – only after 3 a.m.. A mixture of all sorts. There are many popular discos around Plaza de Santa Bárbara.

*La Mala Fama*, Calle del Barco 17, has a pool table and good music. On Calle Campoamor are discos for young people, crowded at night.

*Lola*, Costanilla de San Petro II, Tel: 265 8801 – recently founded and successful cabaret show. The food is good. Shuts 4 a.m.

*Florida Park*, in Parque del Retiro, entrance Avda Menéndez y Pelayo, Tel: 273 7805 – both cabaret and Spanish dancing in a consistantly good spectacular (11 p.m.). Dining both with the glittering show and in the flower-filled patio. Shut Sundays.

*Scala Melia Castilla*, Capitán Haya 43, Tel: 450 4400 – of very high repute, a legs-and-feathers show of excellent quality. The cabaret accompanies the 9 p.m. dinner at about 10.30. Second performance at around midnight.'

*51 La Palma* which is a show including – an unusual little theatre, the extension to San Vincente Ferrer, decorated in dusty dark red where the meal is followed (12–2 a.m.) by 'Noches de Cuple', the singing of traditional songs by Olga Ramós. A 'romantic' evening of special appeal.

*Café Manuela*, Calle San Vincente Ferrer 29 – jazz bar, smokey traditional atmosphere.

*Eligeine*, Calle San Vincente Ferrer 23 – Salsa and folk music often play.

*No. 44*, Calle San Vicentre Ferrer – Lebanese food. Particularly attractive for the tiled exterior. A century ago the building housed a pharmacy, whose advertisements adorn the outside in tile.

**Flamenco** Although Castilla is not the natural home of flamenco, there are fine exponents in Madrid. It is worth choosing the show with care as there is much of lesser quality.

*Café de Chinitas*, Calle de Torija 7, Tel: 248 5135 – one of the most famous flamenco shows in Spain. In very elegant surroundings, with superb dancing.

*Venta del Gato*, Avda de Burgos 214, Tel: 202 3427, 7km (4miles) away – totally absorbing and electrifying. Danced for those who understand the art and sentiment.

*Corral de la Morena*, Calle de la Morería 17, Tel: 265 8446 – with dinner, from 9 p.m.–3 a.m. An excellent performance of high reputation.

*Casa Patas*, Calle Cañizares 10, Tel: 228 5070 – with dancing after midnight. Very genuine, for those who value the dance. Simple food. Open every night, dancing Friday and Saturday.

**Casino** *Madrid Casino*, Plaza Torrelodones, NIV, 28km (17miles) away Tel: 859 0312/(with free bus service from Plaza de España 6) – a gambler's heaven, with three restaurants, six bars and a cabaret to entertain the players. Open 5 p.m.–4 a.m.

*Hipodromo de La Zarzuela*, Ctra de la Coruña, NIV, 7km (4miles) away – the bar is a fashionable meeting-place after the horses have left, and during the spring-autumn weekend evenings. Extremely pleasant.

**A purchase from the Rastro market is homeward bound**

**Shopping** Shopping in Madrid can be a pastime of great pleasure as the choice is exceptional. There are several different shopping areas, each of distinct character and each dedicated to a specific market.

Madrid's specialities are high fashion of clothing and leather goods, and antiques whose quality ranges from the superb to bric-a-brac. Jewellery is not as well offered as in Geneva or London, although there are a number of excellent designers working here. Food shopping is a joy – either from the many municipal markets within which freshness, quality and abundance are absolutely taken for granted, or from excellent delicatessens. Humble local shops are found in the older parts of the city, and here traditional specialist shops (capes, lacework, tayloring, etc.) are unsurpassed.

**Fashion Clothing and Leather Goods** Madrid has gained a high reputation as a centre of fashion design and the selection of Spanish and international fashion offered is superb. There are four fashion areas – Salamanca; around Puerta de Sol and Gran Via; Argüelles; and the Azca Centre.

93

**Salamanca** Running eastwards from the axes of Calle de Serrano and Calle de Goya is the centre of the fashion boutique industry. Calle de Serrano itself is lined on its east side with the most exclusive boutiques, both for shoes and clothes, but shopping here is marred a little by the excessive noise of traffic. (A couple of good cafés offer refreshment on the way.) Goya has less exclusive boutiques and is always lively, with a mixture of designer boutiques and younger fashion outlets. Its cafés – much bigger and noiser – are always full during afternoon shop hours (or *paseo* hours) with opastry eaters and tea drinkers. Many good shoe shops are found here.

Within the smart back streets are more boutiques, but far less concentrated and again more exclusive. Young designer outlets are likely to be found amongst these streets, the grid between the Parque del Retiro and Calle de Goya, and a small number are established on the west side of Paseo de Recoletos – Calle Conde de Xiqueña, and its adjacent streets.

**Argüelles, Azca, Puerta del Sol** None of these are competitors for the Salamanca area in ambience or in quantity of choice. The main shops of Argüelles are along Calle de Alberto Aguilera at its junction with Calle de la Princesa (ARGÜELLES). A small number of excellent shoe shops are here. The Multicentro has a number of fashion boutiques, and there is a department store: a branch of El Corte Inglés. The Azca Complex, a vast commercial development worth visiting for its design alone, contains a selection of boutiques but it is not very lively. Around Puerta del Sol and leading up to Gran Via are numerous shoe and leather shops, some very cheap, some of good quality. The ambience is always cheerful and bustling.

**Antiques** There are three areas for these: between Parque del Retiro and Goya; along Calle del Prado and along the route of the Rastro market – Calle Ribera de Curtadores. Fine antique shops, art galleries and auction houses are in the streets between Parque del Retiro and Calle de Goya. Calle de Claudio Coello is particularly well endowed with antiques, while the galleries are found scattered in the streets just above the Parque del Retiro. Ispaham, Calle de Serrano 5, sells beautiful carpets. The main auction houses are Duran's, Calle de Serrano 12, south of Calle de Goya (with spectacular windows); Sotheby's, Plaza de la Independencia No. 8; and Faberge, Gran Via 1. Fine antiques are

**For refreshment in Salamanca,** there are excellent delicatessens, chocolate shops and cafés, particularly in Calle de Goya and the grid below. Mallorca, and Calle de Serrano just behind Plaza del Descubrimiento is particularly good. Here smoked salmon and champagne are served downstairs beside a very beautiful chocolate counter, and delicacies are sold upstairs or taken from the bar with a beer). Along the far side of Plaza de Recoletos are the welcoming traditional cafés of León, Gijón and Embassy.

94

**Bargains and bric-a-brac at the Rastro**

also sold from several small shops on Calle del Prado which runs down the hill from Plaza Santa Ana to Plaza de la Cibeles.

Two multi-shop antique galleries and bric-a-brac shops live in the street filled on Sunday mornings by the Rastro market. Their quality is variable but very much higher than that of the market itself, whose bargains are offered down Calle Ribera de Curtadores and the nearby streets until 2 p.m. each Sunday. Walking down the market from its head in Plaza de Cascorro, the right branching street leads to a square, Plaza General Vara; here and in the street running down from it are the antique stalls.

**Fashionable Galleries** *Galería Juana de Aizpuru*, Calle de Barquillo 44, Open 10 a.m.–2 p.m. and 5–9 p.m. Shut Mondays. *Jorge Kreisler*, Calle de Prim 13, Open: 9 a.m.–2 p.m. and 5–9 p.m. Shut Mondays. International contemporary art. *Galería Juana Mordo*, Calle de Villanueva 7, Open: 10.30 a.m.–2 p.m. and 4.30–9 p.m. Shut Mondays – eclectic collection.

**Fashionable Antique Shops** *L'Ermitage* – Calle de Villaneuva 27, Open 10 a.m.–2 p.m. and 5–8 p.m. – antique jewellery and clocks. *Fortuny*, Calle de Fortuny 13, Open 10 a.m.–2 p.m. and 5–8 p.m. – art deco and furniture.

Jewellery *Grassy*, Gran Via – an internationally famous jeweller. *Panellato*, Calle de Jose Ortega y Gaset 19, – exclusive design.

**Street Market – The Rastro** Held every Sunday Morning until 2 p.m., with a multitude of stalls. The market runs downhill from Plaza de Cascorro, mainly along Calle Ribera de Curtidores (LA LATINA).

The Rastro market needs to be approached with caution. It is exceedingly crowded and pickpockets glean great profits. There

95

are sections to the market: at the top are cheap clothing and miscellaneous stalls, followed by artesanal jewellery, leather work and more poor-quality clothes and shoes. The mixture continues down to the foot of the road, with an occasional stall selling old clock parts or keys. The two antique galleries are down here. At the foot is old iron – spiral steps, bedsteads, parts of cars; and beyond are a variety of electric goods, records and engines. The side streets are categorized to the west (right off the central downward flow) is junk, painting and ceramics.

To the left, up Calle Cayetano, is the bird market, in which the most lively selling of the market takes place. Here small groups of men will huddle together intently discussing prices and quality. Their colourful offerings range in size from a pigeon downwards. Most men sell without stalls.

**Souvenirs** Souvenirs of Madrid are sold in abundance around Cibeles, and around Sol. Souvenirs and artesanal wares of the provinces of Spain are found in the Artespaña stores, Hermosilla 14 and Gran Via 32 (where, like the big department stores of El Corte Inglés and Galerias Preciados, there are exporting facilities). Beware when buying artesan souvenirs: there is much offered that is produced cheaply by compromising the artesan crafts by less skilled techniques.

**Department Stores** El Corte Inglés and Galerias Preciados are both found in the main shopping areas of the city. Galerias Preciados are near Puerta del Sol on Calle Montera and at the foot of Goya and Serrano. El Corte Inglés is on the Puerta del Sol, at the shopping area of Calle de la Princesa (ARGÜELLES) and at the far end of Calle de Goya. Both stores have exporting facilities.

**Shopping Precincts**

**Puerto de Toledo** has a huge shopping precinct for fashion, artesanal work and antiques. Unfortunately, though recently opened, it is not animated and thus the little boutiques are empty of shoppers. For a peaceful digest of Madrid wares, this is a good focus but lacks all the ambience of the streets. Some of the antique shops are of extremely high quality. The precinct is reach at PUERTA DE TOLEDO metro, and open on Sundays. Most boutiques within are also selling in shops in the city streets. Madrid 2 – La Vaguada, at the north of Paseo de la Castellana, is a huge commercial complex of 350 shops (Metro BARRIO DEL PILAR).

**The bird market at the Rastro**

**Food Shopping** It is easier to buy fruit, vegetables, meat and fish in a municipal market, although there are a number of street shops that also sell food. The biggest, most capacious markets are in the old part of the city: LA LATINA (just up from San Francisco Basílica) and ALONSO MARTINEZ, at the top of Calle de Atocha. The abundance here, and the quantity of stalls and choice is inspiring. The market at La Latina (Calle de la Cebada) has 76 fruit stalls and 29 fish stalls. Fish is flown in daily from both the Atlantic and the Mediterranean. As everywhere, Monday is not a good day to buy fish or meat.

### Specialist Shops

**Book Shops** English books at *Turner*, Calle de Génova 3; and *Booksellers*, Calle José Abascal 48. • Extensive range of volumes – *Casa del Libro*, Gran Via 29 • Antique books – *Luis Bardón*, Plaza de las Descalzas Reales • Second-hand books – daily fair (extended Sunday mornings) Cuesta Claudio Moyano, by Botanic Gardens and Atocha Station. • *Crisol* – Calle de Juan Bravo 38, Open: 10 a.m.–10 p.m. and Sunday 11 a.m.–9 p.m. – books, magazines and records of huge selection. • Book fair – late May/early June, Parque del Retiro.

**Music** *F. Manzanero*, Plaza Santa Ana 12, is a guitar-maker of high repute.

**Flowers** *Campomania*, Calle Campomanes 10 – old-world flower arrangements and soaps. Beautiful. • *Un Jardin en Plus*, Calle de Velázquez 72, – flowers and natural perfume.

**Modern Furniture** *Domestica Sede*, Calle de Hortaleza 116, – designer ware for everything to do with the house.

**Design** *Hazard*, Centro Commercial Moda Shopping, Avda General Perón 40 – exclusive design, clocks, kitchen furniture, etc. • *Items D'HO*, Ronda de Toledo 1 – Alberto Alexi designer office novelties.

**Specialist Artesan** *Sesena*, Calle de la Cruz (near Sol) – maker of capes. • *Casa de Diego*, Puerta del Sol – maker of fans.

97

### Fashionable Hair Designers

*Guiseppe Galli*, Calle del General Moscardo 29. • *Jacques Dessange*, Calle O'Donnell 9

**Health** *Centro de Higiene Vital,* Calle Buen Suceso 8, Open: 10 a.m.–7 p.m. – all treatments.

**Tarot and Fortune Telling** Around Plaza de Cascorro *Karemsa*, Plaza de Cascorro 15 – exhaustive: 3 floors.

**Sunday in Madrid** There are two famous fairs on Sunday mornings: the Rastro fleamarket running down from Plaza de Cascorro, and the stamp market in Plaza Mayor. Both continue until 2 p.m. The Rastro streets (*see* page 95) become extremely crowded, and there are hundreds of stalls. Much that is on sale is of poor quality but there are occasional bargains.

The Plaza Mayor hosts a quieter, less spectacular market, to which earnest stamp, coin and football-card collecters go. This is a delightful place to take breakfast, as the market begins slowly and peacefully.

Elsewhere, the city wakes late. Museums are open normally until 2 p.m. and closed for the afternoon. Lunchtime is a family occasion at home but, both before and after, smart children and parents will be out walking. The parks are full of people all day (particularly Parque del Retiro). Campo de Moro is a popular excursion for families taking a picnic (often via the spectacular cable-car from Parque del Oeste) and for many who enjoy the lake with its boats, the Zoo and the amusement park.

Most *tapa* bars are open for lunch and will fill with pre-lunch parties. Many restaurants close for the evening, and those open during the day are mostly lightly filled.

There are theatre performances on Sundays. In the summer, music is performed in Parque del Retiro. In season there is horse-racing in the afternoon at the Hipodromo (spring and autumn), bullfighting at the monumental ring of Las Ventas de los Toros (spring through to early autumn) and, usually, a football match. All pull enthusiastic crowds.

Many people leave the city at weekends – in the winter to ski, in the summer to the cool of the mountains. The many historic cities and towns which lie less than a couple of hours away attract quantities of visitors.

**Around Madrid** The city of Madrid is surrounded by a thin ring of industrial suburbs. Beyond these extends a varied landscape: to the north-west are the spectacular granite Sierras de Guadarrama, speckled with winter and summer resorts. Northwards along the N1 the landscape is hilly and often rugged, with several large reservoirs. East of this major artery, many of the villages are tiny and very seldom visited by travellers.

The province is bordered on its north-east side by another range of mountains, little penetrated from either Madrid or Guadalajara. South of the range there is more dense population, a number of big industrial towns and beautiful hilly countryside.

South of the capital, roads wind through bright red hillsides, passing many castle ruins and pretty towns. There are substantial industrial towns both here and to the west. Towards the Sierras de Gredos (Ávila) are vine fields and thick pine forests.

The historical prominence of the area is well in evidence: in every direction there are fine Renaissance and baroque churches, and royal palaces of Bourbon ostentation, yet only one Romanesque church remains in the entire province.

**North-West** The Guadarrama Sierra is the eastern end of the great central Cordillera, stretching northwards between the provinces of Madrid and Segovia. La Mujer Muerta (the dead woman, whose outline can be clearly traced from the city of Segovia) forms the southern end. There are two spectacular roads that link Madrid with Segovia; the NV1 crossing the high Puerta de los Leones, and the smaller N601 crossing further north at the highest pass, the Puerta de Navacerrada. The region of Cabeza de Hierro runs northward of this pass, carrying the highest peak

**The reservoir at Embalse de Álcazar**

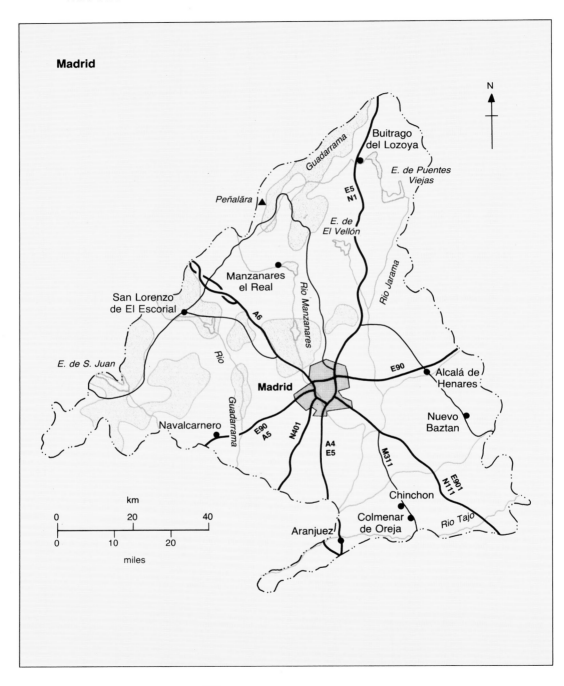

**Madrid**

N

Buitrago
del Lozoya

Guadarrama

E. de Puentes
Viejas

Peñalãra

E5
N1

E. de
El Vellón

Manzanares
el Real

Río Jarama

San Lorenzo
de El Escorial

Río Manzanares

A6

E. de S. Juan

Río

E90

Alcalá de
Henares

**Madrid**

Guadarrama

Navalcarnero

E90
A5

N401

A4
E5

Nuevo
Baztan

M311

E901
N111

Chinchon

km

0        20              40

Colmenar
de Oreja

Río Tajo

0    10        20

Aranjuez

miles

Peñalara, 2,430m (7,972ft) and meeting the third section of the Sierra Morcuera.

The chain is clothed beautifully: thick forests of Scots pine shelter roadflax, ragwort, valerian and wild herbs, while the higher areas carry rock-roses and broom. The mountains are a popular haven in the heat of the summer, with many resorts enjoyed by Madrid families. Mountain activities include good skiing, climbing and a great network of lovely walks.

The main resorts are Nevacerrada, which provides the best skiing, Cercedilla, which has the main train station, and Los Molinos. The funicular ride from Cercedilla to Puerta de Navacerrada and Valcotos is beautiful. The Siete Picos (seven Peaks spread above.

Walks here are spectacular and very beautiful. A historic trail links Cerdilla to La Estación del Espinar, via San Rafael (penetrating into the province of Segovia) – a wonderful but tiring days walk with stunning views. The Pico de Peñelara is the highest mountain peak of the Sierra. Lifts from Valcotos reach up to the beautiful glacial lakes below the peak.

Other walks spread through the area northwards to the pine woods of Valsaín, Rascafría and the monastery of El Paular. A historic walk of abour 5 hours reaches from Milaflores de la Sierra to El Paular via the Puerta de la Morcuera. For all walks, a detailed map is advisable.

The towns of this eastern edge of the Sierras are, again, mostly holiday resorts. The M604 runs spectacularly through the mountains from Navacerrado to Rascafría. Just before the town is the beautiful Monasterio de El Paular, founded in 1390 and still vibrant. Of the original building little remains save the Capilla del Rey. The church, rebuilt after destruction by an earthquake in 1755, has a magnificent alabaster Gothic retable. The façade is Plateresque, designed by Rodrigo Gil de Hontañon. The monastery offers sanctuary to a few male visitors (attached is a luxurious hotel).

Rascafría is a charming quiet town, surrounded by a pine and beech forest. Further east is Lozoya, on the banks of the Embalse de Pinilla. A magnificent Roman bridge spans the river, and the town preserves a church with an unusual ceramic altarpiece by Zuloaga.

**The castle at Manzanares el Real**

From Rascafría a road to Miraflores de la Sierra winds high into the Sierras through heather and broom and granite boulders. Miraflores is a pretty hillside summer resort, clothed in beech and oak. Just north is a zone, Reserva Ecológica-Educativa, where the local natural species of flora have been encouraged in areas where they can be enjoyed easily. (Information in Madrid Tourist Office or in Miraflores.) A *romería* on 3 February, the feast of San Blas, is a lively event. From here another attractive road leads south towards Colmenar Viejo. A turning west leads to Manzanares el Real.

**Manzanares el Real** Manzanares el Real, beautifully situated on the Embalse de Santillana, fills with Madrileños at weekends. It is small holiday resort – a base for fishing in the Manzanares river or for enjoying the extraordinary beauty of its backdrop, the Sierra de la Pedriza. The architectural attraction of the town is its castle, a fifteenth-century fort adapted by Juan Guas into a palace. The exterior of the castle, seen both from a distance and from nearby, is classic, with a square plan, round corner turrets, and battlements. It has been carefully restored, and its

102

several levels, dressed with various period pieces, may be explored. It is used as a conference centre. The long upper level gallery is beautiful. (Open: 10 a.m.–2 p.m. and 3–6 p.m.) The town may be reached from Madrid by buses from Calle Mateo Inurria 11.

## Parque Regional de la Cuenca Alta del Manzanares

The park of La Pedriza has an entrance just to the west of the town. It is part of the huge Regional Park of la Cuenca Alta del Manzanares, on the south side of the Guadarrama Sierra. The area is dominated by strangely formed granite boulders which rise from the water course of the Manzanares at 960m (3,150ft) to well over 2,300m (7,550ft.). Vegetation is sparse – the trees change from Holm oak and pine to Scots pine and juniper as the height increases. During the spring various wild flowers bloom, particularly iris and narcissi. Wild boar and roe deer may be spotted in the park south of the Embalse de Santillana.

Of the two parts to the park, the area of La Pedriza is best known and most accessible. From the information entrance outside Manzanares el Real (open: mornings), a road weaves up through a rocky pass to the tiny village of Canto Cochino. From here there are marvellous walks up the steep paths to various peaks – Peña Siro, Las Buiteras (breeding area of griffon vultures), El Pájaro and Las Torres. Other paths run upwards from Arroyo de la Deshesilla through small meadows and lunar rock mounds. The bare rock formations are extraordinary. Shaped by cavities, deep fissures, and smooth curved faces, the massive towering boulders seem precariously positioned. There is much climbing activity here.

At weekends, La Pedriza is a popular location for family outings, but the paths deeper in the park are quiet. Mountaineering challenges are in the surrounding peaks, Cabezas de Hierro 2,383m (7,818ft.), Valdemartín and La Maliciosa.

## North

## The Palace of El Pardo

is just north of the capital, reached by bus from Calle Martín de los Heros (MONCLOA) leaving every 15 minutes, or via the road Avda de Puerta de Hierro past the Zarzuela race course. Charles V constructed the country house in the old grounds of Enrique III. The palace, burnt within fifty years of construction, was rebuilt by Francisco

**Skiing Information** Puerto de Navacerrada: 12 runs, 7 lifts, (funicular from Cercedilla) with an exciting long run – the Río Frío 'tube'.
Valcotos: 11 runs, 8 lifts, (funicular from Cercedilla). Pines cover the lower reaches.
Valdesquí: with a lit run for night skiing. 8 lifts, 2 baby lifts.

**Landscape of La Pedriza**

de Mora in the early seventeenth century and extended with Italian taste by Philip V and Charles III. The splendid mansion was home to Geralisimo Franco.

The Palace contains a superb collection of tapestry wall hangings. Guided tours will also show the frescoed rooms, fine furniture and a collection of art.

Palace tours: 10 a.m.–12.30 p.m. and 3–5.30 p.m., Sunday 10 a.m.–1 p.m.. Shut Tuesday.

Within the grounds is the opulent Casita del Principe, entered from main road, which was built by Juan de Villanueva, architect also of the cottage of El Escorial.

Nearby is the Convento del Capuchinos, founded by Philip III, which guards paintings (including works by Ribera) and a reclining 'Christ' by Gregorio Fernández.

**Colmenar Vieja** The M607 can be joined from El Pardo, and leads to Colmenar Vieja through part of the Parque Regional de la Cuenca Alta. The tourist reputation of this town rests on its parish church, Iglesia de la Asunción, of Gothic and Renaissance style. Although it has altar paintings by Sanchez Coello and has a fine spired tower, the town is industrial, hilly and with an awkward traffic flow which can make a visit uncomfortable.

From Colmenar, the main road curves towards the Guadarramas or on to Manzanares el Real.

**Patones de Arriba**

**Alcobendas** The main route northwards from Madrid is the NI leading via Buitrago del Lozoya to Soria. An early turning left leads to Alcobendas where there is an important parish church of contemporary design, built to the stark design of Miguel Fisac in 1955. The church, San Pedro Martir, has a central altar.

**Talamanca de Jarama** Talamanca de Jarama sits several kilometres north of Alcobendas, along the straight cereal plateau reached by the M103. The brick walls of this ancient settlement were founded by the Romans and rebuilt by each successive religious occupation. A splendid Roman bridge survives, as does one of the very few Romanesque apses of the province, that of Iglesia San Juan Bautisto (although the main part of the church is Gothic).

**Torrelaguna** Further north is Torrelaguna, a dignified town with old houses, a splendid Gothic parish church and an attractive Plaza Mayor. Cardinal Cisneros was born here, and symbols of his influence can be seen on one of the church towers. Inside the church are a fine Renaissance choir and several tombs.

**Patones de Arriba** A minor road, the M102, leads from here through a plain to Patones and on to a very attractive route into the province of Guadalajara. Patones de Arriba is hidden in the sharp rise of the hills above the modern settlement of Patones. The turning, barely marked, leaves the main road half-way along

**Buitrago de Lozoya**

the village and winds through the ridge for several steep kilometres.

The old town, now almost totally abandoned, consists of three hillsides, two of which are dotted with ruined dwellings, and the third housing an old necropolis. The heart of the village is still alive, with streams running through the awkward stone streets. The houses are all of dark stone and slate. A climb up either hill will show the original size of the settlement and shape of the houses that have since collapsed. The town was, from Visigoth times until the reign of Charles III, an isolated settlement, with its own social systems and own king. Today it is just beginning to attract city visitors, and has two restaurants tucked into the small living part.

The views on leaving the village are spectacular, stretching across the plain below to the cliff rise of the horizontal plateau beyond. Returning to Torrelaguna, the line of mountains in front carry a pipeline of water (the canal of Isabel II) to Madrid city from the reservoir of La Oliva.

Northwards from Torrelaguna, the routes are very attractive, leading spectacularly to either side of the Embalse de El Atazar. In the region north of the reservoir are delightful rural villages, seldom visited and little modernized. Towards Guadalajara are the wonderful beech forests of Hayedo de Montejo. Excepting the narrow twin passes through to Guadalajara through the forests near La Hiruela, there is no viable entrance into the neighbour province further north than Patones.

**Buitrago de Lozoya** The main town of this area is Buitrago de Lozoya, on the main NI road. The small town sits surrounded by water and by splendid old walls, originally Arab. The old quarter is charming, and very pleasant to walk. The Mudéjar castle within, although dilapidated, still has several towers standing. A Picasso museum here shows work by the artist that was donated by his barber, a resident of the town.

Both northwards and southwards, the NI travels through spectacular rugged hilly countryside.

### East

**Alcalá de Henares** is a big, sprawling industrial town on the main east railway line and road from Madrid to Guadalajara and Zaragoza (N11). In its old centre is the architectural jewel of the university, founded by Cardinal Cisneros in 1498. Entrance to the town is slow, but the traffic flows arrive eventually at the old part. If approaching from Madrid by car, the old castellated walls of the Bishop's Palace and Convento de San Bernardo announce the border of the university town. (There is extensive street parking – it is easier to park near the palace than near the university which is several minutes' walk away.)

The centre of Alcalá is lively and has a distinct 'student' atmosphere. The main heart is the Plaza de Cervantes, planted with roses and trees, with bandstand at one end. It is long, thin and partly arcaded. It is linked to the Palace area by a most attractive part-pedestrian street, Calle Mayor, which is arcaded all along both sides with heavy old wood pillars.

The university buildings are just beyond the Plaza. At the top end of the Plaza, to the left of the bandstand, is the Tourist Office (Callejón de Santa María 1, Tel: 889 2694, Open 11 a.m.– 2 p.m.). Good maps are offered.

**The University** In 1836 the main university was transferred to Madrid, and this town has subsequently declined as a university base. Its academic standing was originally established by the publishing of the first polyglot Bible while its founder was still alive, with simultaneous translations into Greek, Latin and Hebrew. Its architectural prestige is formidable and, apart from the magnificent Plateresque façade designed by Rodrigo Gil de Hontañon, the patios, Paraninfo (Senate house) and Chapel of San Ildefonso should be seen. Of the three original patios, two survive, both carrying the swan motifs that symbolize the patron Cardinal.

The Paraninfo has a superb stuccoed gallery, and coffered Mudéjar/Renaissance ceiling painted with reds and blues. (Open: 11 a.m.–1 p.m. and 4–6 p.m.)

The Capilla de San Ildefonso houses the tomb of the Cardinal, worked in Carrera marble. The interior of the small church (open: morning for mass) is a mixture of many styles: Gothic, Mudéjar, Renaissance and baroque. A Franciscan cord and stucco friezes surround the walls. (A guide will take visitors round the historic buildings between 10 a.m.–12 p.m. and 4–8 p.m., Shut Mondays.)

Behind the University, at the back of the old Patio Trilingue is the *Hosterie del Estudiente* (an excellent restaurant) from which the fifteenth-century patio can be appreciated.

**The parks of Aranjuez make a great place for family outings**

**The Bourbon palace of Aranjuez**

**Cervantes Museum** A small museum to Cervantes, born in Alcalá, was built in the arcaded Calle Mayor No. 48, in 1955 to emulate the style of house of his time. It is more interesting for a number of superb examples of old Castilian furniture, and a few early editions, than for recollections of the poet. (Open: 10 a.m.–12 p.m. and 4–8 p.m., Shut Mondays.)

**Gardens** The Palacio Arzobispal gardens are not open to the public. The Parque O'Donnel is just beyond the palace walls, across the busy Madrid road. Well planted with trees and shrubs, it is a welcome rest from the busy town.

Elsewhere, the central part of town has several heavy brick churches and convents, some of which are falling to ruin. Old houses line many of the quiet back streets. Surrounding the old part are busy commercial streets.

Festival Jornadas Musicales Cervantinas is a music festival held in April.

**Meco** Just north of the town, past military barracks, are cereal fields which spread to Meco, a small old town. Its streets are comfortable and wide, and its buildings solid and frequently emblazoned with shields. It is a pleasant town to pass through,

very quiet and dignified, with a massive brick church in its centre.

**Nuevo Baztán** Nuevo Baztán is reached through roads which twist through the hilly agricultural countryside. It is a most unusual village, now increasingly dilapidated, while a modern village of villas is constructed next door. Made up of only a small grid of streets and an imposing church and mansions, it is a quiet reflection of the ideals of its founder, Juan de Goyeneche. It was specifically designed to house Navarrese workers in the eighteenth century, in an attempt to bring increased agriculture and a ceramics factory to the district. Jose Churriguera planned the settlement in 1709, with a market square dominated by a great church and protected by a palace/castle. Within the church is a magnificent marble altarpiece by Churriguera.

The villages East of Madrid are often hillbound, with a large church at the high centre-point. The streets are often awkward to navigate.

### South-East

**Aranjuez Royal Palace** On the banks of the Tajo river, in a lush oasis of gardens and forest parks, stands the splendid Bourbon palace of Aranjuez. The town is 5km (3miles) from the main Madrid–Andalucía road (NIV), less than 50 km (30miles) from both Madrid and Toledo. It is easily reached by bus and rail.

A special direct train runs during the summer weekends – the *Tren de la Fresa* (Strawberry Train) – a replica of that given to Queen Isabel II by the Marquis of Salamanca in 1851 (station: Paseo de la Estación, Tel: 891 0202, west of the Palace).

The small town of Aranjuez, set in the parched landscape between Madrid and Toledo, is a great focus of Madrid family outings, a lovely weekend retreat. During the summer, its restaurants buzz with life and its cool gardens fill with children. The famous local strawberries and asparagus colour many stalls.

A palace has been here since the fourteenth-century, the first built by the Grand Master of the Knights of Santiago. The retreat of Charles V, extended by his son Philip II, was destroyed by fire. The first Bourbon, Philip V, started replacing it in 1727 and his heirs added further to its opulence.

The Royal Palace, completed in 1778 by Francisco Sabatini, is vast – a collection of rooms clad in silk, fine paintings, and magnificent furniture; their ceilings superbly decorated (French, Pompeian, Italian and Spanish styles) and hung with beautiful chandeliers; their floors displaying masterful marble designs and carpets. It is advisable to visit early – the guided tours fill to capacity.

**The gardens at Aranjuez**

Of the many rooms, the Rococo Porcelain Room is particularly remarkable, an extraordinary ceramic display round the walls and ceiling (all produced from the Buen Retiro works in Madrid). The decoration fo the small smoking room imitates that of the room of the Two Sisters in the Alhambra of Granada.. The delightful collection of Chinese illustrations of people and birds given to Isabel II by the Emperor of China is unique. The royal apartments house particularly fine marquetry furniture and are hung with gold and damask. The gardens outside give a lovely perspective. Run by the Patromonio National, Open: Winter 10 a.m.–1 p.m. and 3–6 p.m., Summer 3.30–6.30 p.m., Shut Tuesdays.

**Casita del Labrador** This quaintly named labourer's cottage, built for Charles IV by Isidro González Velázquez (an imitation of the Versailles Trianon) is a compact treasure-house of marble, gold and ornament. The entrance hall and staircase are alone so opulent in their marble splendour that the remaining space is almost uncomfortably small.

As in the Palace, this house displays frescos and canvases by fine contemporary artists, and magnificent clocks abound – particularly one spiral gold fountain clock. Much gold, platinum and filigree ornamentation is used. Some of the marble statues are authentic Greek works. The Casita is a half-hour walk from the Palace through the gardens of Principe, but it is sometimes possible to take a bus ride there. It is still used by the King, for one evening every December, to host a private country party.

**The Gardens** On weekends before lunch and in the late afternoon, these host many contented strolling families, but are extensive enough to remain peaceful. The Jardín de la Isla is older than the Palace; they were planned by Isabel I and laid out by Sebastian Herrera in the seventeenth-century. Within avenues of plane and lime trees are marble and bronze fountains. The park is on the island across the River Tagus next to the Palace.

The Parterre is small and exquisite. Its trees, exotic and beautiful, and its gorgeous beds of flowers stretch between the east front of the Palace and the town. It was begun under Philip V by Francois Boutelou and is French-style garden of fountains, borders and foliage.

The Tourist Office at the foot of the Avda de los Infantas, in front of the Parterre Garden, will provide a map. Tourist Office, Plaza de Santiago Rusiñol, Tel: 891 0427.

The historic city of Toledo is less than 60km (36 miles) from Aranjuez along excellent roads. Eastwards from the royal town, towards Guadalajara, are two delightful small towns: Chinchón and Colmenar de Oreja.

**Chinchón,** home of the powerful anisette liqueur, is much frequented at the weekends and, as a result, is very well equipped with restaurants. Its Plaza Mayor is one of the most famous in the province – entirely surrounded by wood-balconied houses and arcades. During the late summer fiestas, bullfights are held here, the balconies teeming with spectators. An atmosphere of celebration fills the town on summer evenings, when the many restaurants, whose tables are placed out on the balconies overlooking the Plaza, fill with people.

The Iglesia de la Asunción, standing above the Plaza, treasures a Virgin by Goya. Apart from the elegant Parador, in a seventeenth-century Augustinian convent, there is no accommodation. The ruins of a castle, built in the fourteenth-century added to in the eighteenth-century and finally destroyed

**The Jardín del Principe**
designed by Franco is Boutelou, populated by pheasants and peacocks, is a mixture of English and French styles – with a forest of trees, ponds, fountains and follies – which eventually runs into a fine lawned garden which surrounds the Casita de Principe. It is deliciously cool in the summer. A museum of gilt carved ships used by royalty on the Tagus sits in the Jardín del Principe – the Casa de las Marinos.

**Chinchón Plaza Mayor**

by Napoleon, sit on the edge of the high plateau overlooking the dusty agricultural valley below. The view is superb.

There is a fiesta from 20–24 September.

**Colmenar de Oreja** Colmenar de Oreja, close by, has a massive parish church, next to which is a pretty, arcaded Plaza Mayor. Less visited than Chinchón, it is an awkward but charming old town, with marvellous views across the plains outside. Vineyards surround it, and *bodegas* are happy to sell wine to travellers.

Northwards towards Madrid is Arganda, a big industrial town that is not of touristic interest. A spectacular approach to Madrid is the M311 which curves, via Mora de Tajuna, through rugged dark red mountain countryside, clothed sparsely with gorse, rock-rose and herbs.

### West

**El Escorial** The monumental monastery of San Lorenzo sits 45km (28miles) west of the capital in the Guadarrama foothills. Beyond are the provinces of Ávila and Segovia. The small town of San Lorenzo is on a steep slope behind the monastery, while, a kilometre ($1/2$ mile) below is the town of El Escorial to which the trains from Madrid arrive. (A bus meets each train and leaves promptly for the monastery town.)

The monastery, built in just 25 years, was commissioned by Philip II in commemoration of a victory at St Quentin, France on the day of St Lawrence. The building is colossal, resting in the harsh beautiful countryside of grey-black mountains and forests of oak and pine.

The design began with the Italian-inspired plans of Juan Bautista de Toledo, and was continued and finished by Juan de Herrera (completed 1584). The granite building, lined with windows, consists of a square grid plan with great slate roofed towers at each corner and a vast dome over the central Basilica. Sixteen patios, 12 cloisters, 300 cells and 86 staircases give an idea of the scale. Surrounding are splendid gardens which sweep down to the Casita del Principe.

A visit to the monastery will take several hours and consists of a tour of the Basilica, the Panteón de los Reyes and subsequent mausoleums (beneath the Basilica High Altar), the Sacristía, the Salas Capitulars and the Palacio Real. In the Casita del Principe, built by Villanueva for Charles III, there are many Italian frescoes and paintings.

The entrance to the monastery is often enlivened by school children taught by the resident monks at the far side of the austere main façade. A huge statue of St Lawrence stands above the Renaissance columned portal. Within is the oppressive Patio de los Reyes, at the far end of which is the Basilica façade carrying 6 great statues of kings. (The ticket office is to the right of the patio, but a ticket is not required for a visit to the church. Mass is celebrated in a small chapel several times a day. On feast days, at 1 p.m., a choir sings.)

The plan of the Basilica was inspired by the original design for St Peters, Rome. It is awesome in size, with four massive pier-arches supporting the great dome, 92m (302ft) high. The walls and ceiling are frescoed by Spanish and Italian artists (the vaults of the sanctuary and *choro* by Luca Giordano and Luca Cambiaso).

The great central altarpiece of Juan de Herrera encloses paintings by Zuccaro and Tibaldi, and is adorned with marbles. To either side are gilded bronze statues of Charles V with his wife and daughters, and Philip II with three of his four wives (Mary Tudor, his second wife, is missing). These were worked by Pompeo and Leoni. In the centre is a statue of the Virgin,

**The monastery of San Lorenzo**

illuminated by natural light. She glows throughout the day even when the building is dark. Forty-three other altars decorated with Spanish and Italian paintings surround the huge church. A huge white sculpture of Christ stands to the right, worked by Benvenuto Cellini.

Beneath the church is the magnificent Royal Pantheon – an octagonal chamber lined with black marble and jasper, and decorated with bronze. It was built in 1617. In marble casks shelved in the walls are the monarchs of Spain from Charles V onwards. Beyond, in a pale marble room, are the sepulchres of the uncrowned royalty. Don Juan of Austria (half-brother of Philip II and commander at the battle of Lepanto) has an outstanding marble tomb. Another chamber houses the many small caskets of royal infants in a central mausoleum.

The Sacristy and ante-room are frescoed by Castello and Granello. The art collection is notable, including works by Ribera ('Descent from the Cross'), El Greco, Zurbarán, Titian ('Christ on the Cross'), Claudio Coello and Alonso Cano.

The chapter rooms (*salas capitulares*) are further art galleries, frescoed in Italian Pompeian style, with works by Ribera, Carducho, Giordano and others.

The library (*biblioteca*) is at the top of a fine staircase decorated by Giordano. It is a sumptuous gallery carrying a bright ceiling fresco of 'the Liberal Arts' by Pellegrino, Tibaldi, Carducho and Granello. The collection of books is priceless, including Arab, Greek and Jewish manuscripts, and ancient maps and codices from the time of Alfonso X El Sabio (a manuscript of his *Cantigas de Santa María* is kept here).

The Royal Palace, a later addition of Charles III and IV, is decorated in Bourbon style, with tapestries, dramatic frescos and a superb collection of paintings in which Maella, Velázquez and Goya are well represented. Further fine paintings are exhibited in the Palace of Philip II, behind the Basilica, of the Italian and Spanish schools and of works by Hieronymus Bosch, Dürer, and Van de Weyden. A small group of private apartments, finished in 1831, are exquisitely decorated in rich maquetry, used in furniture, doors, panelling and floors. An extra ticket is required to see these.

The private Hapsburg apartments (of Philip II) are of a totally different style from the Bourbon splendours – plain,

**The Cross of Valle de los Caidos**

**Interior ceiling of Biblioteca (Library) of Real Monasterio del Escorial**

small and austere with almost no colour save ceramic tiling.

The New Museums, in the left wing from the basilica, house the majority of the Escorial art collection, including great works of Bosch, Dürer, Titian, Ribera and Velázquez. (El Escorial: open 10 a.m.–1.30 p.m. and 3.30–6 p.m. Shut Mondays.)

The town beside the monastery is a popular retreat from the capital, particularly at weekends In winter it is very cold. There are many restaurants and bars, and the summer ambience is lively but tranquil. The golf course (of Herreria Club de Golf), close to the monastery is one of the most prestigious in the region. A festival of Baroque and Rococo music is held in July. On 10 September the Romería de la Virgen de Gracia is held here.

Across the valley from the town, a small road leads uphill from the road to Ávila (towards El Robledo) to the Silla de Felipe II, 3km (2miles) from the monastery. Here, amongst oak woods, is the carved stone seat from which Philip II watched the progress of the building. On Saturdays, wedding groups may often be found taking photographs here.

**Valle de los Caidos** The giant mausoleum of Valle de los Caidos is often linked with an excursion to El Escorial. In the hostile granite hills less than 20km (12miles) to the north-east, the giant cross, 125m (410ft.) high atop a pinnacle, can be seen from a great distance. Below, tunnelled 262m (271ft.) into the rock, is a great cavern of a church. The whole was built on the order of Generalísimo Franco to the memory of those who died in the civil war, and was worked by the defeated Republicans.

The church, barrel-vaulted with rough-carved stone, lined with tapestries and guarded by mighty Modernist statues has little sculptured decoration. Its impact is created by monumentalism and by the total lack of natural light. At the far end, overlooked by huge stone figures, is a simple altar above which is hung a large crucifix. The plain white tombstone of the Generalísimo is laid behind, and that of José Antonio Primo de Ribera (martyred founder of the Falange party) in front. A chapel is placed in each of the two short transepts. The crypt guards the remains of unknown soldiers killed in the war.

A short funicular will take visitors up to the base of the cross. From here the views of the province of Madrid are wonderful. Behind is a Benedictine monastery, which offers accommodation.

(Church Open: 10 a.m.–6 p.m., tickets sold at the gate at the foot of the hill.)

## NorthWest

West of Madrid the landscape is rugged and forested with oak and pine. The roads are relatively little travelled, except at weekends when the main routes to the Sierras de Gredos fill with cars. Wine is produced throughout the south-west of the region.

The old part of Navalcarnero is attractive, with a Plaza Mayor arcaded with tiers of balconies. The main parish church, La Asunción, has an imposing spire and keeps within one chapel some fine frescoes by Maella.

Close by is the small town of Aldea de Fresno, just outside which is a Safari Park, Reserva El Rincón, designed by Felix Rodríguez. The waters of the Alberche are used well by the town for a water park. Through vineyards and thick pine woods, a turning south leads to Toledo via the fortified town of Escalona.

**Caldalso de los Vidrios** Continuing on westwards is Cadalso de los Vidrios, a small quiet old town, little visited. The streets are lined with old *señorial* houses, amongst which there are *bodegas* proudly selling the good local wine. The sixteenth-century Palacio de Villena, Italian style, was built round the fifteenth-century castle of the powerful Alvara de Luna. The surrounding gardens are very beautiful.

From Cadalso, roads lead on towards the Gredos, or back to the N403 link between San Martín de Valdeiglesias and Escalona. This road is beautiful, running through forests of pine.

**San Martín de Valdeiglesias** is an important but still quite small old town, which has some splendid old buildings and a parish church by Juan de Herrera. Close to the centre of the pleasant town is another imposing castle founded by Alvaro de Luna, covered beautifully with ivy.

Just north is the Embalse de San Juan – a popular place for water sports. (Just across the Ávila border is the reservoir of Burguillo, which is also popular.) Close to Pelayos, on the first small turning to the reservoir after the village, are the great ruins of the twelfth-century Cistercian Monasterio de los Bernardos.

## South

Immediately south of Madrid is a knot of industrial suburbs. The roads are excellent but heavily used. An excursion here is only recommended as a route to Toledo or Aranjuez, not as a pretty journey for its own sake. Getafe is not a pleasant town, but has an important Renaissance church, Santa María Magdalena, showing strong Italian influences. A valuable collection of paintings is housed in the museum, including works by Claudio Coello.

Pinto, again growing industrially, has an attractive old part of the town, in which is a sixteenth-century church with a fine Plateresque retable. Of its castle, a colossal keep remains. The main parish church of Valdermoro is worth visiting if open (mass approx. 9 a.m. and late afternoon). The building is substantial, and within is a retable consisting of works by Goya and Bayeu, paintings by Claudio Coello and several sculptures. The town is attractive, with old *señorial* houses, and narrow streets.

The area is undulating and semi-agricultural, with a number of castle ruins. Just beyond Ciempozuelos, along the NIV, is the oasis of Aranjuez.

### Accommodation and Restaurants

**Alcala de Henares** *El Bedel* San Diego 6, Tel: 889 3700 – in the centre of town, just beside the unversity, 51 rooms, d&b 5300 (AE V).

Restaurant: *Hosteria Nacional del Estudiante* Colegio 3, Tel: 888 0330 – excellent roasts and regional food. Run by the Parador chain. At the back of the beautiful fifteenth-century patio Trilingue of the University, with a señorial dining-room (AE DC MC V).

Restaurant: *La Topeca* 5 Plaza Mayor – a big honest restaurant with a popular bar.

**Aranjuez** Accommodation fills at weekends.

*Isabel II* Avda Infantes 15, tela; 891 1345 – on one of the wooded central avenues, 25 rooms, d&b 4950 (AE DC MC V).

*Castilla* Ctra de Andalucia 28, Tel: 891 2627 – a very pleasant small hotel, family run and well decorated (on the main through road to the NIV, but not noisy) 15 rooms, d&b 2700 (V AE).

*Infantas* Calle de las Infantas 4, Tel: 891 1341 – 40 rooms, d&b 2950.

*Hostal Rusiñol* Avda San Antonio 76, Tel: 891 0155 – basic facilities but pleasant, 18 rooms, d&b 1450.

Weekend lunches are an institution here and the popular restaurants fill completely. On Friday and Saturday evenings the town bars overflow with young Madrileños.

Restaurant: *La Rana Verde* Calle Principe 12, Tel: 891 3238 – a splendid place to eat, on the banks of the Tajo.

Restaurant: *La Mina* Calle Principe 71, Tel: 891 1146 – a huge restuarant with rustic decor, packed with families. Ten minutes' walk from the palace, excellent home cooking.

Restaurant: *Chiron* Calle Real 10, Tel: 891 0941 – smart, intimate. Shut Sundays and during August (AE MC DC V).

Restaurant: *Casa Pablo* Calle Almibar 42, Tel: 891 1451 – a lively, dark Castilian tavern with roasts.

Around the top of Cale Principe and along San Antonio are many bars.

**Cercedilla** *El Aribel* Cueste de la Estacion, Tel: 852 1511 – 23 rooms, d&b 3500.

*Dehesas* Ctra de las Dehasas 4, Tel: 852 0241 – 16 rooms, d&b 9000.

Restaurant: *Los Frutales* Las Dehesas 41.

Restaurant: *Mirasierra* Ctra los Molinos 11 – AE DC MC V.

**Chinchon** Alive at weekends.. Restaurants all round the Plaza Mayor with tables on balconies overlooking the square. Very little accommodation available.

*Parador de Chinchon* Avda Generalísimo 1, Tel: 894 0836 – in a beautiful restored seventeenth-century monastery, 38 rooms, d&b 10000

Restaurant: *Venta Reyes* Ronda del Mediodia 78, Tel: 447 3159 – a familty restaurant with swimming-pool, horses stables and an extensive garden.

Restaurant: *Café de Iberia* Plaza Mayor 17, Tel: 894 0998 – with tables overlooking the square, and inside a pretty patio (1st floor), excellent spit-roasts, Shut Wednesdays.

Restaurant: *Mesén Cuevas del Vino* Calle Benito Hortelano 13, Tel: 894 0206 – in an old mill in the centre of town, with huge old vats, bar rooms and rustic cooking, very popular, bench tables.

**El Pardo** Restaurant: *Pedro's* Avda de la Guardia, Tel: 736 0883 – with a pleasant terrace (AE V).

Restaurant: *La Marquesita* Avda de la Guardia 4, Tel: 736 0377 – sophisticated, with a terrace (AE DC MC V).

**Mansanares el Real** *El Tranco* Tranco 4, Tel: 853 0423 – 12 rooms, d&b 4400, below the peaks of La Pedriza, with a river running by, simple restaurant.

Restaurant: *La Parra* Calle Panaderos 15, Tel: 853 0399 – good for grills and roasts (V).

**Miraflores de la Sierra** *Refugio* Ctra Madrid, Tel: 844 4211 – 48 rooms, d&b 4500, pool and view.

Restaurant: *Las Llaves* Calvo Sotelo 4, Tel: 844 4057 – traditional dishes, suckling pig. Highly regarded and very popular at weekends.

**Navacerrada** *Arcipreste de Hita* Ctra Madrid-Leon 52 (Praderas de San Sebastian), Tel: 856 0125 – 39 rooms, d&b 3400. *La Barranca* Valle de la Carranca, Tel: 856 0000 – 56 rooms, d&b 6500.

**Puerto de Navacerrada** *Venta de Arias* Ctra de la Granja (Puerto de Navaccerada), Tel: 852 1434 – 15 rooms, d&b 3000, restaurant, Shut Tuesdays and during October.

Restaurant: *Fonda Real* Madrid-Segovia road, Tel: 856 0305 – eighteenth-century Castilian decor (AE V MC).

**Rascafria** *Santa Maria del Pauler* Tel: 869 1011 – 58 rooms, d&b 13000, restaurant (AE DC MC V). Exceptional, with superb sports facilities and a very beautiful, tranquil setting.

**San Lorenzo del Escorial** Quality accommodation is plentiful, though frequently fully booked. Cheaper accommodation is almost non-existent. The town is very lively at weekends and on summer evenings.

*Victoria Palace* Juan de Toledo 4, Tel: 890 1511 – 87 rooms, d&b 8200 (AE DC MC V).

*Miranda Suizo* Floridablanca 18, Tel: 890 1511 – 48 rooms d&b 5400, with a fashionable café/bar beneath.

*Jardin* Leandro Rubio 2, Tel: 896 1007 – 22 rooms, d&b 2500, pretty garden, quiet.

*Malagon* San Francisco 2, Tel: 890 1007 – 10 rooms, d&b 1700, almost the only *hostal* in town.

Restaurant: *El Cenedor de Maite* San Anton 19, Tel: 890 4495 – sophisticated cooking. Beautiful garden terrace, very well regarded by Madrileños. Shut Mondays.

Restaurant: *Charoles* Calle Floridablanca 24, Tel: 890 5975 – a gourmet restuarant, very sophisticated in ambience.

Restaurant: *Alaska* Plaza de San Lorenzo, 4, Tel: 890 0889 – a good family restaurant.

Restaurant: As-*Burgas* Cervantes 4, Tel: 890 7319 – a good family restaurant.

**Camping** Most open all year.

| | |
|---|---|
| Madrid: | Osuna, Tel: 741 0510 – Cat 1, 360 people. |
| | Municipal Camping: Tel: 202 2836 – Cat 2, 764 people. |
| Aldea de Fresno: | Tel: 863 7299, – Cat 2, 500 people. |
| Aranjuez: | Soto del Castillo, Tel: 891 1385 – Cat 1, Open 1 April to 30 September, 800 people. |
| Bustarviejo: | El Valle, Tel: 844 3587 – Cat 2, 320 people. |
| Cabanillas de la Sierra: | D'Oremor, Tel: 843 9034 – Cat 2, 720 people. |
| La Cabrera: | Pico de la Miel, Tel 868 8082 – Cat 1, 960 people. |
| El Escorial: | La Herreria, Tel: 890 5617 – Cat 2, 300 people. Caravanning, Tel: 890 2412 – Cat 1, 3000 people |
| Garangilla del Lozoya: | Monte Holiday, Tel: 869 3076 – Cat 2, 1200 people. |
| Manzanares el Real: | El Ortigal, Tel: 853 0120 – Cat 3, 600 people. |
| Navalafuente: | Piscis, Tel: 843 9087 – Cat 2, 656 people. |
| San Sebastian de los Reyes: | Aterpe Alai, Tel: 654 4640 – Cat 2, 523 people. |
| Soto del Real: | La Fresneda, Tel: 847 6523 – Cat 2, 500 people. |
| Valdemorilo: | Tel: 899 0002 – Cat 2, 300 people. San Juan, Tel: 899 0300 – Cat 3, 300 people. |
| Villaciviosa de Odon: | Arco Iris, Tel: 616 0387 – Cat 2, 880 people. |

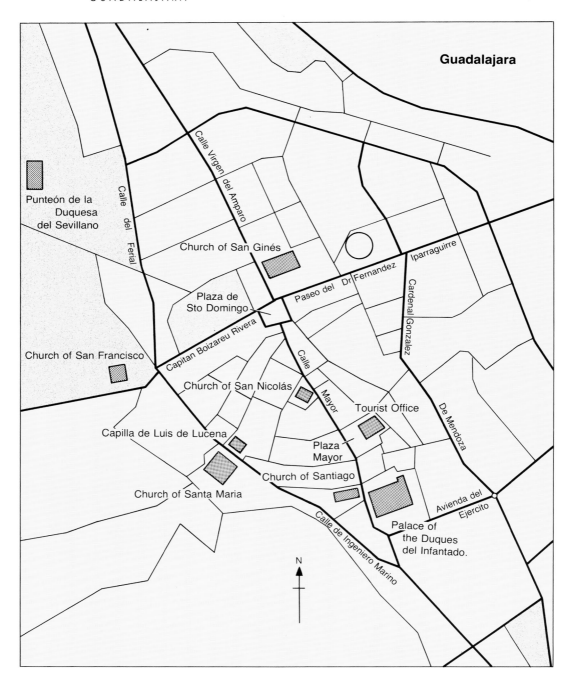

**Guadalajara** is a tranquil, refreshing city set within a dramatic red countryside of undulating plains and sudden hill rises. Its character is akin to that of a wealthy country town, with spacious streets full of light, fine old buildings, and parks that are as expansive as they are beautiful. The small city attracts few visitors compared with the other provincial capitals near Madrid; it has little of cultural or historical interest but its gentle pace and quiet ambience are delightful.

**History** The historical prestige of Guadalajara is strongly connected with that of the resident dukes of Mendoza, whose power rose in the fifteenth-century and subsided in the sixteenth-century. Under the Catholic Monarchs their influence was such that Pedro Gonzalez de Mendoza, cardinal of Toledo, was entombed amongst the kings' sepulchres in Toledo Cathedral. The magnificent Ducal Palace was built at this time. The third Duke received Charles V's prisoner Francis I of France here after the battle of Pavia, and 1559 Philip II married his second wife in the Palace.

Napoleonic troops ravaged the town in 1809, rifling many of the family tombs. Fighting in the civil war caused further damage.

### Outstanding Monuments
Palacio de los Duques del Infantado, Open: 10.15 a.m.–2 p.m. and 4–7 p.m. Shut Sunday afternoons.

### Notable Monuments
Panteón de la Duquesa del Sevillano, Open: 10.30 a.m.–12.45 p.m. and 4–7 p.m., Sunday 10.30 a.m.–2 p.m.
Iglesia de Santiago
Iglesia de Santa Maria
Capilla de Luis de Lucena
Iglesia de San Nicolas
Iglesia de San Ginés
Iglesia de San Francisco
Palacio del Dávalos

**Layout of the Town** The main axis of the city is Plaza de Santo Domingo. From here the old town is downhill to the south, and the newer areas spread to the north and east. Calle Mayor is the social centre of the city and the commercial artery of the old town, within which are most of the notable buildings.

125

Much of this area is pedestrian. The new part of the city, growing gradually as its industrial importance increases, is not interesting to the visitor. The parks extend to the west.

**The Historic City** With the exception of the Panteón de la Duquesa, all the notable buildings are close together in the old quarter.

**Palacio de los Duques del Infantado** The Mendoza family held the town of Guadalajara within their fief in the fourteenth-century. This exotic palace, which sits squarely at the foot of the old town, was built by Juan Guas for them at the height of their political power.

The façade is striking. Built of a golden sandstone in Gothic/early Renaissance style, the flat surface is studded with diamond-shaped bosses. Above is a line of Gothic windows set in turret-like bays, delicately decorated in Mudéjar style. The delicatelly carved doorway is surmounted by a great escutcheon bearing the arms of the Mendoza.

Within is a remarkable patio, entered via the doorway on the left side of the building. The balustrades are supported by twisted carved columns beneath which splendid lions and griffins display the Mendoza and Luna shields.

Damaged by Napoleonic troops (1809) and by civil war bombing (1936), many of the rooms of the palace interior have been lost. Only two downstairs rooms show the original glory of decoration – frescoed on wall and ceiling in Italian style and tiled in *azulejos* (glazed blue and yellow). Of the rooms above, one gallery, closed to the public, is similarly decorated. Much of the interior is now used as the featureless office for municipal archives and for the library.

The provincial art gallery is to the left of the patio, displaying a collection of religious sculptures and paintings, amoungst which are works by José Ribera, Tristán and Escalante.

**Iglesia de Santiago** The church of Santiago is just up from the palace, along Calle Teniente Figueros. Once a convent of the Poor Clares, the restored brick building has a fine wood-panelled ceiling and slender columns which support painted arches. There is a lovely Plateresque chapel.

**Iglesia de Sante Maria** Right along Calle Ramón y Cajál (end of Calle Teniente Figueros) is the unusual church of Santa Maria. Once a mosque, it has a thirteenth-century minaret, baroque façade, neo-Mudéjar horseshoe doorway and a wood canopy which shelters two sides. It was consecrated as a semi-cathedral (*Con-catedral*) thirty years ago. The interior is unremarkable, except for two fine tombs and a statue of the Virgen de las Batallas who was reputedly carried by Alfonsa VI in his crusade against the Moors. A green neon sign labels her chapel.

**Capilla de Luis Lucena** The small brick chapel of San Luis de Lucena, nearby, contains delapidated sixteenth-century frescos by Romulo Cincinato and is kept permanently closed. The round-buttressed corners and patterned façades are capped with superb ornamental brickwork.

**Iglesia de San Nicolás** By the Calle Mayor, San Nicolás, a Jesuit church, looks onto the Plaza Jardinillo. Its interior is dominated by a huge Churriguesresque gilt retable and two florid side chapels. On the tomb of Rodrigo de Campuzano, the alabaster recling figure is similar to that of the famous Doncel, lying in Sigüenza Cathedral. The choir stalls belonged originally to the monastery of Lupianza, 10km(6miles) from the city.

**Iglesia de San Ginés** San Ginés crowns the Plaza de Santo Domingo. Severe damage during the civil war left the Mendoza and Tendilla tombs mutilated, but they are worth a look if the church (undergoing repairs) is open.

**Iglesia de San Francisco (Mendoza Mausoleum)** On the far side of the Parque de la Concordia, along Calle Capitán Boixareu Rivera, are the grounds of the Military Police. Inside is the church of San Francisco, to which visitors are welcome. Entombed in the Gothic crypt are 28 members of the Mendoza family. Among other tombs is that of the Archiprieste of Hita, the literary figure who wrote the *Libro de Buen Amor (Book of Good Love)*. The building suffered damage from Napoleonic troops.

**Panteón de la Duquesa del Sevillano** (also called Panteón de la Condesa de la Vega del Pozo). This fantastic neo-gothic mausoleum, built late last century under the design of Gonzalez Velázquez, is reached by an uphill walk through Parque de San Rogue, or via a bus ride from Santo Domingo. Adoratrice nuns from the convent opposite, make the visit a most memorable experience, such is their pride in the Byzantine riches of the building. If the gate is shut, a doorbell on the right-hand side of the school/convent quadrangle will draw a guide. The

**Palacio de los Duques del Infantado**

127

**Mausoleum of the Duquesa del Sevillano**

high dome and ceiling of the mausoleum are decorated with mosaic· and the walls lined with marbles. The colossal altars are constructed from marbles from the five major sources in Spain. The crypt, in which lies the Duchess and members of her family, houses a magnificent black tomb surmounted by monumental alabaster angels. Splendid bronze lanterns and wreaths surround the sepulchre.

**Plaza Mayor and Palacio del Davalos** The square is dominated by the clean, classical Ayuntamiento, beside which are contrastingly old grey overhanging houses. In the square behind is the Palacio del Dávalos which has a fine Renaissance style. A beautiful Plateresque door is in the far corner, and above are *artesonado* ceilings.

**Shopping** The main shopping street is Calle Mayor, running south off Plaza de Santo Domingo through the old town. It is lined with boutiques, *pastellerías* and elegant shops, and is punctuated by various churches and two attractive squares, Plaza Jardinillo and Plaza Mayor. Further down, the quality of shops lessens and, as the street becomes Calle Miguel Fluiters, it becomes a focus of local shops. There are surprisingly few side-street shops

Behind the Plaza Mayor – recognizable by its distinctive pale pink Ayuntamiento – at the end of Calle Dr Mayoral, is the Municipal Market. It is most lively on Tuesday and Saturday mornings when a street market fills the square outside.

On Plaza de Santo Domingo is a large supermarket which is open until 8.30 p.m. Eastwards from the Plaza, the Paseo del Dr Fernández Iparraguirre is irregularly lined with large show-room shops selling furniture and kitchen goods.

**The Paseo** The evening route flows gently down Calle Mayor, where *pastellerías* serve the local *bizcochos borrachos* (literally tipsy cakes) and cream buns. The Plaza above – Santo Domingo – fills with talking companions and some people drift eastwards down the central tree-lined part of Paseo de Dr Fernández Iparraguirre. The parks are always popular.

**Parks** The lush greenness of Guadalajara's parks is a spectacular contract to the parched red-brown landscape that surrounds the city. Parque de la Concordia is a cool garden planted with trees and shrubs just to the west of Plaza de Santo Domingo. Throughout the afternoons men sit in its shade playing cards.

Parque de San Roque, a minute's walk further west, clothes the hillside with a broad expanse of grass and woodland. In its higher reaches are several schools, and it accommodates their playing fields. The park is very spacious, and thus is both lively and extremely tranquil.

Beside the River Henares is another generous length of garden – the Parque del Río.

**Fiestas** Semana Santa: processions Thursday, Friday, Sunday; Virgen de la Antiqua: 8 September; Autumn fiesta: 25–30 September bullfights and dancing.

**Bars and Tapas** The bars fill during the paseo and at lunchtime. *Tapas*, particularly of fish, are excellent here. The most lively street is Calle Bardales, reached from the Plaza Mayor via Calle San Gil.

**Restaurants** Dinner is taken late, from 9 p.m. onwards.

The region is endowed with excellent hunting and fishing terrain. Local fare is seasonal game, trout, roasts (kid) and grills. Fish is also excellent, as fresh fish is brought in daily by air from Madrid.

There are few bars or restaurants on the main streets in the town. Calle Bardales is lively both at lunchtime and through the evening. It runs between San Esteban and San Gil, Plaza Mayor.

**Guadalajara Plaza Mayor**

129

*Casa Victor* Calle Bardales 6, Tel: 212247 – very popular, with a first-rate *tapas* bar and jovial barmen. The *comedor* (dining-room) is fairly casual (go through behind) and is packed at lunchtime. Roasts are good, and there is a fine selection of shellfish. Shut Thursdays.

*El Figón* Calle Bardales 7, Tel: 211588 – good *tapas*, smarter restaurant upstairs. Good grills, and excellent fish and shellfish. Shut Wednesdays.

*Miguel Angel* (old name: *El Ventorrero*) Lopez de Haro 4, Tel: 212563 – a smart dining-room, full at lunch. A refined ambience both in here and at the bar. The roasts are excellent. Shut Sundays. (DC V).

*Husa Pax Hotel Restaurant* (*see* Hotels) – quality international cuisine, smart dining-room, oriented to the businessman.

### Hotels

The town expects few visitors to stay and is poorly equipped with rooms.

### Category 1

*Husa Pax Hotel* Carretera Madrid/Barcelona (marked from the main road), Tel: 221800 – about ten minutes' walk from the centre of the town, this is the most comfortable hotel here. The uninterrupted views stretch far across the red, hilly landscape. Peaceful yet close to the main town bypass. The majority of the clientele are businessmen.

61 rooms d&b 5400. Restaurant (AE DC MC V).

*Hotel La Cañada* Horche (on the road to Pastrana), Tel: 290211 – welcoming and comfortable. Built with conferences in mind, and with a superb setting. The village is a delight to walk around, with steep narrow streets and a charming market square. Views from the hotel reach across the valley. Ten minutes from Guadalajara by car.

### Category 2

*Hotel Residencia España*
Teniente Figueroa 3, Tel: 211303 – simple and straightforward, close to the Calle Mayor.

33 rooms, d&b 2900. Parking

### Category 3

*Hostal Arroyo* Conzalo Heranz 2, Tel: 211123 – rather shabby with minimal facilities.

25 rooms, d&b 1600.

## Information

| | |
|---|---|
| Area Exchange Code | 911 |
| Estación de Autobuses, Calle Dos de Mayo 1 | 211421 |
|    SE of Plaza Mayor, five minutes walk | |
| Estación de Renfe, Calle Francisco Aritio | 211342 |
|    S of river, fifteen minutes walk | |
| Taxis, Plaza Santo Domingo, Calle Teniente Figueroa | 226358 |
| | and 212245 |
| Tourist Office, Plaza Mayor 7, Open: 9.30–2 p.m., | |
| Shut Sundays) | 220698 |
| Ayuntamiento, Plaza Mayor 7 | |
| *Correos* (Post Office) | |
| Calle Teniente Figueroa 5 | 211493 |
| Cruz Roja (Red Cross), Avda de Venezuela 1 | 226212 |
| Swimming pool: Corner of Parque San Roc/Calle San Roc | |

**Transport** With Madrid: twice-hourly trains, some continuing to Segovia and Valladolid.

Buses: hourly links with the capital

Cars: liberal street parking, but awkward to the east of the Plaza Mayor at market time.

*The parks of Guadalajara make a pleasant place for lunch*

**Around Guadalajara** Guadalajara is a little-visited and little-known province. A great highway, the N11, cuts through it, linking Madrid with the north-east of Spain. Of the huge weight of passing traffic, very few vehicles venture off the main road. The wild, hilly landscape is almost free of travellers and the resulting sense of space and tranquillity is remarkable.

The countryside is hilly throughout. The north is dominated by foothills of the Guadarrama – sharp granite ridges and deep forested valleys, populated sparsely by ancient villages.

To the north-east above the N11, are rolling hills, extensive valley plains, and narrow cultivated plateaus. Of the numerous fortifications, Sigüenza, Atienza and Jadraque are outstanding. South-east, expansive cereal fields sweep and huge forests reach to the great hillside fortress of Molina de Aragon. The beautiful Parque Natural del Alto Tajo is here.

South of the capital is the medieval hillside town of Pastrana, and eastwards lie the extensive resevoirs of the Mar de Castilla and the dignified fortified towns of Brighuega and Cifuentes.

**North** Few passes cross the ridged border into north-east Madrid or Segovia, but a number of roads trickle through the mountainous region to the north of Guadalajara. They follow the river valleys from north to south, and all are breath-takingly beautiful. Dotted along are ancient stone villages, dark with the morning mist. The passes, some cutting through ochre-coloured rock, are clothed by thick forests of lichen-covered oak, beech woods, valleys filled with pine, small meadows, and masses of fern, heather and gorse, covering granite sweeps. (The roads are uncomfortable to drive at night.) There are good walks behind these untouched villages, rewarded by waterfalls (particularly at Valverde de los Arroyos) and otherwise unseen rugged summits.

### Sierra de Ayllón/Reserva Naciónal de Sonsaz

The Reserva Naciónal de Sonsaz, comprising a huge area of the Alta Jarama and the Sorbe valley, protects roe deer and wild boar. Birds of prey include golden eagle, red kite and goshawk. In the northern reaches close to the Segovian border (the Sierra de Ayllón) is the Parque Natural Hayedo de Tejera Negra, forested densely with beech, yew and oak. Lush green meadows lie close to the young River Sorbe. Cantalojas is the nearest village to the park, some 12km (7miles) away. A very beautiful granite

Romanesque church stands in the village, with a solid tower and a most unusual frieze running along one exterior façade. The Romanesque church style is prevalent in the villages of the area. On C114, Cantalojas is a pretty base for the region, close to Atienza and the active Segovian towns of Riaza and Ayllón.

**Cogolludo** To the south of the region is the village of Tamajón, with another lovely church, while San Andres de Congosto Alcorlo and Cogolludo nestle in the rolling hills. Here clothed either with grain fields or wild rock-rose and rosemary. Cogolludo is a favourite visiting place for weekenders, with its warm fresh climate. On one side of the ample main square stands the palace of the Lords of Medinaceli, whose Renaissance façade is quite magnificent. The remains of the patio arches stand behind, but the interior of the palace is empty. The parish church above the village has a good Plateresque façade but the painting by Ribera, so carefully treasured here, is now housed in the Prado while the building is restored.

**North-East** To the north of the N11 the main town is Sigüenza, close to the Sorian border. From the city of Guadalajara, its approach by the C101 via Hita and Jadraque is beautiful. The countryside is mainly dry, with small round hills of rock-rose and rosemary, drawing out into extensive plains around Jadraque. Hita, a popular weekend visit for Madrileños, is a pretty village enclosed by fifteenth-century walls which stand almost in their entirety. Inside, although suffering much damage to its churches during the civil war, the village feels medieval. (From here there is a good route to the Sierras, via the small curving road to Cogolludo).

**Jadraque** The town of Jadraque, on the edge of a plain, is approached from a pass through a ridge of high hills behind it. The town itself is relatively uninteresting, but its high backdrop is utterly breath-taking — a graceful castle placed atop a perfect conical hill commanding an unbeatable view of the dry valley landscape. It is thought that Castle Cid was never completed (it was order to be built by Cardinal Mendoza in the fifteenth-century) but its imposing walls make it one of the most spectacular in Castile. From the town below, in which the church houses a Zurbarán 'Flagellation', wooded roads lead towards the Sierras via La Toba (a very pretty road); or northwards to Atienza; or towards Sigüenza skirting the great red cliff edges of the valleys.

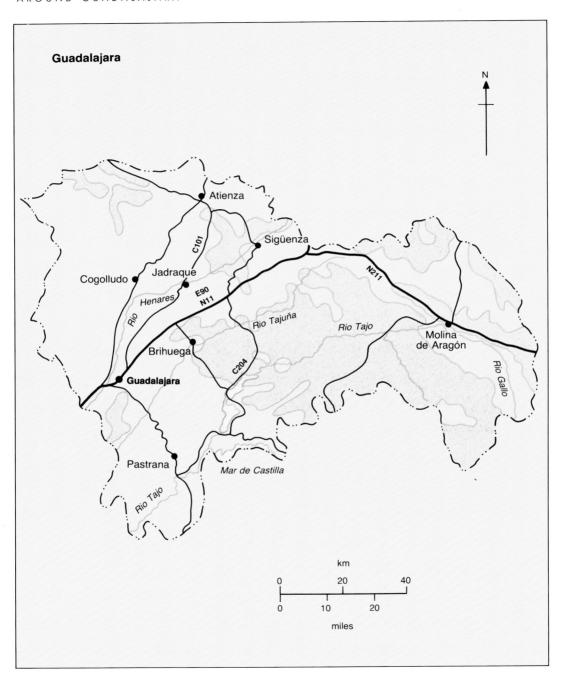

Guadalajara

**Sigüenza** Amongst the treeless rolling plains the severe fortress walls of Sigüenza are a massive interruption. The historic importance of the town is illustrated by the antiquity of the castle – founded by Visigoths – and the status of bishopric that was given in 589 (and is still retained today). The castle became the episcopal palace of the powerful bishops of the Mendoza and then Fonseca dynasties. A key fortress in the battles between Aragón and Castilla, then looted in the peninsular wars, the castle is now well restored and accommodates a Parador hotel.

From the castle to the Plaza Mayor is a steep, pretty street of stone houses. The fine fifteenth-century mansion façade of the Casa del Doncel faces a Romanesque/Byzantine church nearby. The Cathedral, by the arcaded Plaza, is heavily fortified, with two great square crenolated towers either side of the west portal. Built between the twelfth and fifteenth-centuries, it is endowed with an interesting collection of sculptures: flamboyant Gothic choir stalls fifteenth-century tombs, decorous alabaster pulpits and intricate altarpieces. The charming tomb of the Doncel de Sigüenza, where a tranquil youth, perched upon an elbow, lies

**The spectacular scenery around Guadalajara**

135

reading, is very well known. The museum here has an important collection of paintings including works by Zurbarán, Morales, El Greco and Titian (Open: 11.30 a.m.–2 p.m. and 5–7.30 p.m.). The Chapel of Humilladera, in the gardens below the Cathedral, has Visigothic foundations.

North and south of Sigüenza are glorious areas of countryside. South of the N11 a delightful area reaches to the Parque Natural del Alto Tajo, whose dominant town is Molina de Aragón. North-west are the Sierras, approachable from either end at Atienza or Jadraque. Towards Atienza are several attractive villages dotted amongst the pine woodland and dry landscape, particularly Palazuelos, with superbly preserved walls and castle, and Riba de Santiuste, with a pretty castle ruin.

**Atienza** is a dignified town protected by a double ring of medieval walls with several towers still standing. Inside are a number of fine churches (particularly La Trinidad), mansions and two pretty arcaded squares. The castle ruin stands on the hill beside, at the foot of which is the twelfth-century Santa Maria del Rey. On Pentecost Sunday a lively fiesta takes place – the Caballada – during which horses from the region are ridden bareback through the streets commemorating the events of 1162 which secured the reign of the child King Alfonso VIII. From Atienza the beautiful roads of the Sierras are close.

**South-East** In the region between Cifuentes and Molina de Aragón, the sweeping grain plateaus of red-orange earth and the valley forests give a feeling of great space and stillness.

**Molina de Aragón** Surrounded by a dry hilly landscape, Molina de Aragón has a most dramatic fortification: a barren hillside enclosed by a huge ring of high wall with eight square watch-towers. Four of these still stand solid. A solitary keep remains at the crest of the hill. The town, below the walls, has a number of fine Romanesque churches and a pretty bridge crossing the river near the old *judería* (Jewish quarter).

**Parque Natural del Alto Tajo** The Parque Natural del Alto Tajo, shaped like a boomerang to follow the course of the great river, is very little known, but most spectacular for its deep, forested limestone gorges. There are walking trails from the southern point by Peralejo de las Truchas, a pretty old village, right round to Ocentego. Fishing here is superb. A track, barely

driveable, follows the flow of the river from the south up to the GU914 and thereafter the quietness is totally uncompromised. Outside the park are tiny rural communities.

**Jadraque's Castle Cid commands an unbeatable view of the valley landscape**

Northwards, towards Sigüenza, are the ancient cave paintings of Cueva de los Casares and Cueva de la Hoz, both of which make good walking excursions. Southwards, from the village of Villanueva de Alcorón, is a shorter hike to the low peak of La Zapatilla near which there is a fabulous waterfall.

**South** Leaving the capital city to the south, the prettiest road is the N320/C200, which arrives eventually at Pastrana. A few kilometres before Horche a turning east leads along a rocky valley to the lonely monastery of San Bartolomé, Lupiana, a handsome late Gothic building. The cloistered monks will show the extremely beautiful sixteenth-century cloister to visitors on Mondays between 9 a.m. and 12 p.m. Further along, the tiny road GU921 winds up to the pretty, ancient village of Valfermoso de Tajuna from where there are wonderful views of the province. Further quiet roads link eastwards along the tree-lined valley of the Tajuna (eventually the C201), connecting Brihuega and Cifuentes.

Along the N320, the old houses in the awkward village of Horche cluster in the side of a steep hill overlooking a wooded valley. The village is charming to walk through. The countryside is typical of this area, with small oaks in the valleys; rock-rose, herbs and shrubs cladding the hills; and tight terracing surrounding the settlements. The honey from the region is famously delicious. The occasional old villages sit above or below the road, with ample plazas and notable Romanesque churches, many with one porticoed side similar in style to those of Segovia.

**Pastrana** The road approaches Pastrana from above, a beautiful medieval town on the spur of a hill some 40km (24miles) of curves away from the city. The town, surrounded by forests of oak and pine above a valley of terraces, fills at the weekends with families from Madrid. A Roman foundation, it was owned by the powerful Knightly Order of Calatrava until bought by the widow of Diego Hurtado de Mendoza. Under her distinguished descendents, it gained the massive Colegiata (collegiate church) and developed a silk industry of great reputation. Within its walls is a maze of delightful old streets and, in the treasury of the Colegiata, are preserved a magnificent collection of tapestries.

**A farmstead near Lupiana**

A mansion-lined street leads to the Plaza Mayor (where there is

parking space) of which an entire side is taken by the Renaissance palace of the first Duke of the town, today under long-term restoration. The Colegiata, part Renaissance, part fourteenth century, is at the top of the high street tightly surrounded by houses. Its interior walls are lined with retables, and its High Altar crowded with decorative objects. The museum collection is formidable (open: 1–2.30 p.m. and 4–6 p.m.). The four great tapestries, vibrant with colour and energy, recount the war exploits of Alfonso V of Portugal in North Afgrica. The highly detailed patterns, of the Portugese artist Nuño Concalves, were worked in Brussels during the 1470s using the silk of Pastrana. These tapestries are some of the most magnificent in Spain. From the Princess Éboli (of the court of Philip II), black funerary velvets embroidered with silver are displayed with dignity. The rooms also contain religious sculptures from the thirteenth to eighteenth centuries, paintings (including a Morales 'Christ'), silver chalices and a twelfth-century Byzantine enamel casket. There are various momentoes of Santa Teresa and St John of the Cross, both of whom had strong connections with the town by founding convents here.

Continuing southwards from this delightful town, a series of fortified villages sit below the Embalse de Zorita. A fine ruin of dilapidated towers remain of the Calatrava castle (of Arab origin) at Zorita de los Canes, in which sits a barrel-vaulted Romanesque church. Nearby is the archaeological site of Recópolis, a Visigothic town. Almonacid de Zorita is a little further south, surrounded by agricultural fields and orchards of fruit and almond trees, where a well-preserved fourteenth-century wall surrounds the lively community. The late Gothic parish church is splendid. Northwards are a series of great reservoirs.

**Mar de Castilla** Known as the Sea of Castile, the hydroelectric product of this string of reservoirs constitutes a vital part of Guadalajara's economy. From the hills on the west side, clad in pine forest, are glorious views of the waters. A particularly spectacular route climbs a pass between cliffs to descend into the resort of Sacedón. The communities here expand in the summer months as many come to enjoy the coolness of the steep west hills or the beaches and water sports of the east side. Durón and Alocén are pretty resorts.

**Cifuentes** is the major town above the Embalse de Entrepenas. Sitting high above is the proud ruin of the castle, from where the town walls were built to surround the whole town. The sturdy keep and square defence towers still stand. The centre of the compact town is spacious, with an attractive Plaza Mayor, arcaded and triangular, which leads up to the Renaissance portal of San Salvador. Inside, the church is Romanesque/Gothic with fine vaults.

Towards Brihuega is the hilltop village of Yela, at the summit of which sits a beautiful Romanesque church. It is unusual in having colonnades on both sides, and the pillar capitals of its main door are graced with sculptured leaves.

**Briheuga** is an important historic town. It is beautifully approached from Cifuentes, the road running beside a river under glades of eucalyptus, poplar, hawthorn and honeysuckle. The town was once a resort for the Moorish kings of Toledo, and is a refreshing place with a fortifying wall built only last century. The ruined castle walls are draped in ivy and sit to one end of the town. At the higher end is the circular pink shell of Charles III's royal cloth factory (La Real Fabrica de Paños). Although in great disorder within (the private owner has only restored the façade), the gardens of the factory are exquisitely arranged and beautifully kept, with fine views over the woods beneath and the dusty brown hills further away. The town has a number of notable Romanesque churches in varying states of repair, particularly San Felipe which is set back off the main curve of the road.

Back on the main N11 is Torija, whose square thirteenth-century fortress, with tall sturdy keep, has been well restored.

## Accommodation and Restaurants

Cantaloja
*Hayedo de Tejera Negra*, Camino de Rubial,
Tel: 303028 – 8 rooms.
Valverde
Restaurant: *El Corzo* – family eating house, roasts.
Sigüenza *Parador Castillo de Sigüenza*, Plaza del Castillo,
Tel: 390100 – 77 rooms, d&b 8500. Beautiful; in the castle/Episcopal palace at the top of the town. Good restaurant.
*El Doncel*, General Mola 1, Tel: 391090 – 20 rooms, d&b 3000.
Restaurant: *El Moderno* General Mola 1, Tel: 390001 – shut June, July and Sunday afternoons, country decor.

Atienza

*Fonda Molinero* Calle Hector Vazquez 11 Tel: 399017.

Molina de Aragón

*Rosanz*, Paseo de los Adarves 12, Tel: 830836 – 33 rooms, d&b 2400.

*El Giraldo*, Plaza de San Francisco 16, Tel: 831291 – 12 rooms, d&b 2800, simple restaurant.

Pastrana.

Restaurant: *Hosteria Princesa de Ebol*, Calle Monja – shut weekend evenings, simple cooking.

Restaurant: *Meson Galindo's*, Calle de Teracón, Tel: 370161 – 90m (100yds) beyond the town, roasts. Ring before for their superb *cabrito asado* (roast kid).

Sacedón

*Mari Blanca*, Matires 2, Tel: 350044 – 27 rooms, d&b 2500.

Brihuega, *El Torreón*, Paseo Cristina 6, Tel: 280300 – 20 rooms, d&b 2500.

Cifuentes

*San Roque*, Ctra Comarcal 204, Tel: 810028 – 28 rooms, d&b 2500, simple restaurant.

**Camping** By Parque del Alto Tajo: orea, 6km (3$^{1}/2$ miles) from Casco Urbano, Tel: 836001 – Cat 1, open 1 April to 30 September, 72 people.

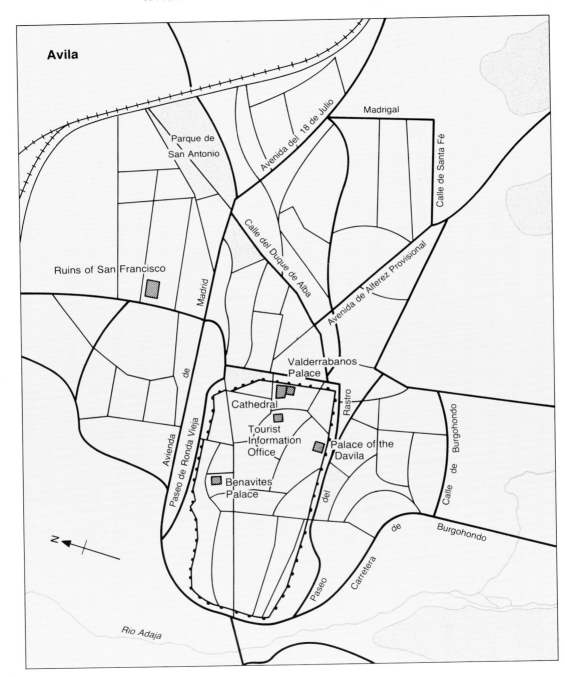

Avila

Parque de San Antonio

Madrigal

Avenida del 18 de Julio

Calle de Santa Fé

Ruins of San Francisco

Calle del Duque de Alba

Madrid

Avenida de Alferez Provisional

de

Avienda

Paseo de Ronda Vieja

Valderrabanos Palace

Cathedral

Rastro

Calle de Burgohondo

Tourist Information Office

Palace of the Davila

Benavites Palace

del

Paseo

Carretera

de

Burgohondo

N

Rio Adaja

**Ávila** The great walls of Ávila can be seen from many kilometres away, crowning a hill above the Río Adaja. The small provincial capital, magnificently fortified, is peaceful, quiet and refreshing. Views extend across the countryside from many of its streets. It is an important centre of religious tourism being the birthplace and home of Santa Teresa, and fills particularly at the weekends and summer months with visitors. Its spacious streets, and the wide scattering of its monuments, accommodate them easily.

Ávila is small enough to be visited comfortably in a day, and is particularly beautiful in the late afternoon when the setting sun tinges the walls with gold and the churches with a rose hue. Being the highest city in Spain at 1,131m (3,711ft.) it is extremely cold in winter, and very hot in summer.

**History** There was an important settlement here in Celtic times. Religious prominence began with the first-century AD missionary powers of San Segundo, the first bishop of the town. It gained its fortifications after being retaken from Moorish occupation by Alfonso VI. Count Raymond of Borgoña, who had the walls built, repopulated the town with noble families from the north, members of which subsequently took part in the discoveries of the New World a few centuries later. The city

**The magnificent walls of Ávila**

flourished in the fifteenth and sixteenth-centuries, when many *señorial* palaces were built, and flowed into a steady decline from the seventeenth-century onwards. The religious prominence of the town continues with the memory of Santa Teresa, born here in 1515. (The composer Thomas Luís de Victoria (1548–1611) also came from Ávila.)

Santa Teresa, patron saint of Spain, started her distinguished religious career at the age of 20 when she became a nun. With her confessor, San Juan of the Cross, she was responsible for reforming the Carmelite order along the principles of subsistence without possessions through charity. Her foundations are spread through Castile. By the time of her death in Alba de Tormes on 17 October 1581, she had founded 17 convents for women and a further 15 for men. Her mystical writings, originally inspired through the Confessions of St Augustine, had a profound influence on religious thought at the time. She was cannonized in 1582.

### Outstanding Monuments

Walls

Cathedral, Open: 10 a.m.–1.30 p.m., 3–5.30/7 p.m., Sunday 11 a.m.–5 p.m. Shuts summer Sundays 1.30–3 p.m. Within walls.

Iglesia de San Vicente, Open 10 a.m.–1 p.m. and 4–6 p.m. Just outside the walls to the east.

Real Monasterio de Santo Tomas, Open: 10 a.m.–1 p.m. and 4–6 p.m. Outside the walls, ten minutes' walk downhill south-east from the Cathedral.

### Notable Monuments

Monasterio de la Encarnacion, Open 9.30 a.m.–1 p.m., 4–6 p.m. Outside the walls, ten minutes' walk downhill north of Cathedral.

Museo Provincial, Open 10 a.m.–2 p.m. and 5–7 p.m. Shut Sunday afternoons. Just outside the walls, east of the Cathedral.

Convento de Santa Teresa, Open 8 a.m.–1 p.m. and 3.30–9 p.m. Within the walls.

**Layout of the Town** Apart from *señorial* houses and the Cathedral, most of Ávila's monuments lie outside the walls. The most notable buildings within the walls are to the east end, scattered close to the Cathedral, whose apse is built into the defensive walls. There are two centres to the old town: Plaza de la Victoria, inside the walls to the east end; and Plaza de Santa Teresa, the main social centre, just outside the main Puerta del

Alcázar, by the Cathedral. Between these two plazas are the shopping streets of the town. To the west end of the walled town new buildings are replacing the old – there is a surprising spaciousness. Puerta del Puente leads from this west end across the River Adaja.

Outside the walls, a number of churches and convents are scattered to the east of Plaza de Santa Teresa. The small new town spreads below .

**The Historic City** The surrounding fortifications are monumental. Built between 1090 and 1099, they are 2.5km (1 1/2ml.) in circumference, 3m (9ft.) thick, 12m (36ft.) high and interrupted by 88 turrets and 9 gates. The most important gates are both at the east end: the Puerta de San Vincente, to the north of the Cathedral; and the Puerta del Alcázar which opens on to Plaza de Santa Teresa, the other side of the Cathedral. The entrance to the Parador hotel, in the north side of the walls, is spectacular; that opening on to the bridge over Río Adaja (west end) is pretty. Just outside, above the river, is the Romanesque Ermita de San Segundo, which contains a beautiful statue of the saint at prayer, by Juan de Juni.

The Puerta del Alcázar is double arched, and was rebuilt by the Catholic Monarchs and Philip II. (Within is an attractive little square, from where the early Gothic windows of the Cathedral can be seen.)

**Cathedral** The apse of the Cathedral is an integral part of the wall. Heavily fortified, the vast cylindrical structure is encrusted with three layers of battlements and is known as the *Cimorro*. The Cathedral has a solid, heavy exterior, without Gothic elegance or Romanesque majesty. Constructed from the early twelfth-century to the late fifteenth-century, and added to subsequently, it displays a discordant mixture of styles and materials. Although the apse is Romanesque, the bulk of the Cathedral was designed in Gothic by the French architect Fruchel who was thus responsible for first Gothic church in the peninsula.

The main west portal is Gothic, guarded by two figures (Pierres and Caco) who stand to either side. A baroque embellished pediment was added in the eighteenth-century. Of the two planned towers, only the left has been built.

The north side carries the door of the Apostles, a fine thirteenth-century portal carved with five arches of beautifully sculpted figures. It was the main west doorway until moved by Juan Guas in the fifteenthcentury. Its Gothic elegance is sadly compromised, however, by the brick and stone additions which surround it.

Inside, the mottled red and white stone of the Romanesque parts contrast with the white stone of the later building. The shape is unusual, with a very narrow high nave relative to the aisles. Much of the original stained glass of the Gothic windows was lost during the Lisbon earthquake of 1775. In style, the apse is Romanesque, the left aisle is pure Renaissance and the vaulting is early Gothic.

The High Altar retable is a masterpiece of Pedro Berruguete, completed by Juan de Borgoña and Santa Cruz. To either side are pulpits of gilded iron relief, and two splendid Plateresque altars stand in the transepts. The retrochoir is lavish.

Amongst the sepulchres, the intricate Renaissance alabaster tomb of Bishop Alfonso de Madrigal (El Tostado), behind the High Altar, is the most important. It was crafted by the Tuscan Renaissance sculptor Vasco de la Zarza. The oldest tombs, of the twelfth-century, are housed in Capilla Nuestra Señora de Gracia.

The Chapel of San Segunda, to the right of the high altar through a closed door, is dark but sumptuous.

The museum, housed in the Capilla del Cardenal, guards a collection of religious artefacts amongst which are two small works by El Greco and Morales (an *Ecce Homo* custodia door), and a magnificent gold monstrance by Juan de Arfe. It is entered via the Sacristy, which contains a mighty Plateresque altarpiece in alabaster. The fifteenth-century cloisters can be reached from the museum.

**Señorial Houses** Surrounding the west entrance of the Cathedral are *señorial* houses including the Palacio de Valderrábanos (now a hotel), and Palacio del Rey Niño, in which Alfonso XI spent his childhood.

**Convento de Santa Teresa** Westwards into the old town, past Palacio de Dávila and the Plaza del Rastro, is the Convento de Santa Teresa. It was built over the site where the saint was born, and has a large church with sculptures by Gregorio Fernández and a museum which treasures a small number of Santa Teresa's possessions.

**The walls of Ávila have 88 turrets and 9 gates**

Across to the north side of the town, past the gardens of the Parador, is the Capilla del Mosen Rubí, an imposing sixteenth-century church decorated with the typical ball motif of the city. Puerte de San Vincente is at the end of the palace-lined street.

## Outside the Walls

**Iglesia de San Vincente** The church of San Vicente is just outside the gate of the same name. It is a splendid building, Romanesque tinged with Gothic, with high transepts and two beautiful portals. Beneath a portico, the south door as a decorated pediment showing the battle of Sin against Virtue. The west portal is surrounded by Romanesque figures. Inside, the stone is falsely mottled to imitate that used in the Cathedral. There are fine tombs, particularly the canopied thirteenth-century sepulchre of San Vicente de Huesca, martyred in 304. The carved reliefs surrounding his tomb are magnificent.

**Palacio de los Deanes** The provincial museum is between San Vincente and Plaza de Santa Teresa. It records the history of the area with archaeological finds, ceramics and artesanal craft traditions.

**Plaza de Santa Teresa** The Plaza de Santa Teresa, arcaded along one side and always full of life, is the social centre of the town. At one end is the Puerta del Alcázar which shadows a statue of the Saint worked to commemorate the Pope's visit in 1982. At the other end is the beautiful church of San Pedro. It was built in the twelfth and thirteenthcenturies, with Romanesque apses, a lovely Gothic rose window, and a fine Romanesque entrance. Inside, religious paintings decorate the walls. The retable is by Juan de Borgoña.

**Real Monasterio de Santo Tomás** A few minutes downhill from the square (Avda de Alférez Provisional) is the Dominican monastery of Santo Tomás. It was founded by the Catholic Monarchs, and their motif is emblazoned throughout the buildings. The pomegranate symbols decorate the façade in celebration of the recent victory of Granada. The church is vast, with a unique architectural feature of a raised sanctuary and choir. The altarpiece is a masterpiece of Pedro de Berruguete, depicting the life of Thomas Aquinas. Below is the beautiful tomb of the Prince Don Juan, the only son of the Catholic Monarchs, who died aged 20 in Salamanca. The intricate animal and flower sculptures are the work of Domenico Francelli. The epitaph describes a perfect youth.

Two other fine tombs rest in the church, one of Nueñez de Arnalte, worked by Vasco de la Zarza, and the other of the attendants to the prince, Juan Dávila and his wife. In the sacristy is the tomb of the Grand Inquisitor, Torquemada.

There are three cloisters, of which the Claustro de los Reyes and the Claustro del Silencio are notable.

A museum of artefacts brought back by Dominican missionaries from the east, is displayed in a gallery at the far end of the monastery.

**Convento de San José** The Convento de San José is in the centre of the new part of town, five minutes north of the Real Monasterio. It was the first foundation of Santa Teresa in 1562. The convent, since rebuilt in Renaissance style, has a large church with several fine tombs. The museum has dozens of trinkets of the Saint.

**Convento de la Encarnación** The Convento de la Encarnación, is far over to the north of the town, across a new area of houses and vegetable fields. The Saint spent nearly thirty years here, and the cell where she levitated with St Juan of the Cross is visible. A small museum here commemorates her.

**The Plaza de Santa Teresa is always full of life**

**Shopping** Being a small town, Ávila has little to offer the traveller commercially. Its short shopping thoroughfare is, however, pleasant to walk through, and it has a good municipal market.

The shopping area is mainly in the streets between the Cathedral and Plaza de la Victoria: Calle de los Reyes Católicos, Calle de Allemania, Calle Comuneros de Castilla and Calle Caballeros.

La Flor de Castilla, a *pastissérie* in Calle Santo Tomé, makes the local sweet speciality, *yemas de Santa Teresa,* a small golden delicacy of sugar and yolk. These sweets are exported widely from this shop, and are one of the most well-known offerings of the town.

The municipal market, open both morning and evening (except Saturdays – morning only) is just off Plaza de la Victoria, near the Ayuntamiento. A small street market is held on Tuesdays near the small Plaza del Rastro. The Mercado del Ganadia, a lively weekly animal market, takes place on Friday mornings, in grounds between the walls and the Convento de la Encarnación.

**The Paseo** The evening *paseo* (stroll) is gentle here, bathed in the warm glow of the late afternoon sun which colours the pale stone. The centre is Plaza de Santa Teresa, which fills with lively young schoolchildren and strolling local people. One of the two routes, inevitably, follows the main shopping streets – Calle Reyes Católicos, Calle Alemania, Calle Generalisimo, Plaza de Santa Teresa – to finish a little way up Calle San Millán and Calle del Duque. The other route follows the walkway, Paseo del Rastro, just beneath the walls to the left of Plaza de Santa Teresa. From here there is a glorious view of the rolling hills and dry landscape of the provincial countryside. The café Grand el Grande, under the arcade in the main square, offers excellent tea and cakes.

**Parks** Parque de San Antonio, pretty and well kept with plenty of trees, lies to the east of the walled town, between the bus and rail station. It is popular during the late afternoons. Parque del Rastro is small, nestling beneath the walls to the south, where part of the Paseo walks (Paseo del Rastro). Surrounding the walls are grassed banks.

**Sunday** Being close to Madrid, Ávila fills with visitors at the weekends. The religious monuments are open through the day, and restaurants stay open for the traditional family lunchtime. The ambience is most pleasant.

**Restaurants** Compared with Madrid or Segovia, the evening meal is taken early here, between 8 and 10.30 p.m. There are plenty of restaurants around, the majority scattered in the area near the Plaza Mayor.

The evening *paseo* with views over the countryside

Restaurant: *Piquio* Calle de Estrada 2, Tel: 211418 – well patronized, just off Plaza de Santa Teresa. The comedor is upstairs. Good Castillian fare, and *tapas* (AE DC MC V).

*El Fogón de Santa Teresa* (*see* Hotel Palacio Valderrábanos).

*Parador Raimundo de Borgoña* (*see* Hotel Parador).

*Mesón del Rastro* (*see* Hostal El Rastro) – a large clientele of regulars. Fills with Castilians every lunchtime. Big light room, very lively, with a straightforward menu and a country decor. Well recommended for its ambience.

*El Torreón* Plaza de la Catedral, Tostado 1, Tel: 213171 – housed in the lower ground floor of a Renaissance palace, there are three *comedors* and a bar at the entrance. Low, dark ceilings and stone walls give a rustic, cosy atmosphere. Food is local fare – *tipico* (AE DC MC V).

*La Posada de Santa Teresa* Plaza Pedro Dávila 8, Tel: 222863 – a good family restaurant, (AE DC MC V).

*El Tabernón* Calle Don Segundo 41 – a great hall with barn door entrance, just outside the walls near the Plaza Santa Teresa. Cheap, very cheerful and much patronized. Small tables, check tablecloths and bustle. Shut Wednesdays.

**Hotels** Relatively few people choose to stay a night in Ávila. Being so close to Madrid, it is more frequently chosen as the focus of a day visit.

### Category 1

*Palacio Valderrábanos* Plaza de la Catedral 9, Tel: 211023 – a genteel and handsome hotel within the Palacio de Valderrábanos. It is one of the many fortified Renaissance palaces of the fifteenth century, built for Gonzalo Dávila, chief magistrate of Jerez and active conquistador in the decisive 1462 battle to win Gibraltar from the moors. Hall-like rooms, with some fine beamed ceilings. Placed opposite the Cathedral, by the Puerta del Alcázar.

Restaurant: *El Fogón de Santa Teresa*: A varied menu, with a quiet and dignified atmosphere.

73 rooms d&b 8500–7000 (AE DC MC V). Parking.

*Parador Raimundo de Borgoña* Marqués de Canales y Chozas 16, Tel: 211340 Smaller and simpler than many in this famous chain. Placed in a quiet position, just a few minutes' walk from the Cathedral, with a pretty garden whose roses climb the city wall. It has unique access to the only section of wall that may be walked by the public.

62 rooms d&b 9000–7500 (AE DC MC V). Parking. Restaurant.

### Category 2

*Reina Isabel* Avda José Antonio 17, Tel: 220200 Outside the walls, close to the train and bus stations. Ten minutes' walk from the Cathedral. It has a pink and white façade. Bar and disco.

44 rooms d&b 4000–3500. Restaurant.

*Hotel Jardín* San Segundo 38, Tel: 211074 In an attractive position just outside the walls close to the Cathedral and Plaza de Santa Teressa. Simple and family-run.

26 rooms d&b 2600–2400. Pension.

*Hotel Rey Niño* Plaza de José Tomé 1, Tel: 211404 Within the walls, central.

24 rooms d&b 3500–2800 V.

*Hostal Continental* Plaza de la Cathedral 6, Tel: 211502 Opposite the Cathedral, simple.
54 rooms d&b 3000–2500 Pension.

## Category 3

*Hostal El Rastro* Plaza del Rastro 1, Tel: 211218 Within the walls, a large entrance hall with beamed ceiling, heavy old furniture and a huge fireplace. Simple rooms.
16 rooms d&b 2400–2200 (AE DC V).
Restaurant: extremely popular locally.
*Hostal Las Cancelas* Cruz Vieja 6, Tel: 210063 Near Cathedral. Minimal facilities.
14 rooms d&b 1700.
Restaurant: Ooven cooking. Much patronized by tour groups.

## Information

| | |
|---|---:|
| Area Exchange code | 918 |
| Cruz Roja (Red Cross) | 224848 |
| Renfe, Information | 220188 |
| *Estación de Autobuses* | 220154 |
| Tourist Office, Plaza de la Catedral 4 | 211387 |
| Police, Avda José Antonio 1 | 211188 |
| *Correos* (Post Office), Plaza de la Catedral 2 | 211370 |
| Taxis, Plaza de Santa Teresa | 211959, 220278 |

The area of banks is behind the Iglesia San Pedro (Plaza de Santa Teresa) in the Plaza de Ejército.

**Transport** Cars: There is plenty of parking near the walls to the east, around the new town, and within the walls at the west end. Inter-city transport: regular buses and trains connect with Madrid, Valladolid, Segovia, Salamanca.

**Around Ávila** The province of Ávila is divded between the cereal plains to the north and the spectacular dominating Sierra de Gredos to the south. Within the plains are agricultural villages, some very pretty, and a couple of important and attractive centres – Arévalo, with a fine castle, and Madrigal de las Altas Torres, with a superb surrounding wall. While the countryside here is preoccupied with commercial agriculture, the towns of the southern mountains serve mostly as cool, refreshing holiday refuges for quantities of visitors.

**North** Travelling to the north and west of the capital, the countryside is spectacular for its sweep of vast cereal fields. The

N501 towards Salamanca via Peñaranda, although busy, gives a good impression of the little-populated expanse of agriculture. A prettier route west, slower and far less used, is the AVIII heading towards Gallegos de Sobrinos, from where there are constant views of the rising Sierra de Ávila.

**Arévalo** Midway between the capital and Medina del Campo (Valladolid) is Arévalo, the second major town after Ávila itself although its foundation appears to make it the most ancient in the province. Like many of the towns and villages in the corn plains, Arévalo is an important centre of Mudéjar architecture. Two churches are important. San Martín, (thirteenth–fourteenth-centuries) has a splendid pair of square brick towers and, inside, guards a retable of Gregorio Fernández. Santa María, with a Romanesque apse, was restored in the seventeenth-century, adding significantly to the Mudéjar decorations. It has a beautiful wood-panelled ceiling. A third church, San Salvador, is remarkable mainly for the Juan de Juni retable.

The castle, home to the young child Isabella the Catholic, has been frequently restored but its brick-built solidity is impressive. Within the great keep, the rooms are furnished with sixteenth-century pieces. Of the other fortifications, the walls have almost totally disintegrated with time and only an archway remains.

The town's streets display some fine old houses and convents, and the squares are all porticoed.

Just outside the town are two attractive Mudéjar bridges and, on the minor AV820 road is the very beautiful ruin of Ermita La Lugareja – one of the most highly regarded examples of thirteenth-century Mudéjar religious architecture. Three Romanesque apses topped by a sturdy square tower are decorated with elegant slender blind arches and brick tracery. Its Cistercian nuns now live in the Convento de Santa María, in the centre of town.

A serious lure of Arévalo is its reputation for traditional cooking – the roast suckling pig (*tostón*) is outstanding. Restaurants are particularly full at weekend lunchtimes.

A cultural festival and cattle fair is held at the beginning of July.

**Madrigal de las Altas Torres** Madrigal de las Altas Torres is west of Arévalo, close to the Salamancan border, and, as its name suggests, its spectacular feature is the great brick and rubble defensive wall connecting 23 square watch towers, each of which is

154

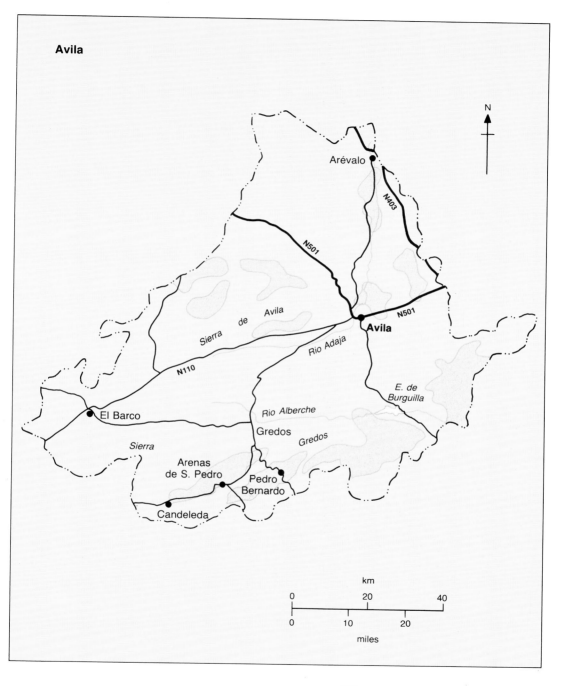

Avila

N

Arévalo

N403

N501

Sierra    de    Avila

Avila

N501

Rio Adaja

N110

E. de
Burguilla

El Barco

Rio Alberche

Gredos

Gredos

Sierra

Arenas
de S. Pedro

Pedro
Bernardo

Candeleda

km

0          20          40

0      10      20

miles

crowned with battlements. Built in the eleventh and twelfth centuries, the walls have been kept in superb condition. The future queen Isabella I was born here. The small town is tranquil and pretty, again with much reminiscent of the Mudéjar style.

Its fiestas in, mid-September, involve bull running.

**Fontiveros** Amongst the agricultural villages in the plain beneath Arévalo and Madrigal, sits Fontiveros, a small pilgrimage centre. Here, in 1532, was born Juan de Yepes, to become St John of the Cross, confessor of the mystic Santa Teresa and himself also a writer of mystical tracts. An eighteenth-century hermitage is placed over his birthplace, and the village also boasts a twelfth-century Romanesque/Morisco church and a Carmelite convent founded in the same era. On the day of St. Juan, 14 December, the fiesta's traditional food is *cocido* (chickpea stew).

### South

**Piedrahita** There are several approaches to the Sierras de Gredos from the capital. The N110 to Barco de Ávila is relatively unspectacular, and passes through the town of Piedrahita. The main historic building is the eighteenth-century palace of the Dukes of Alba. The parish church and monastery of Santo Domingo preserve a mixture of styles from the thirteenth-century onwards. Like El Barco de Ávila, Piedrahita is in sparse granite countryside, with few trees to break the harshness. North from the town, in Bonilla, are pretty remains of walls.

**Valley of the Alberche** Other routes to the Sierras cut either side of the small Sierra de la Paramera, joining through the pretty but narrow granite valley of the Alberche, which runs just south of the Paramera. On the C502 10km (6miles) from Ávila, is an extensive Iron Age site, the Wilderness of Ulaca. It is difficult to find, beyond Villavicosa, the neighbouring village to Solosancho. The grey stone walls ring a huge field in the bleak hilly area, laid out like a skeleton town. The granite boars, found in several Castilian cities, came from here. (Remains of an Iron Age settlement, with rings of walls and 1,500 sepulchres are found just north of Ávila town, in Cardeñosa.)

The roads of the Alberche are beautiful. The river itself, a fisherman's paradise, fills the reservoir of El Burguillo, in which watersports of all sorts are enjoyed. Westwards along the valley are the warm peach groves of Burgohondo, leading on to the Scots pine and chestnut forests of Hoyacaseros and up into the Alpine heights of the Gredos.

**El Tiemblo and Cebreros** East of the reservoir, joining the main southerly route from the capital (N403), are the pretty villages of El Tiemblo and Cebreros whose delicious product is a full-bodied aromatic wine, and olives. Outside El Tiemblo is a scruffy small field in which four ancient pre-Roman granite bulls stand in a humble surrounding. These *Toros de Guisando* are famous, but little visited. Cebreros is reknown for its celebration of carnival.

To the south-east of Ávila, in the area ringed by the two main roads N403 and C505, is a small range of peaks, pine-clad and cut through by a spectacular narrow road crossing the Puerto del Boquerón and Arrebotacapas. A tract passes from San Bartolomé to the reservoir accompanied throughout by a lively stream.

**Sierra de Gredos** The massive range of the Gredos is part of the long chain of mountains that divide the South Meseta from the North, running west to east. Near Madrid the range is continued by the Sierra de Guadarrama. At the foot of the range, to the south, the mighty Tajo River sweeps along, finally to course through Portugal.

The southern rise of the range above the sub-tropical region of the Tiétar Valley is dramatic – so swift that snow-capped peaks are only a few hours' climb away. The views of the valley are spectacular, as it falls 1,700m (5,500ft.) below. The north side is far less steep and colder, affording the totally different wildlife of a sub-alpine vegetation. The former supports palms, citrus trees, holm oaks and tobacco cultivation; the latter is clad with pine and meadowland.

Skiing, climbing, walking, and hunting are all regular pastimes in these Sierras. The main villages have developed in chalet clusters which fill with weekenders from the big cities, and holiday resorts offering refuge from the summer heat. A few walkways have become very popular, (particularly the route to the highest peak of the range, Almanzor, reached via the road to El Plataforma off the C500), but the vast and marvellous region is otherwise barely touched.

There are few roads in the heights of the mountains. To the south, a route winds from Arenas via Candeleda to Jarandilla and on the Plasencia (Extremadura). To the north, a route curves to Barco de Ávila from where one pass continues to Plasencia and another to the further mountain town of Béjar. The two roads only join at the east end near Arenas de San Pedro.

Linking together around the peaks are a myriad of walking trails and several ancient *cañada* routes still used by transhumant shepherds.

**Piedralaves** The summer resorts of the south side begin in Piedralaves, on the road from Madrid to Arenas de San Pedro. With streams rushing through it, and marvellous valley and mountain views, it is packed with second homes and offers good food and accommodation. Walks up into the thick pine forests abound.

The pretty road continues straight to Arenas de San Pedro, but first there is a fabulous diversion of tortuous roads, little used, which ring round the beautiful stone villages of Pedro Bernardo, San Esteban del Valle and Serranillos; there are breathtaking views from these.

**Arenas de San Pedro** Arenas de San Pedro is set in a bowl of pine trees and Pyrenean oak, carpeted with fern and Spanish lupin, with a backdrop of mountain ridges rising to the north, and the young Tiétar cutting through. Historically it was prominent in the fifteenth-century when its castle was home to the wife of Juan II's executed advisor Álvaro de Luna. It is aptly called 'El Castillo de la Triste Condesa'. Today only the mighty tower and turreted corners remain, set over the river by the centre of town. The Infante Don Luís de Bourbon also took refuge here when exiled from Madrid by his brother Charles III, and a small sumptuous eighteenth-century palace still stands. The Gothic parish church is important chiefly for the tomb of San Pedro de Alcántara. The town is the commercial heart of the Sierras and the biggest centre from which to enjoy the mountains. It is full of people at the weekends, but is not particularly attractive, with surprisingly few places to eat and sleep. The main street offers plenty of shops, and a useful information centre advises on the many walking routes in the mountains nearby.

The Cuevas del Aguila are 4km (2 1/2 miles) below Ramacastañas (neat Arenas). They are a glorious series of natural galleries decorated with crystal and figures formations. Tours: 10.30 a.m.–6 p.m.

**Guisando** Guisando, hidden in a cut high above Arenas, is a delightful village closed in by forest with several streams splashing steeply through. Although it, too, is mostly a resort, it is small, and the mountain tranquility is uncompromised. A few hostels and restaurants cater for mountain visitors. From here, and the neighbouring El Hornillo and El Arenal, are walks which wend towards El Plataforma and on to the Circo de Laguna Grande and the peak of Almanzor. The ancient trail of the Pass of the Horses connecting Toledo to Valladolid runs by.

**Candeleda** Candeleda is further to the west of Arenas on the C501 which then runs into the Valle de la Vera, passing Valverde de la Vera and Jarandilla. Placed within the rapid rise of the mountains between the Tiétar valley and the high peaks, Candeleda is a surprising small town of wood-beamed houses, basking in a sub-tropical climate with an abundance of palm trees and tobacco plants. Beneath it, in the valley, the small bird population is extensive: bee-eaters, golden orioles, azure-winged magpies, stone-curlews, and warblers.

From Candeleda there are trails up towards Almanzor peak and the lakes via the Sanctuary of Nuestra Señora de Chilla, or via one of several streams. A further starting point is from El Raso and from Madrigal, villages to the west of Candeleda, from where trails can stretch across to Bohoyo and Navalperal, or lead to below Almanzor via Portilla Bermeja Pass. The Trocha Real, a route sanctioned by Alfonso XIII, leads to Venteadero. Crossing the Reserva National by the Circo de las Cinco Lagunas, it is possible to sight the splendid mountain goats *Capra Pyrenaica Gloriae*.

**Mombeltrán** Travelling towards the northern side of the Sierras from Arenas, the pass via Puerto del Pico is an excellent road. Mombeltrán preserves the walls of a fourteenth-century castle, a perfect square fortress nestled in the mountain scenery. Further round are sturdy stone village bases for walking or riding explorations of the mountains. The views here are totally different from the sheerness of the southern slopes. The vistas are of might rolling granite summits clothed with gum cistus, broom and scrub, and thick gentle slopes of Scots pine forests.

Walking in this colder area the wild plants are gorgeous – Alpine plants are sprinkled about the meadows and forests, with pale-yellow snap-dragons, columbine, and star-of-Bethlehem. A little further down, the forests of Hoyocaseras are fragrant with

**The ancient trail of the Pass of the Horses**

lily of the valley, peonies, St Bernards Lily and, in summer, purple knapweed.

The main walking bases are Navarredonda (near which is the famous Parador de Gredos), Hoyos del Espino, Navalperal and Bohoyo, from which trails pass southwards through the spectacular peaks of the range. From the peak near the Parador – Alto del Risquillo – wonderful views stretch to the Tormes valley and the region of Piedrahita and Béjar.

Apart from the approach to Almanzor (the highest peak at 2,592m/8,504ft.) via the asphalted road up to El Plataforma from Hoyos del Espina, the main walking paths are not crowded. At Almanzor, black griffons and vultures are often to be seen.

**El Barco de Ávila** Further along, the road reaches El Barco de Ávila, a crossing point for the main route between Extremadura (the beautiful Valle de la Jerte) and Ávila, and connecting with the Sierra de Béjar. It has a fifteenth-century castle ruin and porticoed streets, but is a quiet and otherwise rather heartless small town.

The Gredos peaks are the home of several birds of prey: eagles (at least five kinds, including the great Imperial), kites (black and red), goshawks and black storks (although these are seldom seen).

Few buses travel along the range; most traverse via the main routes through, running from Ávila to Arenas de San Pedro and down to Talavera, or across to El Barco de Ávila and down to Plasencia, or from Arenas de San Pedro to Jarandilla (a slow but pretty journey).

**Country Trails** There are several historic trails to be walked and a multitude of rarely visited paths. The Editorial Alpina maps, 1:50,000, illustrate the routes clearly.

The refuges in the Gredos vary in condition. It is best to check with a Tourist Office or hiking shop before depending on them. (Particularly good refuges are Albergue José Antonio Elola, Laguna Grande; Refugio Victory, at La Apertura, at the foot of La Mira; Refugio de La Mira, in the meadow of Los Palayos.)

**Riding** A superb way to visit the Gredos is on horesback. The experience is marvellous, without the limitations of walking, and without the interference of traffic. There are various organizations whose excursions last from a day to a month, often taking the ancient shepherd trails used to move sheep between the pastures of northern and southern Spain. Accommodation varies from mountain huts to comfortable hotels according to preference.

Arrangements can be made from Madrid or locally:

Gredos al Caballo, Tel: Madrid 519 2644, or book at Parador National de Gredos.

La Isla, Navaluenga (Gredos – based in Madrid) Tel: 91 633 3692

Rutas a Caballo, Hoyos del Espino, Tel: 348110

Grecaba, Navarredonda de Gredos, Tel: 918 348010 – for experienced riders.

**Hunting** Coto Nacional with strictly limited hunting. The Ibex is under careful protection, and can often be seen from the peak named La Mira, above La Apertura. The hunting season of Ibex (*Cabra Montes*) is 1 April to 15 May and 10 October to 30 November and stalking is organized in Arenas de San Pedro, Cuevas del Valle, Villarejo del Valle and San Esteban del Valle. Information, Tel: 918 212100. Fallow deer, wild boar, and small game (red patridge, rabbit, etc.) also abound.

**Fishing** ICONA, Méndes Vigo 6/8, Ávila, Tel: 918 221686. The Parador de Gredos also issues hunting and fishing permits.

## Accommodation and Restaurants
## Arenas de San Pedro

*Don Álvaro de Luna* Florida 4, Tel: 371650 –
34 rooms, d&b 4000 (AE DC MC V).

*Avenida* Los Regajel Tel: 370716 –
18 rooms, d&b 3200.

*Lumi* Avda Pintor Martínez Vázquez 1 –
7 rooms, d&b 2500, family-run hostal.

Restaurant: *El Bodegón – asador* (spit-roasting) in a cellar restaurant, with an outside terrace by the castle.

## Arévalo

*Fray Juan Gil* Avda Deportes 2, Tel: 300800 –
30 rooms, d&b 4400.

For superb roast lamb and suckling pig:

Restaurant: *Goya* Avda Emilio Romero 33, Tel: 300362 – Shut Thursday evenings and during September. (AE DC MC V).

Restaurant: *La Pinilla* Teniente Garcia Fanjul 1, Tel: 300063 – Shut Sunday, Monday evenings and end of July. (AE DC MC V).

### Candeleda

*La Pastora* Avda de las Piscinas, Tel: 380146 –
20 rooms, d&b 2500.
Restaurant: *Don Finardo* Gredos 9, Tel: 380822 – roasts.
Restaurant: *El Paraiso* Aduanas, Tel: 380472 – shady garden,
roasts.

### Guisando

*Pepe* Linarejos 4, Tel: 370908 – 16 rooms, d&b 3500, in the
depths of the forest. Restaurant.
*Los Galayos* Paraje del Husero, Tel: 370908 –
6 rooms, d&b 1900, simple, above the town. Restaurant.

### Navarredonda de Gredos

*Parador de Gredos* Tel: 348048 – the first of the distinguished chain
to be established, deep in mountain forest with wonderful views
and tranquility.
77 rooms, d&b 8000, (AE DC MC V). Restaurant.

### Piedrahita

*Grand Duque* Pastelería 17, Tel: 360077 –
21 rooms, d&b 2500., good restaurant.

### Piedralaves

*Almanzor* Progreso 4, Tel: 8665000 –
59 rooms, d&b 3000, Shut mid-October to mid-December, with
garden full of trees, pool.
*Del Bosque* Generalísimo Franco 84, –
15 rooms, d&b 250, family-run house.

### El Tiemblo

*Los Toros de Guisando* Avda Madrid 5, Tel: 8625011 –
30 rooms, d&b 4600, good restaurant. (MC V).

### Camping

Guisando: Los Galayos, Ctra Linanejo, Tel: 370921
– Cat 2, Open all year, 200 people.
Hoyos del Espino: Gredos Puente del Duque, Tel: 348085
– Cat 3, Open: 1 March to 31 December, 700 people.
Mombeltrán: Prados Abiertos Ctra Ávila/Talavera, Tel: 386061
– Cat 2, Open all year, 500 people, pool.
Navaluenga: La Bellota Herren de la Virgin, Tel: 286230
– Cat 2, Open 1 June to 30 September, 190 people.
Peguerinos: Ctra Peguerinos/Alto de los Leones, Tel: 8983074
– Cat 3, Open all year, 180 people.

**The walls of Ávila**

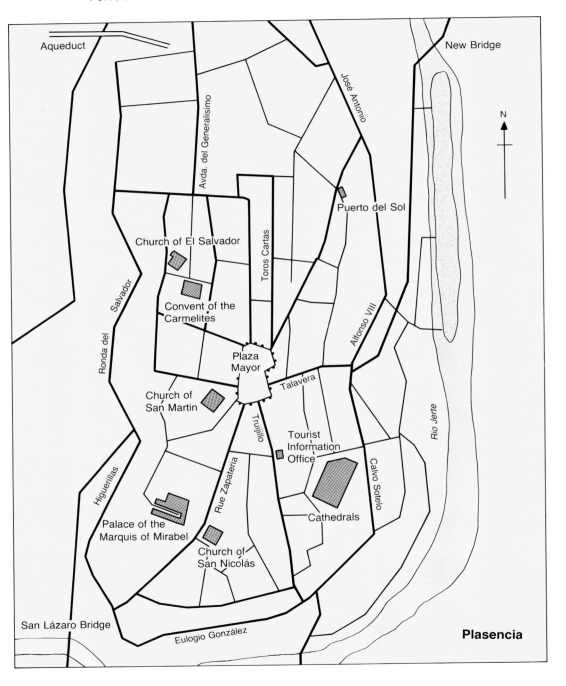

Aqueduct

New Bridge

N

Avda. del Generalísimo

José Antonio

Puerto del Sol

Church of El Salvador

Toros Cartas

Convent of the Carmelites

Ronda del Salvador

Plaza Mayor

Alfonso VIII

Talavera

Church of San Martin

Trujillo

Tourist Information Office

Rio Jerte

Higuerillas

Rue Zapateria

Cathedrals

Calvo Sotelo

Palace of the Marquis of Mirabel

Church of San Nicolás

San Lázaro Bridge

Eulogio González

**Plasencia**

**Plasencia** is not greatly frequented by tourists. Its cultural sites are little match for the monumental old city of Cáceres, or the romantic ruins of Trujillo further south, and it makes little attempt to interest visitors in its history. A busy, provincial centre, with bustling streets, a dominating Plaza Mayor and a rather eccentric pair of cathedrals, the town's greatest lure is its air of continuity and normality. It is well worth a visit – its energy and vivacity complement the fine *señorial* buildings and pretty streets, and there is no hint, anywhere, of a museum town.

**History** Plasencia, built strategically on a bluff protected by the curve of the River Jerte, was rebuilt by Alfonso VIII (late twelfth century) after suffering serious damage during the reconquest. Of the massive walls, punctuated by 68 semicircular towers and 6 gates, a substantial amount remains.

The town became prosperous through the buoyant international wool market of the fifteenth century, when it benefited from the overwintering of sheep from the Gredos mountains. Most of its fine buildings date from this era. Today, it is very much smaller than its provincial capital Cáceres, but is the commercial hub of the north of Extremadura.

### Notable Monuments

Catedral/Iglesia de Santa Maria, Open: 8 a.m.–1 p.m. and 4–6 p.m.

Convento de San Vicente

Iglesia de San Nicolás

Palacio del Mirabel

Casa del Dean

**Layout of the Town** Town life radiates from the Plaza Mayor, centred within the oval walls. The main streets lead off the Plaza, named by their gateways or by the towns to which they ultimately lead (e.g. Trujillo, Talavera). The small *barrios* (districts) are named after their dominant parish churches. Outside the walls, the town is not of much interest or character. Here are the rail and bus stations, and a thin spread of industrial buildings. The town's beautiful park is on an island in the river below.

**The Historic Town** Plasencia is best enjoyed by strolling through the streets. There are a few buildings to be aware of, most built during the boom years of municipal wealth reflected in

**NOTE:** On Tuesday morning the historic market is held.

The area surrounding Plasencia is one of extraordinary natural beauty, the lush green hills and rivered valleys have bathed in a generous climate. The Extremaduran sun, usually relentless, is softened by the ample protection of the Gredos foothills.

167

The link between the Old
and New Cathedrals in
Plasencia shows the contrast
in architectural styles

the ambitious Cathedral designs. They are to be found on a curve to the south of the Plaza Mayor.

The foot of Rua Zapatería which radiates southwards from the Plaza opens to an attractive area surrounded by *señorial* houses and dominated by two important religious buildings. San Nicolás, early Gothic with a beautiful rose window, faces the Convento de San Vincente, a Dominican monastery with a sacristy brightly tiled in *Ázulejos* from Talavera. To the right are splendid steps which lead up to the palace of the powerful Zuñiga family, the beautiful Renaissance Palacio del Mirabel. Following the curving streets southwards is the Cathedral. Opposite is the Casa del Dean, with its opulent, proud corner balcony.

A walk within the walls, much of which remain (although often obscured by buildings), will pass through some very peaceful streets, and some full of life and bustle. Some are pretty, others very ordinary, but the whole is an attractively natural mixture within a historic town which maintains its cultural heritage with unself-conscious dignity.

Known also as the Iglesia de Santa Maria, the Cathedral is made of two buildings, one late thirteenth-century Romanesque, the other Gothic. The flourishing wool trade of the fifteenth century provided Plasencia with the wealth and optimism to construct a new cathedral. That great symbol of civic status, to be built as the old church was removed, remains unfinished. A string of the finest church architects worked on the Cathedral (Juan de Álava, Alfonso Covarrubias, Dievo de Siloé, Rodrigo Gil de Hontañón...) but the result reaches only to the shortened choir. The design is graceful and beautiful – delicate star vaults supported on soaring, unbroken columns – and the abrupt plastered wall is a sad interruption. Behind the wall is the Old Cathedral, now used as a museum and entered from within the New Cathedral.

The strange contrast in style between the two buildings, roughly joined through the cloister walls, is reflected also by the north façade. A splendid Berruguete-style Plateresque portal, arrayed with fine carving around four tiers of columns (completed 1558), balances a second north portal – Romanesque – belonging to the old building. (The old church also has a west entrance.) Beside the high Gothic roof, terminated with a wall of brick, the neighbour seems squat and flat.

Clothing the interior of the new Cathedral, the list of craftsmen is exceptional. The vast apse is filled by a powerful florid retable of the Baroque master Gregorio Fernández, and the panels painted by Francisco Rizi. To the left of the main door is the Capilla del Transito whose retable was the work of the Churriguera family – José, Joaquin and Alberto. The choir stalls, of Roger el Alemán, are beautiful.

Through the early Gothic cloisters to the left, past the untidy stone and wood stitching which joins the two buildings, is the Capilla de San Pablo, within which mass is heard daily. Small, with a central lantern similar to that of the Salamancan Torre de Gallo (Old Cathedral), it is dominated by a huge thirteenth-century polychrome Virgen of Paloma. Further round is the Chapter House within which are two Ribera canvases and a small Morales 'El Divino'. Gil de Hontañón's long spiral staircase windows leads to a terrace. The old church itself with alabaster and sculpted capitals, now houses a small museum of ecclesiastical treasures and old hymnals.

**Shopping** Plasencia displays the commerce of a busy provincial town, with shops selling a jumble of local necessities. There is little obvious segregation into areas of goods, but several prominent streets radiate from the Plaza Mayor: Calle Sol (running SE from Plaza), lined with small shops, Calle Talavera (S from the Plaza) and Calle Trujillo (W from the Plaza).

The generous, lively Mercado Municipal (fresh food stalls) has entrances at the top of this street and in Plaza San Esteban. The selection of local craft goods is best at the Tuesday market.

The Plaza Mayor is the commercial and social centre of the town, hosting, every Tuesday morning (since granted permission by Alfonso VIII) a spectacular fruit and vegetable market. The superb quality of the produce is ensured by the haven of lush, fertile hills surrounding the town. The extension of the fair curls through Calle Santa Clara to the Cathedral square where stalls sell locally produced ceramics, clothes and *rastro* bric-a-brac.

**The Paseo** This is not particularly marked here. The usual evening walk passes along the main shopping route of Calle Sol but without the tranquil ambience that accompanies the stroll in Castile.

**Garlic sellers in Plasencia market**

170

**Parks** Beneath the walls is an island joined to the town by several small bridges. Meandering past is the Rio Jerte. Well tended, full of trees and grasses, this is the pretty parkland which hosts the local families during the weekend walks.

**Fiestas** The market becomes the focus, once a year, of the fiesta Martes Mayor which is held on the first Tuesday in August. Beckoned in from the previous Saturday with evenings of traditional dancing, music and fireworks, the Tuesday morning is filled with dozens of competitions involving: vegetable/fruit growers and sellers; the artesan skills of craftsmen working wood, bone, pottery, textiles, leather, etc. The beat of *tamborileros* (musicians with drums) can be heard through the streets. The festivities finish with the drinking of *pitarra* (local artesanal wine) and a full-scale bullfight.

**The spring Fiesta** lasts for a week early in June, during which a series of corridas are held, with evening entertainment of fireworks, dance and music. The town is decked with colour, and local costume is often to be seen.

**Bars and Tapas** Lively bars are scattered throughout the town, bursting with jovial local people, particularly on market day. They are to be found in quantity round the Plaza Mayor (Café Español is very popular); along Calle Vidrieras and Calle Pedro Isidro (both running north from the Plaza) and in CallePatalón (off Calle Talavera from the Plaza). There are excellent *tapas*, and several bars have eating rooms at the back which serve a good lunchtime menu. In the evening, the bars fill noticeably early.

Café Nueva Riviera, on Calle Pedro Isidro (north off the Plaza) is a good bar for breakfast. For excellent Extremaduran ham, Don Jamón, 17/19 Calle Sol (the main shopping street) has a magnificent selection.

### Restaurants

*Alfonso VIII* (*see* Hotels).

*Mi Casa* (*see* Hotels) – good Extremaduran fare served in a huge *comedor* (dining-room) always well filled with families.

*El Refugio* Calle Patalón 1, Tel: 416350

Popular *asador* (spit-roasting) serving lamb and beef.

*Restaurant Extremeña* (*see* Hotels) – Good smartish food, quiet cultured ambience.

*Blues Mery*

Santa Clara 6, Tel: 417293

By the Cathedral, quite suave, with a fashionable clientele. Refreshing garden terrace.

**Hotels** The selection of accommodation is very small.

### Category 1

*Alfonso VIII*Calle Alfonso VIII 32, Tel: 410250 – smart and suited to business people. On the main road flowing beneath the walls on the east side of the town.

Rooms: 57 d&b: 7800–6700. Restaurant – good international and regional cooking. Parking (AE V MC DC).

### Category 2

*Hostal Mi Casa* Calle Maldonado 13 (also named Calle Patalón), Tel: 411450 – Near the heart of the town, well run, with a very popular restaurant and bar.

Rooms: 40 d&b: 2690/2340.

*Hostal Rincon Extremeno*

Calle Vidrieras 6, Tel: 411550 – just off Plaza Mayor, surrounded by bars. A little pretentious but comfortable. Restaurant.

Rooms: 30 d&b: 2200–2000.

### Category 3

*Hostal La Muralla* Calle Berrozana 6, Tel: 413874 – Modern, comfortable rooms, family-run.

Rooms: 13 d&b: 1800. Pension

### Camping

La Chopera 2km (1mile) from town on N110, Tel: 416660 – Cat 3, Open 1 May to 31 October, 171 people.

### Information

| | |
|---|---|
| Area Exchange Code | 927 |
| *Estación de Autobuses*, 10 minutes SE of centre | |
| RENFE: 15 minutes west of the walls | 412004 |
| Cruz Roja (Red Cross) | 412679 |
| Correos (Post Office) opposite Puerta del Sol | |
| on Calle Alfonso XII | 412277 |
| Tourist Office, Trujillo 17 (Casa de la Cultura) | 412766 |
| Open: morning and afternoon | |
| Banks, around Plaza Mayor | |

### Transport

Madrid – Bus: three times daily (3 hours)

Train: twice daily

Cáceres Bus: every $1^1/2$ hours

Salamanca: four times daily

Valladolid: three times daily

Seville: three times daily

Trains: more awkward and slower, connecting with Cáceres and Madrid.

Cars: allowed into the walled part of town through a narrow single direction system. Parking inside is extremely awkward – it is better to park in the street outside the walls.

**Around Plasencia** Plasencia is surrounded by beautiful countryside. South of the town is a national park whose forest, rocky peaks, pasture vegetation and water basins provide the habitation of a superb range of birds of prey. The harsh plains and hills of Extremadura stretch south the the Tajo valley, where the fascinating old towns of Cáceres and Trujillo and the monastic shrine of Guadalupe can be visited.

To the west of Plasencia is the small old town of Coria, encased within a great wall and treasuring a magnificent Cathedral. Northwards, far from easy communication, in the beautiful wooded country of Sierra de Gata and Sierra de las Hurdes, nestle a scattering of little-visited hamlets.

North-east are three routes penetrating the Sierra de Gredos to the provinces of Salamanca or Ávila. Two of these are particularly attractive for their small villages and gorgeous countryside: the Valle del Jerte and the Valle de la Vera.

## South

**Parque Natural de Monfragüe** The park of Monfragüe covers an area of nearly 18,000ha between Plasencia and Cáceres, within which the Rivers Tiétar and the Tajo join. Its major glories are the numerous species of birds of prey that breed within its boundaries. Some species overwinter here, but the park is most interesting from March onwards, when breeding and spring migrations begin. It is at its most spectacular in May, the time also of the local fiestas and *romerías*. Ancient *cañada* (sheep track) routes pass through the park, and the traditional movement of sheep flocks between the pastures of the south and the north can be seen as the seasons change.

The tiny village of Villarreal de San Carlos contains a small information centre which has maps and suggestions for walking routes. These are well marked through the park. It is best not to stray far from the paths – the acid soil is highly erodable and the habitat easily damaged.

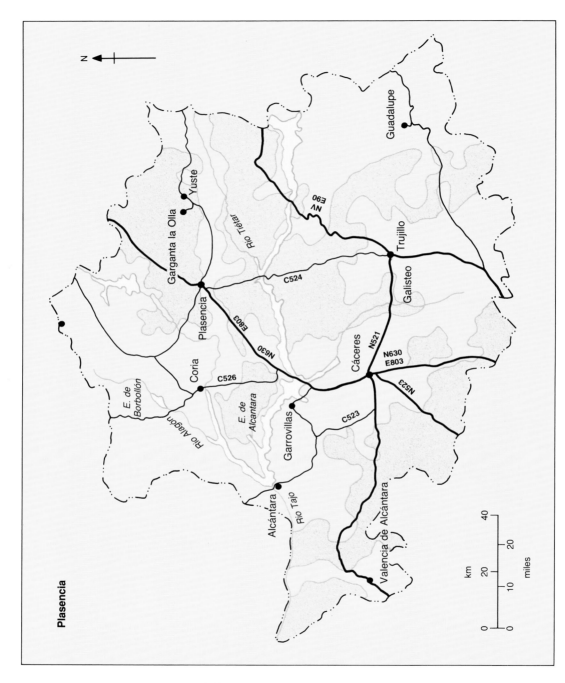

Plasencia

**The lush country around Plasencia**

175

**The castillo and hermitage of Monfragüe offers a dramatic point for watching birds such as these griffon vultures**

The *castillo* and hermitage of Monfragüe, overlooking the dammed Tagus at the western end of the park, is a most dramatic point for watching birds of prey. Set in the long quartzite ridge that runs across towards Portugal, atop the Sierra de las Corchuelas, is the castle. Once an important strategic fortress, it is now a well-restored folly from which the activities of griffon vultures and eagles on the Peñafalcon rock can be watched. The extent of the park can be viewed from here - south to the sunscorched Dehesa landscape (from where sounds of goat bells emenate), north to the shade-protected forests. Further viewing points are along the Rivers Tiétar and Tagus.

The Dehesa vegetation to the south side of the park is found only in the Iberian Peninsula and in the north-west Africa, made up of cork and holm oak and pasture. North of the Corchuelas ridge is thickly covered by some of the most ancient Mediterranean forest in Europe. Evergreen shrubs – wild olives, Kermes oak, turpentine trees, strawberry trees and stone pines – cover a layer of cistus, lavender, broom, bladder senna and wild herbs. (Since the area was designated a Park Natural in 1979, the planting of eucalyptus and pine was stopped.)

Black vultures and Spanish Imperial eagles (both under threat from extinction) breed here in the ancient cork and holm oak areas. Goshawks, sparrowhawks, booted eagles and various owls can also be seen. On the ridge of Peñafalcon, nest Griffon and Egyptian vultures. Golden eagles, Bonelli and Short-Toed eagles, peregrines, kestrels, ravens, and choughs may pass by the ridge. The rare black-winged kite is more difficult to see. Black storks and black vultures nest mostly in the plains to the south, but are often spotted near Peñafalcon.

Smaller birds are plentiful: hoopoes, woodchat shrikes, bee-eaters, golden orioles, and azure-winged magpies, and water birds include great crested grebes, collared pratincole, cattle egrets, spoonbills and greylag geese.

The mammal and reptilian life is also important here. The rarest animal is the Spanish lynx, which is very seldom sighted. Snakes (none fatally poisonous), salamanders and small reptiles abound. Amongst the mammals are wild cats, fox, badger and Egyptian mongeese.

Information office 9 a.m. – 7 p.m., Villarreal de San Carlos.

176

Best visited in May for flora, April–June for birdwatching. With a licence from ICONA in Cáceres, hunting (deer and wild boar) and fishing is permitted.

### West

**Coria** Still surrounded by a mighty solid wall of granite blocks, much of it remaining from Roman times, the quiet town of Coria retains formidable evidence of its past importance. A fifteenth-century pentagonal tower built into the wall near the central point is all that remains of the twelfth-century castle. The fortifications, in places over 12m (40ft) wide, protect a white town of low houses in long rows, dotted with fine *señorial* houses and a few convents.

The Cathedral, still an episcopal seat, stands proud above the tobacco and cotton fields, making an impressive sight from afar. It was built mostly in the sixteenth century and is unusual for being single aisled. The choir stalls are finely carved. The exterior seems vast, with Plateresque work adorning the west door and decorating the unusual Baroque bell tower that sits by the north entrance. Damage from the Lisbon earthquake is demonstrated by huge fissures in the walls, which are hung with various religious works. The main apse displays a Churrigueresque altarpiece by Juan and Diego de Villanueva, and the quantity of sculptured figures almost crowds its sides. Sadly, the cloister is shut for lengthy repairs. The sacerdotal will proudly show a fine collection of church vestments if asked. Mass is normally heard at 6 p.m., but the building is open from 9.30 a.m. – 6.30 p.m., closing 1 – 4 p.m.

Coria, famed for its bull-running festivities, celebrates the Fiesta of San Juan from 23–29 June with bulls and dancing.

**North** The generous waters of the Rio Alagón, twice dammed to form the Embalse de Gabirel y Galán (in which much water sport is enjoyed) and the lesser Embalse de Valdeobispo, separate Plasencia from the extensive mountain regions of Gata and Las Hurdes. The two Sierra regions are distinctive in countryside and in village style, and neither are equipped for tourist visitors. Sierra de Gata is far out of the way, although a pass leads northwards to the valley region of Ciudad Rodrigo (Salamanca). The villages of Las Hurdes, still somewhat off the beaten track, lead to the lovely Sierra de Francia, in which are the most prominent, famously attractive mountain villages of the Salamanca Province (La Alberca, Miranda del Castenar).

Apart from the peaceful streets of Coria, the plains to the west and north of Plasencia are without particular recommendation, supporting sturdy farmsteads and growing villages. The reservoirs and waterways provide good vistas, but the landscape is otherwise either rather barren or well worked.

**Sierra de Gata** A drive through light *encina* (holm oak) forest and boulder-strewn plateaus opens to spectacular views across the meadowed valley to the Sierra. The winding mountain roads are all extremely pretty, and the little traffic is mainly local – school buses, elderly cars and flocks of sheep or goats. The colours are beautiful, the thick forest and pasture layered in the autumn with orange-yellows and many greens, and lush with freshness in the spring. Small market gardens and orchards surround the villages. The houses vary – some are old and humble, some modern. While the villages are not wealthy, they are lively and a good deal of new building work will be seen in each one.

**Valverde de Fresno** Valverde de Fresno is the last town before the Portuguese border. Steeply built, with narrow streets of crisp white balconied houses, it is a thriving place and attractive to walk around during the bustle of the morning market. Cars can

**The countryside of Sierra de Gata**

negotiate the main streets fairly easily. Nearby are Elijas, steep and pretty at its crown, and San Martin de Trevejo, rural and charming, both with surprisingly large schools.

**Villamiel** Perched on a jut of rock 3km (2miles) beyond Villamiel is the castle of Trevejo, with wonderful views of the valley all around. The route to it, populated by working donkeys and shepherds, becomes increasingly rocky. Few people live in its tiny, ancient, village – the small houses are of dark stone, the streets of roughly laid slabs. (The severity of conditions here is alleviated by telephone and television.) Amongst the stooping black figures, there are some entrepreneurs who will offer *castañas* (chestnuts) or honey to travellers.

**Hoyos** Hoyos is a fine village with *señorial* houses, one a dwelling for an archbishop, and religious buildings (a convent and a Romanesque church) to illustrate its historical prominence. Wholesome meals can be found here. Nearby is the main pass curling over the Sierra through rock-rose, gorse and lavender fields, which drops into the rough pasture plains of Ciudad Rodrigo.

Eucalyptus, pine and oak (and occasional citrus trees, bright in the autumn) clothe the road to the next cluster of villages, again healthy and lively. The dignified church of Torre de Don Miguel, treasuring three paintings by Morales, is graced with palm trees. Gata, prosperous with cafes and flower-filled squares, is extremely pleasant, with pretty walks just outside.

Towards Sierra de las Hurdes, high on a hill beside the main route is Santibañez el Alto, with marvellous views over the Embalse de Borbollón. Its glory is at its crown, where remains of old walls and the small ring of a castle ruin are worth a detour. A narrow road leads from this area towards Ciudad Rodrigo, passing small villages surrounded by mountain woodland and pine.

Apart from touring through the area it is pleasant to stop, walk in the fragrant woods, visit some of the small religious sanctuaries and swim in one of the delightful natural pools (particularly outside Valverde, Hoyos, Acebo and Descargamaría) beside which are fountains and tables. Good fishing for trout and eel may be had in the abundant rivers.

**Sierra de Las Hurdes** For fifty years the poverty of this area, highlighted in the writing of Unamuno and in the films of Buñuel (*Land without Bread*) has been notorious. The villages still

179

have the problem of an almost unworkable steep slate terrain, but new housing, schools and modern communication have raised the general standard of living. Honey flavoured by the herbs and heather of the hills, and olives from the flatter meadows, constitute the economic resources, although both are unreliable, the former prone to bad harvests, the latter suffering fluctuations in demand. There is plenty of water, and the microclimates of small areas produce pockets of fertility.

The main villages in Las Hurdes are Pinofranqueado, an old centre with a growing modern surround, and Caminomorisco, a pretty place with glorious fragrant climbing roses, locked in a small valley of olive trees. Nearby are the ruins of the Convento de Los Ángeles – a lovely walk. The surrounding villages of this valley are tiny, their farming methods unchanged for centuries. Behind these, in the hills, are the ancient villages of Horcajo, Nuñamoral, El Gasco, Casares de Hurdes and Ladrillar, each with circular clustered houses whose slate roofs run together like the scales of a fish. The older houses are of stone, many in a ruinous

**The tiny and ancient village of Trevejo**

state, while there are numerous new dwellings under construction. The sharp river valleys give excellent views of these from the roadside.

Off the arrow winding roads are lovely walks, particularly around the caves and rocky hillside of El Gasco, amongst the pine forests and meadow of Caminomorisco, and between Ladrillo and the tranquil nature reserve of the Valley de las Batuecas.

### East

**Valle del Jerte** This is a lovely valley pass – a lush moist green throughout the year; a glory of fragrant white cherry blossom in early spring; a mixture of deep crimson, orange, yellow and copper in the autumn. The River Jerte cascades from the height of the Puerto de Tornavacas (bordering with Ávila at the important crossing of Barco de Ávila), down to Plasencia, coursing through the villages and collecting in a reservoir just outside the city.

The road N110 to Ávila, formally an ancient route of the *cañadas* ( a shepherd's transhumance trail) accompanies the river all the way. The valley is steep, cut between high hills, and the

**The rooftops of Casares de Hurdes**

terrain curving up from the river way varies from rich meadows, to terraced orchards above which are forests of elder, ash, holly, walnut and oak. Fruit grows in abundance – citrus, olives, pomegranates, kakis and figs. Pretty haystacks, built round tall poles and circled by a protective stone wall, speckle the pasture. A drive through the valley is a delight, and buses pass through here regularly between Plasencia and Ávila.

The villages offer a mixed history. Tornavacas was a rich artesanal town making cloth, patronized by the Count of Oropesa. Its wealth has left a substantial village of fine houses crowned with escutcheons and granite-supported arcaded fronts. Marvellous views stretch down the valley from here. The bravery of Jerte and the small El Torno caused the virtual destruction of both by fire during the Napoleonic invasion, Jerte has a fine baroque church as a result of its rebuilding. Cabezuela is pleasant to explore, shaped by the river, it is many-levelled with timber-framed overhanging houses. Above the river is the old Jewish quarter, a tight-cornered puzzle of narrow ways. 14km (8$^1$/2 miles) north along a lovely winding mountain road from the left, is Hervas – a village famous for its superbly preserved *judería* (Jewish quarter). (It is more easily reached from the Béjar pass.)

Sixteen km (10 miles) from Plasencia, above the reservoir, are four unkempt twisting roads penetrating the steep hills on either side of the valley. Up these are delightful uncompromising mountain villages often bedecked with climbing roses and drying peppers, water coursing down the streets – Rebollar, Cabezabellosa, Cabreros, Casas del Castañar, Piornal, etc., – amidst beautiful utterly peaceful scenery. From these long, winding roads it is possible to cross to either the pass between Plasencia and Béjar, or the Valle de la Vera.

A well-timed *romería*, at the sanctuary Nuestra Señora de Peñas Albas, coincides with the explosion of cherry blossom on 25 March. At Navaconejo, again with typical houses over the river, San Sebastián's day (20 January) is celebrated with vivacious dancing.

**Valle de la Vera** This pass, winding along the abrupt southern rise of the Gredos through a wide forested valley is populated by small villa towns, e.g. Jarandilla and Jaraiz, and substantial quiet villages many of which are seldom interrupted by travellers. The vegetation, generously watered by the River

Tietar, supports a striking variety of trees and shrubs – ash, pear, chestnut, oak, quince, cherry, walnut, laurel, citrus and white hawthorn. The banks of the river are lined with poplar. The cultural gem is the secluded Monasterio de Yuste, in which Charles V spent his last year. The pass eventually joins the province of Ávila at Candelario, basking in the sub-tropical climate of the south Gredos, its population waxing with mountain walkers from spring onwards.

From Plasencia, the route C501 becomes pretty after a few kilometres. Small dignified rural villages lie beside the road, or penetrate the foothills a short way, and farmsteads speckle the countryside. A fine Romanesque church stands close to the turning to Pasarón. Beyond the busy commercial centre of Jaraiz is the picturesque village of Cuacos de Yuste, which nestles beneath the main road. It is a much visited place, with its ancient traditional timber and adobe houses which sometimes have two tiers of overhanging balconies. Just off the Plaza Mayor is the house in which lived the son of Charles V, Don Juan of Austria. Cars can park in the pretty Plaza, but it is more comfortable not to drive into the village.

*The countryside is a walker's paradise, and a few peaks (El Calvitero, El Torreón) offer challenges to climbers.*

**Monasterio de Yuste** Across the main road, steeply uphill, is the track to the monastery of Yuste. (Open: winter 9.30 a.m.–12.45 p.m. and 3.30–6 p.m.) Summer 9.30 a.m.–1.45 p.m. and 3–6.30 p.m.) The Emperor Charles V died here in 1558 having withdrawn to its tranquility less than a year earlier, leaving his son Philip II to rule the extensive empire. Winter visiting is preferable – the small rooms are simple and not enhanced by large groups of visitors. There is no electricity in the old quarters so good daylight is important. Architecturally unremarkable, the building is surprisingly humble; it is surrounded by dense oak woodland with a small garden of citrus trees and a pool in which Charles V would bathe mounted on his horse. The magnificent eucalyptus trees which stand sentinel are relatively modern additions.

Only the quarters of the monarch are shown – rooms with a little furniture, a wheelchair/cot, a desk, a few paintings. His bedroom, placed to the side of the church altar so that he could watch the constantly celebrated mass, remains hung with black. Whatever the change caused by the Napoleonic devastation here,

**Monasterio de Yuste**

the austerity is a tangible reflection of the last year of the gout-ridden Emperor. (A view of the two fine cloisters is given, but the present Jeronimite order is closed and admits only a few visiting men within its doors. If the building seems closed during visiting hours, ring the bell of the main monastery.)

Lovely walks wind along streams through these wooded hills.

**Jarandilla** Further along the valley, Jarandilla makes a good resting point. The attractive fifteenth-century castle of the Counts of Oropesa, its cloister hung with ivy, is today inhabited by a Parador hotel. The vivacious town is a cool summer resort, with a small selection of hotels and restaurants.

The route passes several villages, each of which have restaurants on the main road, but continue life unmolested away

184

from the thoroughfare. Losar, Valverde, Villanueva and Madrigal are all substantial villages, with good streets – often ridged and running with fresh water – and chains of white houses, some overhanging, some decorated by geraniums. Each is distinctive, the most attractive possibly being Valverde. Neither quaint nor old-fashioned, these are hospitable, lively places, full of boisterous children. (It is still more comfortable to park on the main road.)

Fiestas are notable particularly at Valverde on Maundy Thursday where penitents process with heavy crosses roped to their backs (*empalaos*), and in Villanueva which celebrates its Pelo Palo festival amid a carnival atmosphere on Shrove Tuesday.

Roads turning southwards from this route sweep rapidly down into the Tiétar valley, providing striking views. (The towns of Talayuela and Navalmoral are commercial centres, of little tourist interest.)

**Towards Béjar** The N630 towards Salamanca via Béjar is comparatively uninteresting, running along a railway line rather than water. Apart from a couple of extremely pretty roads crossing the Montes de Tras la Sierra to the Valle de Jerte, the village of Hervas is better visited as an addition to the lovely Béjar Sierras. Baños de Montemayor, closer still to Béjar, is a spa town of Roman origin, offering sulphurous waters. The link roads across the peaks of the Salamancan boundary to the pretty town of Candelario are spectacular.

**Horse Riding** To ride through the Valle de la Vera, horses may be found in Pueblo Nuevo de Miramonte, 'Pequeño Rosanto'.

**Hunting** Big game: deer and wild boar. Wolves are protected. The hunting of wild boar using horses and hounds, called *la Ronda* is to be found only in Extremadura.

**Fishing** In the Rivers Jerte, Tiétar and Alagón.

**Local Specialities**

Alcohol:

Pitarra – artesanal wine

Gloria – Liquor of grape and anis (orujo)

Beso Extremeño – liquor of acorn

Food: cured ham is the Extremaduran speciality – pigs are fed from acorns to produce the excellent flavours. Roasts of kid and lamb; heavy chickpea stews (*cocido*). Summertime – a rough but delicious gazpacho. Cheese from the Valle de la Vera is renowned. Artesanary – copper goods, jewelery, furniture, ceramics.

### Accommodation

### Coria

*Los Kekes* Avda de Calvo Sotelo 49, Tel: 500900 – 22 rooms, d&b 3000, modern, comfortable.

*Montesol*, Ctra Cáceres/Ciudad Rodrigo, Tel: 501049 – 16 rooms, d&b 2200. Peacefully on the river bank just outside the town.

### Sierra de Gata: Valverde del Fresno

*Palmera* Avda Santos Robledo, Tel: 510323 – 22 rooms, d&b 2600, lively restaurant.

### Sierra de las Hurdes: Camino Morisco

*El Abuelo* Ctra de Salamanca, Tel: 436114 – 17 rooms, d&b 1350, with hearty restaurant.

### Valle de la Vera: Aldeanueva de la Vera

*Chiquette* Calle Extremadura 3, Tel: 560862 – 16 rooms, d&b 2600.

### Jarandilla de la Vera

*Parador Nacional Carlos V* Tel: 560117 – 53 rooms, d&b 8500. Magnificent, in the ivy-covered fifteenth-century castle of the Counts of Oropesa. A good restaurant. (AE MD DC V).

*Marbella* Calvo Sotelo 103 , Tel: 560218 – 10 rooms, d&b 3000, café/restaurant.

### Towards Béjar: Baños de Montemayor

*Balneario de Montemayor* Avda Calvo Sotelo 24, Tel: 428005 – 95 rooms, d&b 3340/2175 (Spa Open 1 June to 15 October).

**Peasant in Sierra de Grata**

## Camping

Madrigal de la Vera:

Alardos Ctra Candelario/Madrigal, Tel: 565666 – Cat 2, 150 people, Open all year.

La Puente, Tel: 565333 – Cat 2, 74 people, Open all year.

Santibañez el Alto: Borbollón – Cat 2, Open: 1 March to 30 September, 301 people.

Jarandilla:

Jaranda, C501, Tel: 560454 – Cat 2, Open 1 May to 31 October, 250 people.

Aldeanueva de la Vera:

Yuste, C 501 – Cat 2, Open 1 April to 30 September, 500 people.

Cuacos de Yuste:

Carlos 1 Avda Ceralejo, Tel: 461002 – Cat 1, 240 people.

**Countryside of Sierra de Grata**

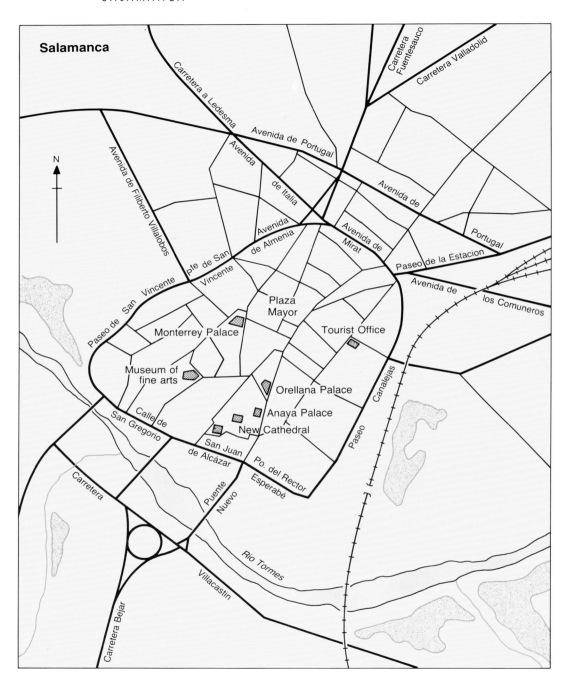

**Salamanca** is very beautiful. It rises above the Río Tormes, in a rich golden cluster of churches, convents and palaces, dominating the surrounding wheat plains. The city is built of sandstone, the tone of which, suffused with the varying strength of the sun, glows from a pale yellow to a deep orange. For centuries the university was patronized by the monarchs and aristocracy of Castile, and respected by the academics and ecclesiastics of Europe. The intellectual magnetism of Salamanca is still extraordinarily powerful: the graceful opulence of its fine buildings is tempered with a profoundly religious tranquillity uncompromised by the city's contemporary vivacity.

The city changes with the seasons. Winter is bitterly cold with crystal clear skies. Spring is delightfully warm and pleasant. The storks return to their nests of the previous year (at sunset they stand atop the many pinnacles and towers, their slender silhouettes gracefully adding height to the city). Summer is hot. The character of the city alters as many Salamancans leave the town for holiday and the university fills with foreigners taking language courses. With the September fiestas and the coolness of autumn, the city, returns to its vivacious normality. Throughout the year, the difference in ambience between day and night is remarkable.

**History** The city has a long history, passing to the victorious hands of Hannibal in 217BC and thereafter falling successively to Romans, Vandals, Visigoths and Moors before Alfonso VI triumphed here in 1085 – the great year when the line of Christian reconquest passed south of Toledo. Under the King's son-in-law, Raimundo de Borgona, the town gained great defensive walls and an Alcázar.

Its historical prestige, unlike the courageous town of Zamora, is based not on war but on intellectual prominence. As a centre of learning, it was nurtured from the thirteenth century onwards, leading religious and humanist thinking until its prominence began to recede in the sixteenth century – dulled by the zeal of Christian purity and by the challenging prestige of Valladolid. Ravaged twice by French troops in the Peninsular Wars, both before and after Wellington's victories over Napoleon Salamanca pitched further into decline until the late nineteenth century.

The historical reputation of the University as defender of independent thinking had rested on, amongst others, the controversial defender of the American Indians, Fransisco de Vitoria, and the resistance of Luis Fray de Leon to the power of the Inquisition. This reputation re-emerged in the 1920s with the celebrated debate between Miguel Unamuno and Primo de Rivera's dictatorship (leading to the former's imprisonment).

Today Salamanca is prosperous, living with dignity from its historic university, from its splendid buildings, and from the surrounding wealth of agriculture. Even now, it remains a religious centre of magnitude, with over 60 convents within the town, 13 of which are cloistered.

### Outstanding Monuments

**Plaza Mayor** Catedral Nueva (New Cathedral) Open: 9.30 a.m.–1.15 p.m. and 3.30–5.45 p.m., Sunday morning only.

Catedral Vieja (Old Cathedral) Open: as above.

Universidad & Escuelas Menores (University buildings) Open: 9.30 a.m.–1.30 p.m. and 4.30–8.30 p.m. Saturday and Sunday morning only.

San Esteban Church Open: morning and afternoon mass. Convent open: 9 a.m.–1 p.m. and 4–7.30 p.m.

Domincas Dueñas Open: 10.30 a.m.–1 p.m. and 4–5.30 p.m.

### Notable Monuments Colegio del Arzobispo Fonseca

Open: 9 a.m.–2 p.m. and 4–6 p.m.

Casa de las Conchas (Closed for repairs) • Palacio de Monterrey (façade only) • Palacio de Anaya (Patio) • Calatrava (Façade only) • Torre del Clavero (Façade only) • Museo de Belles Artes Open: 10 a.m.–3 p.m. and 5–8 p.m., Shut Sundays and Mondays.

Puente Romano • Casa-Museo de Unamuno Open: 4–6 p.m., Saturday and Sunday 11 a.m.–3 p.m.

Churches:    Clerecia (Closed for repairs)
             La Purisma (Closed)
             Las Ursulas Open: 9.30 a.m.–1 p.m. and 4–6 p.m.
             San Marcos Church Open: morning and afternoon mass
             Sancti Spiritus, Church Open: morning and afternoon mass
             Santo Tomás de Canterbury, Church Open: Sunday 12 p.m. mass.

**Layout of the Town** Within the ring road Avda Alemania/Paseo de Canalejas is the unwalled old part of Salamanca. In the centre is the huge Plaza Mayor, from which radiate lively shopping streets to the north and quiet unbustled pedestrian streets to the south. Here, in the tranquil area between the river and the great square, are the University buildings, the Cathedrals, palaces, gardens, and numerous fine churches and convents. The arcaded Gran Via (also called Calle España) is the main artery which runs east of the Plaza, reaching from the main bridge of the river to Plaza España, and there joining the inner ring road.

**The Historic City** Much of old Salamanca is unmolested by cars and is very pleasant to stroll around. Many of the notable buildings stand in the pedestrian arc south of the plaza, and a gentle walk can encounter most. Everywhere, the use of red, (originally with a base of bulls' blood) attractively signs the building and street names. All round the remaining University buildings are symbols which commemorate the gaining of doctorates by students.

**Plaza Mayor** Mention Salamanca to any Castilian, and his immediate response will be to praise the glories of its Plaza Mayor. The reputation is well deserved – of all the Plazas in the region, it is the most magnificent and the most memorable. The heart of the city both geographically and socially, its cobbled arches are passed through by an extraordinary variety of people.

**Of all the Plazas in central Spain, the Plaza Mayor in Salamanca is probably the most magnificent**

The cafés – each with a different character – are never still, and throughout the year chairs and tables surround the sides of the arcades. It is essential to take a refreshment here to appreciate the character of the city.

The huge trapezoidal Plaza is a fairly modern addition to the university city, whose architectural heyday was in the sixteenth century. Built during Philip II's reign, it was designed by Alberto Churriguera and Andrés Garcia de Quiñones, the latter responsible for the Ayuntamiento on the north side. The work continued from 1729 to 1788. The surrounding terraces, three storeys high, are mostly lived in. The medallions decorating each arch span of the arcades display figureheads – monarchs to the east by the Pabellón Real arches, historical leaders to the south. Generalísimo Franco is the most recent addition (east) and several are still to be filled.

**The cathedral, seen from San Esteban**

It takes time to enjoy the beauty of the Plaza; the gold hues and shadow lines change with the time of day, as does the ambience. Particularly special times, apart form the geniality of the *Paseo,* are the calm of early morning, sunset, and evening as the lamps are lit. At night, groups of students don traditional garb, sit at café tables with guitars and sing *tunas*.

San Martín, an early twelfth-century church, is confusingly incorporated into the south side of the Plaza Mayor. The south portal is Renaissance (and a favourite nesting spot for storks), the fine Romanesque entrance is inside the Plaza. The heavy interior has an ungilded altarpiece by Alberto Churriguerra (designer of the Plaza).

Linked to the Plaza Mayor by the Rua Mayor (south) is the lovely Plaza de Anaya, the palace of which is dominated by the raised Catedral Nueva.

**The Cathedrals** Unlike Plasencia, whose double Cathedral is the unplanned result of insufficient funds, the adjoining Romanesque and late Gothic cathedrals of Salamanca are both complete and fine examples of their styles. The later building, buttressing the weakened north side of the Old Cathedral, was begun at a time when civic prestige and wealth, often demonstrated by great works of ecclesiastical architecture, was at its peak.

**Catedral Nueva** It took over 200 years from the placing of the foundations in 1513 to complete this vast Cathedral. Even

then, an earthquake left the building without the planned tower
(to be like that of Toledo Cathedral) and the drained coffers
forced plans for much sculptural embellishment to be abandoned.
The north façade, decorated with great mythical gargoyles and
with dozens of late Gothic pinacles, lacks the statues that should
be housed beneath them. Inside, the main chapel is hung with red
velvet in place of ornamentation (Gregario Fernández's
'Assumption of the Virgin' hangs alone), and behind it the
prepared stone surface will remain unadorned.

The exterior facades, however, live up to the contemporary
Salamancan fashion. The west and north portals are heavily
decorated – the north with a sculpture of 'Christ's entry into
Jerusalem', and the west with Churrigueresque archivolts, arches
of statues and a tympanum sculptured with an 'Adoration of the
Magi' (Juan Rodríguez).

After the ornate facades, the inside can seem surprisingly sober.
The Renaissance/Baroque choir, clad in various coloured
marbles, predominantly green, with sides intricately carved in
floral motifs, stands as an imposing block in the nave surprisingly
far from the High Altar. It is the design of Alberto Churriguera.
Juan de Juni worked the statues of the retrochoir – San Juan
Bautista and the Virgin with Santa Ana.

193

**The splendid fifteenth-century altarpiece by Nicolás Florentino**

There is plenty of adornment, however, but much is in a more disciplined style than that of the exterior. Looking upwards, there is a delightful flamboyant Gothic freize of beasts and hunting scenes which runs round the building at gallery level. Medallions, similar to those in the Plaza Mayor, sit at intervals along the walls. The dome, lit by Renaissance windows, is delicately polychromed and the vaulting of the High Altar, and the cuffs of the capitals are decorated in dark blue and gold.

The Capilla del Carmen behind the High Altar is richly carved, gold and silver twisted Churrigueresque columns almost drowning the little eleventh-century crucifix with opulence. (The image is said to have been carried by El Cid during his campaigns – hence the chapel's other name 'Capilla de las Batallas'.) In the chapel of all saints ('Todos Santos') near the west end, Juan de Álava covered the walls with a profusion of sculptures – the images of 110 saints. The Cathedral was built from west to east, and the two other chapels on this side reaching to the west end, and the first two opposite, are the work of the building's original architects, Juan Gil de Hontañón and Juan de Álava.

**Catedral Vieja** The old Cathedral is entered through a chapel next to the Todos Santos chapel. With heavy, pure Romanesque columns supporting early Gothic vaulting, headed by three apses, the character of this Cathedral is powerfully distinct. It was built for Jerónimo de Perigueux (chaplain to El Cid), over 300 years before its neighbour. The magnificent fifteenth-century altarpiece is by Nicolás Florentino – a collection of 53 scenes from the lives of both Jesus and Mary painted on wood tablets, capped by a fresco of 'The Last Judgement'. Centred within the tablets is a beautiful image of the patron saint of Salamanca – La Virgen de la Vega, from the beginning of the thirteenth century, worked in copper and Limoges enamel. The whole impact is wonderful.

In the main apse and to the right are thirteenth to fifteenth-century sarcophagi, supported by lions, inset in polychromed, pointed niches. Less easy to find is the Capilla San Martín, whose walls were decorated in 1262 by Anton Sánchez. The chapel is well hidden to the right of the west-end portal. Its entrance is through a dark passageway whose light-switch is just inside to the left. The paintings are in superb condition.

**The cathedral seen from the cloisters of Las Dueñas**

Through the cloister are further chapels. The most attractive is the first, El Salvador (or Talavera), twelfth century and very small, its square base capped with a bright-blue painted Mudéjar octagonal vault. The Mozarabic Rite is heard here, except when, annually on a late July Sunday, the historic mass is celebrated with great ceremony in English, Castilian, French and German in the old Cathedral. The larger chapels, Santa Bárbara and Santa Catalina, were used in the early days of the University as tuition and examination rooms. Capilla de Anaya (or San Bartolomé), recognizable by its alabaster tomb, quietly houses one of the oldest organs in Europe, dating from 1380.

The Diocesan Museum is notable for a superb collection of paintings by the fifteenth-century master Fernando Gallego, to whom much of the museum is dedicated. Fine work by Juan de Flanders is also displayed. The few dignified rooms are a pleasure to visit.

From the Patio de Chico at the far side of the Cathedrals, reached by a pretty but indirect route, the extraordinary exterior of the old Cathedral and the juxtapostion of the two buildings can be appreciated. The Torre de Gallo, with its scaled Byzantine/ Romanesque dome, is rare – apart from in Zamora and Toro (NE of Salamanca) there are almost no others like it.

Off this patio is Calle Arcediano whose end garden is said to have been the garden refered to in Fernando de Rojas' satirical play *La Celestina*, the garden of Calixtus and Melibea. References to the play are frequent in the city.

Back towards the Old Cathedral, the narrow route falls to a town gate. Outside is the river, crossed by an old bridge. The 15 arches closest to the walls are Roman and were part of the great commercial route, Via de la Plata, which ran northwards from Mérida. The stone bull placed in the middle is a symbol of the city, although by no means a unique sculpture of its types in the Meseta. Lazarillo de Tormes, character of an early Castilian picaresque novel, is celebrated here with a statue.

One street west of the New Cathedral in the quiet Calle Libreros is the famous sculptured façade of the University.

**The University** The city has three universities, the Civil university – renowned for its architectures today, and at its peak, recognized for its teaching of law (also letters, philosophy, science and medicine); the Pontifical University, teaching theology, philosophy and Canon Law; and the University of the Dominican Fathers, specializing in theology. Today, the first is the largest, and still holds a good reputation in the peninsula (despite the near collapse of the faculties in the eighteenth century). The courses in the Spanish language for foreigners are extremely successful, partly accounting for the large number of resident foreigners during the summer.

The original University, based in the Old Cathedral, was founded in 1212 and supported by the subsequent Kings of Léon. Alfonso X 'El Sabio' founded the Law faculty, soon after the University absorbed its neighbour foundation in Palencia. Until its decline in the seventeenth century, it was a celebrated arbiter of international learned disputes and enjoyed a reputation comparable to that of the universities of Oxford, Bologna and Paris. The list of humanist professors is as formidable as the list of those who consulted them. Its independent thinking, vulnerable to the accusations of the Inquisition and severely discouraged thenceforth, led to the confiscation of books and the banning of

**The magnificent façade of the University is one of the best examples of Plateresque sculpture in the peninsula**

controversial subjects like maths and medicine and the near demise of the foundation.

The fifteenth-century University, patronized by the Catholic Monarchs and consulted by the great explorers of the time, is what is seen today, although only one-fifth of the colleges survived the ravages suffered during the Peninsular War. The façade of the University is one of the most admired displays of Plateresque sculpture in the peninsula. The three-tiered design is marvellously worked – a medallion of the Catholic Monarchs, surmounted by the coat of arms of Charles V with his two double-headed eagles, above which is a Pope flanked by cardinals, Hercules and Venus. Surrounding these main figures is a profusion of sculpted decoration – floral motifs and grotesques. The derivation of the style is from the decorative craft of the silversmith.

There are a few rooms to visit inside. The Lecture Hall of Luis de León – the brilliant humanist who suffered imprisonment by the Inquisition (his translation of the 'Song of Songs' led to his arrest in 1573) – is kept with its original furniture of rows of thin wood benches and a dark hooded pulpit (although today the windows are larger). Two panels by Juan de Flanders can be found in the Music Room, and the Old Chapel displays works by Fernando Gallego. At the end of a patio gallery upstairs (with a splendid coffered ceiling) is the magnificent library, home to 50,000 old volumes varying from eleventh-century codices to eighteenth-century tomes.

Off the small plaza is the fine Plateresque doorway of the Escuelas Menores. The inner patio, typically Salamantine, leads to a lecture room which houses an important fresco by Fernando Gallego which originally belonged to the Old Library – 'Cielo de Salamanca' ('Sky of Salamanca'), illustrating the multiple signs of the zodiac.

Beside is the Museo de Belles Artes, a collection of archaeology and fifteenth-to-seventeenth-century sculpture and art.

Just along from the University, towards the Plaza Mayor, are a group of handsome buildings including the monumental Clerecia of the Pontifical University and the Casa de las Conchas.

**La Clerecia** is a famous, monumental, singe-aisled Baroque church, originally commissioned as a Jesuit school by Philip II, with massive gilded retables and a very fine 'Christo Flagelado' by Luis Salvador Carmona.

**Casa de las Conchas** The Casa de las Conchas is renowned for the rows of sculptured scollop shells (*conchas*), the shadows of which, changing continually throughout the day, decorate its façade. The house was built for a counsellor of the Catholic Monarchs (who was also a Knight of Santiago, hence the symbolic shells) and is a classic example of the Renaissance style of its time. The Spanish Gothic window grills are notable and, should the door be open, the inner patio is arcaded in a typical Salamancan style similar to the patio of the Escuelas Minores.

The Dominican convents of San Esteban and Las Dueñas are at the foot of Gran Via but are spectacularly approached from the Plaza in front of the New Cathedral, Plaza de Anaya, via the curving lane El Tostado.

**San Esteban** Magnificent outside, collossal within, San Esteban was designed by Juan de Álava (also author of the Cathedral and that of Segovia) in the sixteenth century and extended by Rodrigo Gil de Hontañón and Juan de Ribera. Approached through the gardened terrace, the west façade is spectacular − a glorious, intricately carved, golden wall crowned by a massive arch. The Plateresque scenes are of the martyrdom of St Stephen etched by Ceroni. The splendour continues inside the huge single-aisled church, where a massive gilded altarpiece, a masterpiece of José Churriguera, presides. The Claudio Coello canvas placed in the middle section is almost dwarfed by the thick twisting columns adorned with vines and foliage. Above the entrance is the choir − entered via stairs of the Dominican convent whose simple arches are to the right of the church − from which a differing aspect of the church can be seen. The choir stalls are quietly beautiful, and the fresco, by Palomino, is pertinent to the strength of the Order.

The Claustro de los Reyes ('Monarchs' cloister) in the convent has Isabelline doorways and arcades decorated with medallions.

**Convento de las Dueñas** Opposite San Esteban, this Dominican convent has opened its delightful Renaissance patio to visitors. It is small, of an unusual shape, with remarkable capitals of fantastic animals and monstrous human forms. The lower arcade has smooth, rounded arches contrasting those above. At a counter off the entrance patio the nuns sell pastas − various little almond and spice cakes that are utterly delicious.

**East of Gran Via** Here are a number of lovely buildings. Just up the hill from the Tourist Office is Sancti Spiritus, a sixteenth-century church of the Italian Renaissance era. The chapel of Cristo de los Milagros (once the choir) is unusual for this city — very dark and sombre with a striking Mudéjar pannelled ceiling.

By San Esteban, at the foot of Gran Via, a wide street rises eastwards passing a splendid diocesian seminary, constructed by Joaquín Churriguera for the Calatrava military order. Further up is the tiny church of Saint Tomás de Canterbury. With a single aisle and three apses, it was dedicated to the saint in 1175 by two Englishmen.

Another seminary is hidden by the parallel street of Santa Clara. Down from the convent is a tranquil place, one side of the square being the raised classical façade of the San Román seminary.

**West of Gran Via** In the triangle between Gran Via, San Esteban and the Plaza Mayor is the Plaza Colón — a formal garden. Standing to one side is the Torre del Clavero, an attractive Baroque fortification, and to the other, old Renaissance palaces.

**West of Plaza Mayor** Surrounding the lovely gardens of San Francisco are a number of splendid buildings. At the foot of Calle Prior (leaving the Plaza beneath a west arch) is the Monterrey Palace, an attractive sixteenth-century building, its crested façades, sculpted chimneys and towers are typical of the Spanish renaissance. Opposite is the vast Herrera-style church, La Purisma, falling sadly into decay.

Left of the gardens along Calle Fonseca is the Renaissance Collegio del Arzobispo Fonseco (once the seminary of the Irish order of nuns). Its chapel has a fine reredos by Alonso de Berruguete. The quiet patio is beautiful. During the summer months a delightful series of music concerts, 'Fonseca de Noche', are held in the open patio. It is advisable to arrive very early for the tickets.

Down the other side of the gardens is the chapel la Vera Cruz, once a synagogue, and now a chapel of the convent of sister adoratrices. It has a rich baroque interior liberally decorated with gold and silver, whose atmosphere is made particularly special by the constant presence, directly in front of the altar, of a white-habited nun in prayer,

Next door is the Convento de las Ursulas. The exterior of this building is impressive – a Renaissance tower with a sculptured terrace, attractively lit from within at night to enhance the effect. Within is Diego de Siloé's splendid marble tomb f the Archbishop Alonso Fonseco. In the choir the nuns have put together a small but fairly unremarkable museum.

**North of Plaza Mayor** At the top of Calle Zamora sits San Marcos, a lovely round Romanesque church, intimate, cool and spacious inside, with early Gothic frescos.

**Shopping** Being a wealthy, thriving city, the shopping network is extensive. There are four main shopping areas:

**North of Plaza Mayor –** Fashion and shoes: in numerous shops surrounding the Plaza Mayor and in the fan of streets leading northwards towards the inner circuit road (Avda Alemania), in particular, Toro, Zamora and Azafrana. There are further small roads crossing towards Gran Via.

Books: 'Cervantes', Plaza Santa Eulalia.

**South of Plaza Mayor –** Souvenirs: lining Rua Mayor, the main street leading from Plaza Mayor to the Cathedrals. Artisanal things: leather, silversmith work – Calle Meléndez (between the Plaza Mayor and La Clerecia).

**East of Plaza Mayor** to Gran Via. Excellent produce is sold during the morning in the Mercado Municipal directly east of the Plaza. Small grocery and ham stores surround it and are also found in the streets leading towards Gran Via. Another market is beside the bus station north of the Avda Alemania. Each morning stalls in the plaza San Justo (SE of the main market, sell vegetables and garlic. Excellent bread can be found in the Boutique de Pan, Calle Azafranal near the top of Gran Via.

**Gran Via** This is a splendid, arcaded street, long enough to contain several areas of different character. Good-quality clothes shops, *patisseries*, and groceries are offered amongst the cafés and bars. Police, Post Office and Tourist Office are also here.

**Sunday Street Market** Plaza del Puente, by the Roman Bridge – more amusing for its liveliness than for its stalls.

**The *Paseo*** The shape of this *paseo* is most unusual. In other towns the evening stroll usually takes place through the main shopping streets, and the cafés of the main square fill as the strolling ceases. In Salamanca the huge Plaza Mayor is host

throughout. The surrounding streets fill with people flowing towards it arches, within which the social walk is taking place. Disciplined by the splendid lamps standing at the four corners of the inner square, companions tread the traditional ring in a single direction, at an unhurried pace, without heed of time.

The character of a Castilian *paseo* can be seen here better than anywhere in the region as the stroll continues in an unbroken circle. From a café table, one can watch the subtle changes of its components – a familiar pair joined by another acquaintance; a group talking now more fervently; a new addition to the stream. It is restful to join the *paseo*, the pace and atmosphere being conducive to reflection and gentle conversation.

The character of the *paseo* changes according to the time of year and the day of the week. During the high summer, which many Salamancans spend away from the city, the *paseo* lacks its regular components. Spring and autumn are the most comfortable times of year – warm and lively, accompanied in spring with ice-cream and in autumn with the aroma of roasting chestnuts. If it rains, the flow continues beneath the arcades. As usual, weekend evenings and Sunday mornings after mass witness the most popular *paseos*.

On Mondays in the morning, quantities of men meet here. Their walk is usually within the arcades and tends to be lively and crowded, especially near the clock, where many stop to participate in intense discussion. The small dark cellar-bars under the east side of the Plaza, beside the market, are packed with locals.

**Parks** There are a number of pretty gardens here. Near the centre is Plaza Colón, a small rose garden beneath the Torre de Clavera. West of the Plaza Mayor is the cool, many-levelled garden of San Francisco, with trees and a fountain. By Plaza España is a refreshing park which fills with families each evening. Far to the east of the Plaza Mayor, past the ring of artery of Paseo de Canalejas is a young park with rose arcades, trees and flowers which will become extremely beautiful – the Jardín Huerta los Jesuits.

**Fiestas** Semana Santa – processions and decorated city. Bulls. Summer Fiesta – the town celebrates solidly for three weeks, beginning in late September with the feast of their patron saint the Virgen de la Vega, with almost daily bullfights (fought in the Plaza Mayor until the mid-nineteenth century).

**Sunday** This is a gentle day here. A bustling street market is held between the river and the gates of the town each Sunday morning. Most monuments are closed in the afternoon. The Plaza Mayor is extremely quiet until late morning when its café tables begin to fill. The *paseo* gatherings here are particularly filled with families who stroll before lunch and after evening mass. Children, beautifully turned out, play around the centre of the Plaza; parents stroll with friends while keeping a proud eye on their young, and grandparents walk nearby. Large families will settle later at one of the cafés here or in the Plaza de la Libertad, next to the Plaza Mayor.

Most restaurants and bars are open for lunchtime, although in general families will eat at home and friends will gather for tapas rather than a full meal. The Plaza Mayor is the centre of activity rather than the parks, although some people while away time rowing on the river.

**Bars and Tapas** Salamanca has superb *tapa* bars. Most of the restaurants have bars in front for *tapas*. (Those recommended in the Restaurant section are extremely popular.)

Cafés abound – each in the Plaza Mayor has its own atmosphere, e.g. *Berysa* – smart; *Novelty* – traditional. Outside there are many others: Gran Via – a street full of cafés, particularly fashionable at night. (*Café Moderno* – No. 75, *Scherzo* – nearby).
Cuesta de Espiritu Sancti (curving east off Gran Via by the tourist office) – a delightful hidden enclave of cafés. Plaza Libertad (Off Calle Zamora north off Plaza Mayor) – particularly *D'Angelos*.
Plaza Colón – west of Plaza Mayor, a tranquil little garden outside Las Ursulas. Lovely for afternoon peace.
Calle Libreros – the finest fresh *horchata* served at El Trigal, No. 20.

The bars beneath the east side of the Plaza are old, tiny, and full of character.

Being a university city, there is plenty of night activity • *Its* – up Calle Toro beside the Hotel Alfonso – a genuine spanish-style place to dance, filled with Salamancans. • *Number 1* – on Plaza España, red and plush – often preferred by visitors. • *Titos* – Espoz y Mina, with dancing round a pool.

**Restaurants** Most serve a similar menu of Salamancan or Castilian cooking. The evening meal is taken late, from 9.30 p.m.

onwards. Salamancan food is heavy and satisfying: roasts of suckling pig and kid, game, beef. Stews: *chanfaina* (a spiced pepper/aubergine mixture with meat); *Calderillo* (a thick potato and meat stew); *hornazo* (*chorizo* or tuny-filled pastries); *Farinato* and *Embutidoes de Guijuelo* (local sausages); stuffed chicken; garlic soup; excellent ham.

*Parador* (*see* Hotels)

*El Fuedal* (*see* Hotels) Gran Hotel.

*Chez Victor* Espoz y Mina 26, Tel: 213123 – superb French cuisine, of the highest reputation. Shut Sunday evenings, Monday and during August (AE V).

*El Candil* Ventura Ruiz Aguilera 14–16 , Tel: 217239 – *Tapas*. A great old *tapa* bar, with superb Castilian and Salamancan food. A restaurant is behind.

*Candil Nuevo* Plaza la Reina 2. Tel: 215058 – continuing the reputation of El Candil for excellent suckling pig and Salamancan fare (AE DC MC V).

*El Mesón* Poeta Iglesias 10, Tel: 217222 – *tapas*. By the Plaza Mayor in a basement, lively.

*Rio de la Plata* Plaza del Peso 1, Tel: 219005 – *tapas*. By Plaza Mayor, Shut Monday evenings and during July. Very popular, good fish and Salamancan cooking with good cellar.

*La Posada* Aire y Azucena 1, Tel: 217251 – *tapas*. Fashionable, lively and casual. Shut 1–15 August. Along Calle Toro north of Plaza Mayor (AE DC MC V).

*La Olla* Plaza del Mercado 17 Tel: 268658 – tranquil first-floor restaurant decorated in pretty rustic style. By the market. Shut Sunday evenings (AE DC MC V).

*Le Chapeau* Calle España 20 (Gran Via), Tel: 271833 – tapas. Art nouveau decoration and very lively (AE DC MC V).

**Hotels** The quantity of visitors here is such that hotel accommodation of every level abounds. it is strongly recommended, especially in high season, to reserve in advance.

### Category 1

*Gran Hotel* Plaza Poeta Iglesias 6, Tel: 213500 – a prestigious hotel, just outside the beautiful Plaza Mayor. The restaurant is good. Very comfortable. Rooms: 184 d&b: 11000–96000.

Restaurant: *El Fuedal* (AE DC MC V). Parking.

*Parador Nacional de Salamanca* Treso de la Feria 2, Ctra a Caceres, Tel: 268700 – a 20-minute walk/short taxi ride from the centre, but the inconvenience is compensated by a fine view of the city from across the banks of the Tormes River. A good restaurant, and a swimming pool. A modern building. Rooms: 206 d&b: 9000–8500 Restaurant (AE DC MC V). Parking.

*Monterrey* Azafranal 21, Tel: 214401 – in an old building, a dignified hotel close to the Plaza Mayor. Rooms: 153 d&b 10300–8000. Restaurant (AE DC MC V). Parking.

## Category 2

*Alfonso X* Toro 64, Tel: 214401 – Joined to Monterrey – the lesser brother. Rooms: 126 d&b: 7500–5000. Restaurant (AE DC).

*Amefa* Pozo Amarillo 18, Tel: 218189 – Close to Plaza Mayor, comfortable. Rooms: 23 d&b: 5000–3000 (AE DC MC V).

*Condal* Plaza Santa Eulalia 2, Tel: 214705 Modern, just across from Monterrey. Rooms; 129 d&b: 4975–4375 (AE DC MC V).

**Category 3** Comfortable, no cards. There are many hotels and hostals of this type. If sleep is important, note carefully the road when choosing other accommodation – night activity here is noisy, and lasts in summer, until well into the morning.

*Emperatriz* Compaña 44, Tel: 219200 – rather old-fashioned, in an attractive walled street close to the Monterrey Palace. Rooms: 66 d&b: 3800–3300.

*Clavero* Consuelo 21, Tel: 218108 – simple. Opposite the Torre del Clavero beside a small park. Rooms: 47 d&b: 3600–3400.

*Las Torres* Plaza Mayor 47, Tel: 212100 – overlooking the Plaza Mayor, with a very popular café downstairs. Delightful views, but noisy at night especially in summer when the square is quiet only after 4 a.m. Rooms: 47 d&b 3650–3400.

*Gran Via* La Rosa 4, Tel: 215401 – simple hotel half-way up Gran Via. The café below is pleasant for Sunday breakfast. Rooms: 80 d&b: 4500–4000.

**Category 4** Straightforward, honest hostals.

*Mindanao* Paseo San Vicente 2, Tel: 263080 – close to Fonseca Palace and Bus Station, on inner ring road. Rooms: 53 d&shower 2560–2300.

*Barcelona* Paseo San Vicente 24, Tel: 264528 – similar to Mindanao on inner ring road. Rooms: 62 d&b: 3250.

*Gabriel y Galan* Plaza Gabriel y Galán 3, Tel: 221774 – on inner ring road.

Rooms: 45 d&b: 2650–2500.

*Laguna* Consuelo 19, Tel: 218706 – opposite Torre de Clavero, quiet.

Rooms: 26 d&b: 2600.

## Camping

*Regio*, Ctra Salamanca Madrid, 4km (2$^1$/2 miles) from centre Tel: 220250 Category 1, 1,126 people, open all year.

*Don Quixote* Ctra Aldealengua, 4km (2$^1$/2 miles) from centre – Category 3, 480 people, open: 20 January to 10 December.

## Information

Area exchange code 923

| | |
|---|---|
| Banks | Clustered in Calle Toro, 100m (100 yd.) north of Plaza Mayor |
| *Correos* (Post Office) | – Gran Via 39 |
| Police | Ronda de Sanctus Spiritus 2, Tel: 245311 (or 091) |
| Tourist Office | Gran Via 25, Tel: 243730. 9.30–2.00 and 4.00–7.00, shut Sun (booth) Plaza Mayor 10.00–2.00 and 4.00–7.00, shut Sun |
| Bus Station | Avda Filiberto Vilalobos 71, Tel: 222603 (10 minutes north of Plaza Mayor) |
| Renfe: | Information – Plaza de la Libertad 10, Tel: 212454 station (15 mins NE of centre, along from Plaza España) Tel: 225742 |
| Cruz Roja (Red Cross): | Plaza San Benito, Tel: 215642 |

Parking for cars – liberal street parking – difficult to obtain close to the centre. Parking beneath Calle Santa Eulalia (just off Gran Via/Calle España), or beneath Plaza de los Bandos (off Calle Zamora)

## Transport:

| | |
|---|---|
| Madrid | bus: every 2 hours (takes approx 3$^1$/2 hours) train – frequent, slower |

Bus connections to all major local towns; Ávila, Soria, Valladolid, Pasencia, Barcelona

Train connections Extremadura, Ávila, Zamora, Leon.

### University language courses

La Universidad de Salamanca, Patio de Escuelas, Tel: 923 216689
Universidad Pontificia, Compana 5, Tel: 218316

**Around Salamanca** The countryside of the region is extremely varied – a strip of green fertility lines the banks of the Tormes while corn plains stretch to the east and north to join those of Valladolid, Zamora and Ávila. Towards Extremadura rises the western end of the Central Systema, the Sierras of Béjar and Francia.

Rugged bull-raising pastureland dotted with *encina* (holm oak) trees flanks the splendid old *señorial* town of Ciudad Rodrigo south-west of the capital. The landscape then becomes treeless, and boulder-strewn towards the spectacular Düero gorge that divides Portugal and Castile.

**North** Between the city of Salamanca and the border of Zamora, the countryside is a mixture of rough pasture and corn flats, sprinkled with olive and cork-oak trees; and small fields of green sugar beat and yellow sunflowers. Small, extremely humble farming communities live within. The ample River Tormes, lined for several kilometres west of the city with trees and greenery, provides nourishment for superb local vegetable and fruit produce. It is dammed closed to the Portuguese border (where it meets the River Duero), and the expanse of the reservoir, Embalse de Almendra, spreads back to the old walled town of Ledesma. The town, 40km (24miles) from the city along the river, has a fine parish church at its crest, and a small park beside has fine views over the crags of the river and its two bridges. (On the river close to the town is the spa Balneario de Ledesma.)

**Castillo de Buen Amor** Directly north of the city of Salamanca is a delightful castle. On the N630, 13km (8miles) within the provincial border, a small abrupt turning to the east leads bumpily to the Castillo de Buen Amor, a privately owned castle which belonged to three generations of the great Fonseca family. Visitors are shown round the furnished, cared-for-rooms by a proud housekeeper whose husband tends the garden. The vaults below are Romanesque, while above are rooms (some later additions) with decorative ceilings. Similar to the castle of Guadamur, Toledo – also furnished for living – it is possible here to see the fortress/palace as more than a ruin. Open 10 a.m.–1 p.m. and 4–6.30 p.m.

**Salamanca**

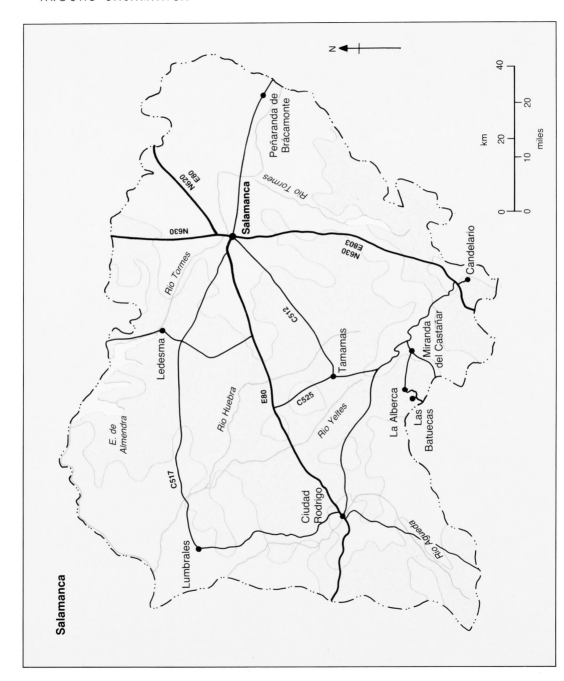

## East and South-East

**Alba de Tormes** South-east from Salamanca is Alba de Tormes – a golden chip off the block. The patron saint of Spain, Santa Teresa, died here in October 1582 and lies in the sepulchre of the Convento de la Anunciación, which she founded in 1570. The town is an important focus of pilgrimage. There are a number of attractive churches, Romanesque and later, and the beginnings of a mighty church that was to be raised to the memory of the saint. The ruins of the circular Torreón de la Armería, a small fortress of the Dukes of Alba, presides over the town and *señorial* buildings line the street. The town is small, with a few shopping streets and a tranquil pleasantness.

**Peñaranda** Peñaranda is placed between Ávila and Salamanca amidst the huge corn plains. An idea of the vastness of the plains, which stretch for hundreds of kilometres northwards, can be gathered from a journey along the N501. The town itself is a provincial market centre, uninterested in tourist visits and attractively lively, particularly in the central plazas which are well served by bars.

**There are a number of attractive churches in Alba de Tormes**

209

**The Plaza Mayor in Béjar**

**South** The south of the province offers strikingly pretty villages, a variety of vegetation from dense forest to bleak granite plateaus, spectacular walks and good winter sports. They are, in summer, the cool haven of the Salamancan people.

The two mountain regions of Béjar and Francia are very different. Sierra de Francia rejoices in famously traditional villages, its highest peak crowned with a convent whose views are unimpaired, its valleys (particularly Las Bateucas) rich in wildlife, vegetation and hidden sanctuaries. The character of Sierra de Béjar, dominated by the active commercial town, is contrastingly energetic, its rolling granite heights more extensive, its pleasure resources exploited.

**Sierra de Béjar** Béjar is a busy town, with a lively economy and a pride in its history. Wool textiles have been the basis of its economy since the thirteenth century (it has extensive summer pasture for sheep). Its shape, stretched like a round arrow-head, is protected at its western crest by walls originally built by the Moors. Close to the crest is the Plaza Mayor, far from the municipal park which joins the modern area to the older streets. A long narrow street runs from here up to the Plaza Mayor, lined all the way with shops of every description (including good hiking/climbing shops), and bustling with life. A few cars can squeeze through.

In the Plaza itself sits the Ayuntamiento (from which the Tourist Office works out of season), and dominating the square is the dignified sixteenth-century Palace of the Duques de Zuñiga, the lords of the area for five hundred years until the traumatic 1812 laws of Cádiz which abolished fuedal powers. The fortress-like building is now a college. San Sebastián, a thirteenth-century church, sits prominently near it.

Béjar's gardens are beautifully kept: La Antigua, just within the western curl of the walls, the park in the centre, and the historic sixteenth-century garden of El Bosque with its ancient trees and small palace. The town, awkwardly laid-out, can seem unwelcoming with its rim of towering blocks and net of grey narrow streets, but its lack of compromise to the tourist, and its general vibrance are refreshing. Looming over it are high peaks of Candelario which are nearly always snow-capped.

Béjar is a good base from which to go exploring the wild mountain countryside – experienced advice can be found within. Hotels here are adequate, and the most popular restaurants offer food fit for energetic walkers. It is best to park in the new part of town.

The region of Béjar extends northwards into wooded foothills, full of nestling villages, small pastures, and streams. The Embalse de Santa Teresa collects water from the young Tormes River — born amongst the Gredos peaks. The banks near Puente del Congosto provide good fishing, and the village itself has an attractive sixteenth-century bridge and castle.

To the west of the region, near Lagunilla, the thick vegetation becomes similar to that of Sierra de Francia, the great River Alagón dividing the two. Marvellous walks and picnic spots exist around Lagunilla and El Cerro, from which the views reach deep into Extremadura. Nearby is Montemayor del Rio, a village with fine castle ruins, 3m (10ft) thick fortifying walls and an attractive plaza Mayor with a thirteenth-century church.

To the south of Béjar, the majestic rise of the mountains provide more strenuous walking, and old villages well built to withstand heavy snows. Immediately above the town (along N630) is the Sanctuary of Nuestra Señora del Castañar, a baroque building amongst elm and chestnut trees with one of the oldest bullrings in Spain (originally constructed 1667). Further along, via Llano Alto and a trackway, is Peña de la Cruz — a point with fine views.

**Candelario** The grand hikes are found near Candelario, a famous, picturesque mountain village 8km (5miles) from Béjar, which is snowbound in winter and much visited in summer (several daily buses connect the two). The white houses, with corners and bases of granite, have wood shuttering and attractive flower-laden balconies. The large double-layered front doors are unusual — the outer one is trimmed like the lower half of a stable door and used alone in summer. The village is substantial, with steep streets and a dramatic surrounding countryside of mountain peaks and thick woodland.

From here there are a multitude of walks. A winding road, often undrivable in winter, leads up to the area of El Travesa (good for skiing). Nearby are waterfalls signifying the beginnings of the River Cuerpo de Hombre. From this area walks lead westward across the high peaks to El Calvitero 2,425m (7,956ft) in the Solana, or eastwards towards the crest of Canchal Negro

**The distinctive doors of Candelario**

211

2,369m (7,772ft) in La Covatilla. From the small village of Hoya, north-east of Béjar, a long track also leads upwards to La Covatilla. The views from these walks are breath-taking.

Driving in the region, the main road N630 tends to carry heavy traffic. However, southwards to the province of Cáceres, past the spa town of Baños de Montemayor, there is a turning left towards Hervás – a small town renowned for its remarkably preserved *judería* (Jewish quarter).

This winding road continues for many spectacular kilometres to arrive above Cabezuela, one of the villages of the beautiful Valle de Jerte which wends down to Plasencia. (Barco de Ávila, east of Béjar, heads the road through this valley, and also provides the link to the passes of the Sierra de Gredos.) Another spectacular road crosses from Candelario to La Garganta. Narrow and little used, it passes over great bare granite heights with extraordinary vistas of granite rolls and forest valleys on either side.

Heading for Salamanca, it is more pleasant to keep off the main road to Guijuelo. Precipitous villages such as San Esteban de la Sierra, and Linares del Riofrio are attractions on the way.

Towards the Sierra de Francia, the road to Aldeacipreste (from where roads can lead to Montemayor or Colemar) follows the section of the river Cuerpo de Hombre called El Tranco de Diablo – a superb rush of white water.

**Right**
**La Alberca**

**Below**
**The ancient houses of La Alberca**

Leaving Béjar eastwards towards Barco de Ávila, the entry point for the main Gredos range, the quiet road passes high Alpine villages, rough pasture and stone-walled paddocks.

**Sierra de Francia** The rolling countryside of the Sierra de Francia is forested with oak, chestnut, walnut and strawberry trees. The convent of Peña de Francia sits upon the highest granite peak, at 1,723m (5,653ft) it is far below the Béjar peaks. The picturesque villages tucked in to the tight high valleys, the expansive woodlands carpeted with yellow and purple in spring, and the many brooks of fresh water, have given this area a reputation of great beauty. Here there are wonderful walks.

**La Alberca** is very attractive. Its construction is well protected from deterioration by its status as a National Historical Monument. Although this ensures that it is flooded with tourists, especially in summertime, the status also gives a visitor licence to look everywhere and enjoy the extremely rustic nature of the village. (Elsewhere, the traditional beauty and humble nature of village life can be difficult to look at – what makes a delightful sight to a visitor is often an unromantic necessary to a local person.

The most well-known area of the Sierras is near the border with Cáceres where the most famous villages cluster, and from where the beautiful valley of Las Batuecas falls. Every village in the region will boast of its good water.

The houses of La Alberca are of a wood skeleton, infilled with adobe or clay, the upper storeys protruding further than the ground floor. Often the living area will be upstairs, the ground floor reserved for the family livestock. Verandas, built into the upper floors, are substantial.

The village is at the foot of a hill crossing a stream, and the narrow, cobbled streets wind through. At the Plaza Mayor, cafés sit beneath the proud old buildings. Many of the inhabitants are elderly, but the status of the village is such that there are plenty of small enterprises selling local ceramics, *turrón*, and marvellous almost-black honey. It is more pleasant to visit La Alberca early in the day and on a weekday. The smallholdings just outside are very pretty.

The summer fiestas here, 15 and 16 August (celebrating the Ofrenda a la Virgen, and La Loa) are amongst the most decorative and visited in the region. The traditional dress, displayed then, is adorned with gold and silver artesanal ornament, and illustrates the considerable historical wealth enjoyed by the village.

**Mountain Villages** The main other historic villages which cater for visitors are Miranda del Castañar, San Martín del Casteñar, Cepeda and Sequeros. They are all extremely attractive.

213

Miranda is a splendid old town encased by thick thirteenth-century walls (within which run passageways) with a steep, winding main street. A fifteenth-century castle sits at the top, and fine buildings are scattered throughout. San Martín also has a castle, and a church with unusual thirteenth-century Morisco arches within.

Sequeros and Cepeda are dignified clusters of timber and clay houses in a surrounding countryside of fruit orchards and forest. Embossed leather wineskins and honey are sold.

Mogarraz is seldom visited, falling below the roadside. Long, narrow and steep, its quiet streets are as well clad with the ancient traditional houses as the well-known villages. A walk through is most pleasant. (Its summer fiesta on 5, 6 and 7 August, with little bullfights and dancing, is a delight.)

Throughout the area are walks – particularly Herguijuela southwards through thick woods to Rebollosa, and Monforte Southwards to Madroñal, the latter being most beautiful when its orchards of cherry trees are in blossom. A fiesta in July celebrates the harvest.

**Peña de Francia** The convent of Peña de Francia is the crowning glory of the Sierras, encircled by thrilling views. Dominicans arrived here in 1437, and a few (from San Esteban, Salamanca) still inhabit the convent in the summer months. The sanctuary is an important focus of pilgrimage – the original figure of the Virgen, in poor condition, is encased within the altar sculpture seen today. The buildings were much restored in the nineteenth century. It is possible to stay in the Hostal here, and heavy country food is produced in the *comedor.*

**Las Batuecas** The monastery overlooks the valley of Las Batuecas, a National Reserve of hunting, and full of wildlife and thick vegetation. Wolves, lynx, roe deer and wild boar roam the forest, and Imperial eagles and black vultures soar above. Few tracks penetrate this beautiful isolated valley.

Quite close to the road from La Alberca to Las Mestas is the monastery of San José, founded to exorcise the valley of evil spirits in 1599. Although abandoned in the dissolution orders of 1836, the monastery is today inhabited by strictly cloistered aged monks of the Carmelite order. A lovely walk follows the river from below the monastery. Hidden in the valley are the ruins of other sanctuaries, and caves with neolithic paintings of goats, lions and other animals.

North-east from here are the Quilamas peaks, across which a network of tracks pass, linking together almost every village of the wide circle which surround it (Linares, Escurial, Navarredonda, Cereceda, etc). Within the circle are three important peaks – Pico Cervero, Los Calamorros and Codorro – several rivers (good trout fishing, some natural pools for swimming) and delightful valleys untouched by roads. Walks here can be many kilometres long, and the tracks are punctuated, near villages, by good water fountains and park areas equipped with tables. The town of Linares, grower of beautiful strawberries, has plentiful cafés and shops, and makes a good starting point with many tracks into the meadow/forest of the Sierras.

Driving to the north and east of the range, between Salamanca and Linares del Riofrio, rough oak pastures and farming hamlets (husbanding cattle and pigs) line the straight roads. The foothills begin outside the curve of Tamames, Linares and San Esteban. San Esteban, a spectaculary steep old village plunging into the valley is surrounded by fragrant hills of wild herb. Linares and Tamames are more substantial. (On the road from Linares to San Miguel, 1km (1/2 mile) from the town, is a water fountain, reputably the most delicious in the region.) To the west of the range rise the wilder Sierra de Gata and Sierra de las Hurdes in the province of Cáceres.

The plains of Cuidad Rodrigo, north-east of Peña de Francia, can be approached spectacularly from the mountain road via Monsagro, plunging through Las Batuecas and over hillsides of herbs and pasture to drop suddenly into orchards and grain flats (the C515 is a more straightforward route).

## West and South-West

**Ciudad Rodrigo** To the south-west of the city of Salamanca, through the characteristic dry oak and pasture landscape, is the town of Ciudad Rodrigo. This countryside is known for the raising of brave fighting bulls for the rings of Castile, and excellent pigs for the famous cured Salamancan hams. (Enthusiastic spectators flock to attend its festival of *Corridas*.)

The town is a superbly preserved relic of the fifteenth and sixteenth centuries – splendidly walled and built upon a rise in the surrounding plains. There is a small modern addition outside the walls, but within remains the living evidence of a powerful city of the Middle Ages – a network of streets full of fine *señorial* houses, a cathedral, and a castle. It is possible to walk almost the entire circuit of the 8m (25ft) high wall; the defences are in good repair and the towers were only added in the eighteenth century. Three roads lead through the walls – two entrances (Calle Madrid, leading to the Plaza Mayor is the most prominent gate; the other leads to the Cathedral, further round to the north) and one exit. It is easiest to leave cars by the main entrance or next to the Cathedral, although there is also parking by the Parador/castle.

Ciudad Rodrigo is dignified and quietly bustling, with local shops, narrow streets and plenty of people. It is most pleasant to wander round. Amongst the many old houses (the old town is little interrupted by modern building) are a superb Romanesque Cathedral, the Palacio de Montarco and the Casa de los Vázquez (now an eccentric and delightful Post Office). The sixteenth-century Palacio, in a small Plaza off the main high street just inside the walls, has a splendid doorway with spiral columns either side, and windows adorned with Plateresque designs. Next to it is an austere *señorial* house.

On down the main street is the Plaza Mayor – long and irregular, filled with bars and capped with the sixteenth-century Ayuntamiento, and, next to the main street, a house decorated with an attractive freize. (Bar El Sanatorio, No.12, is filled with photographs commemorating the bullfights of the town.) Rua Sol leads straight out of the old town to the left of the Ayuntamiento. To its right is Calle Ledesma in which is the delightful Post Office. It is worth buying a stamp in order to see the decoration inside this sixteenth-century mansion; heraldic shields in stained glass, beautiful coffered ceilings, walls decorated with tiles of hunting scenes and a beautifully carved staircase.

Curving right from this road, past a great Herreran church and an old hospital, the castle is placed by the wall overlooking the plains towards Portugal. Now a Parador, it was a Roman and then a Moorish fort before becoming a stronghold of Henry II Trastamara, the victor of the Castilian civil war against Pedro I the Cruel in the late fourteenth century. The Torre de Homenaje is austere.

Amongst the religious buildings are several of heavy Herrara style (the designer of El Escorial, Madrid) and a number of the Romanesque era.

**The Cathedral** is extremely important. At 11 a.m. each day mass is held accompanied by the organ. Constructed between 1165 and 1230, it has two magnificent Romanesque portals lined with sculptures of saints. The west doorway is enclosed by an outer door, but can be seen by pushing the heavy door from inside the Cathedral – it is unlocked for this purpose. The south doorway is again remarkable: twelve Old and New Testament figures stand above the tympanum in which Christ and four disciples are carved. The windows, seen both inside and out, are beautiful Romanesque examples allowing a pale light into the Cathedral. The main apse, by Rodrigo Gil de Hontañón, is lofty and graceful, and decorated simply by a painting of Fernando Gallego. The choir stalls of Rodrigo Alemán are very lovely. A sacristan will approach offering permission to look at the cloisters. They are a further treat of Romanesque and Gothic style with delightful capitals, each graced with four tiny figures. In the arcade to the left an unusual, highly decorated capital hangs without the support of a column. Beneath is a well, the cause of the daring omission. The Cathedral opens: from 8 a.m. for mass, from 10 a.m.–1 p.m. and 4–6 p.m. for visitors.

The Tourist Office is beside the Cathedral.

**A detail of Cuidad Rodrigo cathedral**

**Los Arribes de Duero** Onwards towards Portugal, the landscape becomes harsh, rugged and desolate, spotted with small humble stone villages. The River Tormes also loses its clothing of green to run through rocky country until the dam of the Embalse de Almendra. There is a sudden change in countryside after the dam, where the extraordinary crags and deep pitched cuts of Los Arribes de Duero appear. The long gorge, varying from 200m to 700m (650 to 3,000ft) in depth, runs the length of the River Duero that divides Portugal from Zamora and the Salamanca. Within it are remarkable microclimates where protection from the harsh sun creates a Mediterranean warmth in which almonds and oranges can be grown. There are beautiful and spectacular sights, but it is generally necessary to approach on foot from Mieza, Saucelle or Adeadavila.

Between Lumbrales (an old town north of Ciudad Rodrigo) and Saucelle, is the beautiful road SA330 from which the spectacular Puerto de la Molinera can be approached. San Felices de los Gallegos is just south of Lumbrales – a lovely old walled village.

**Frontier Crossings to Portugal** Just within the Zamora border where the Tormes meets the Duero at Barragem de Bermpost, near Fermoselle. Near Lumbrales: across the Salto Saucelle dam – limited hours; via the bridge crossing of Muella de la Vega, only open during the weekends for foot or bike travellers – there is no road connection,

These crossings are spectacular for the hovering birds of prey and the hostile majesty of terrain. Directly west of Ciudad Rodrigo: an important main crossing point: Colonia de la Estación.

**Horse Riding** Excursions by horse in the region:
Salamanca a Caballo, S.A., Perez Oliva 9, Salamanca, Tel: 256726 – visits around Peña de Francia, Ledesma, Batuecas, etc.

**Alba de Tormes**

*Benedictino,* March to October, 6 Beritas, Tel: 300025 – Open: March to October. Restaurant. Comfortable and quiet, up at the back of the town.
40 rooms d&b 3000 (V DC).
*Alameda* Avda Juan Pablo II, Tel: 300031 – old-fashioned, across the river from the town. Restaurant.
34 rooms d&b 3000 (V DC).
*Hostal America* La Guia, Tel: 300071 – recommended restaurant for fresh-water fish.
30 rooms d&b 2200 (V).

**Béjar** (Tourist Office – P de Cervantes 6, 403005)
*Colón,* Colón 42, Tel: 400650 Comfortable, central and long-established.
54 rooms d&b 4900 (AE DC MC V).
*Comercio,* Puerta de Ávila 5, Tel: 400219. In the outskirts, modern.
13 rooms d&b 3500 (AE DC MC V).
*Yuste,* Ctra de Salamanca 24, Tel: 401152. Central, noisy and very modest. For walkers. Bar downstairs.
22 rooms d&b 1800.
Restaurant *Argentino*, Ctra Salamanca 22, Tel: 402692. A big *churrasco* restaurant, serving excellent roast and grills brought to the table on wooden platters. Terrace (AE DC MC V).

**Fiestas in Béjar**

| | |
|---|---|
| May: | Corpus fiesta |
| September 8: | *Romería* to Hermitage of Castañar |
| Summer fiesta: | end of September |
| Carnival | spectacular and lively |
| Summer Festival | Encierros (bull running) and Corridas SpringCattle Fair |
| La Alberca: | 15 and 16 August |
| Mogarraz: | 5 and 7 August |
| Madroñal: | July |

## Candelario

*Cristi*, Plaza Bejar 1, Tel: 413212 A good hotel, with tavern–style restaurant (Tóston, Chorizo).
40 rooms d&b 2970 open June/Sept.

## La Alberca

Las Batuecas, *Ctra las Batuecas,* Tel: 437030 Quiet, just outside the village.
24 rooms d&b 4100 V
Restaurant: El Castillo, Ctra de Mogarraz, Tel: 437481 – big country restaurant, popular at weekends.

## Ciudad Rodrigo

*Parador Enrique II*, Plaza del Castillo 1, Tel: 460150 – in the fifteenth–century castle, lovely gardens and very comfortable.
27 rooms, d&b 9000 (AE DC MC V). Good restaurant.
*Conde Rodrigo*, Plaza del Salvador 9, Tel; 461404 – old–fashioned and dignified , by the Cathedral. Restaurant.
35 rooms, d&b 4500 (AE DC MC V).
*El Cruce*, Ctra de Lisboa, Tel: 460258 – on the main road (plenty of choice), comfortable.
40 rooms d&b 3400 (V).
Restaurant: *El Rodeo*, Calle Gigantes 6, Tel: 462685 – near the castle. Typical food of the region (good roast kid)
Shut Thursdays (AE V).
Restaurant: *Mayton*, La Colada 9 Tel: 460721 – roasts in flamboyant style, by the Plaza Mayor. (AE DC MD C).
Shut Monday evenings and end of October.

## Camping

*Candelario:* Cinco Castañas, Tel: 414495 – open all year, Cat 2, 440 people.
*Fuente de San Esteban:* El Cruce, Tel: 440130 – open: 15 June to 30 September, Cat 2, 225 people.
*Nava de Francia:* Sierra de Francia, Tel: 449419 – open: 14 March to 5 April and 15 June to 15 September, Cat 2, 320 people.
*Puerto de Béjar:* Puerto de Béjar, Tel: 229305 – open 1 July to 30 August, Cat 3, 320 people.

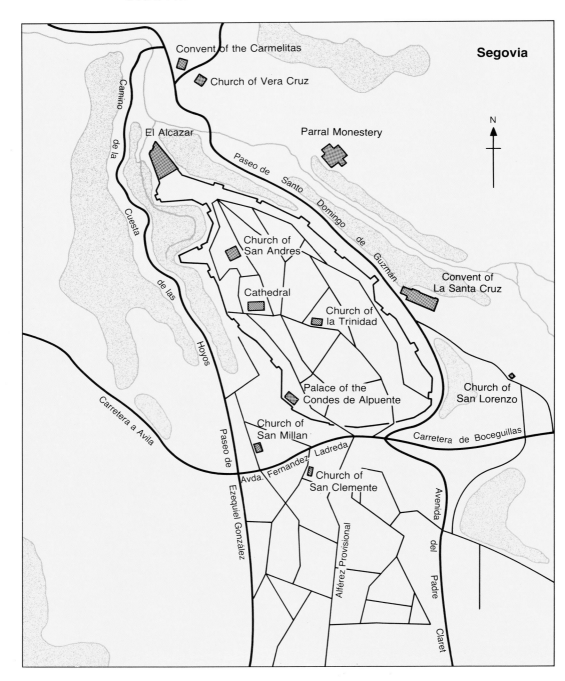

Segovia

Convent of the Carmelitas

Church of Vera Cruz

Parral Monestery

N

Camino de la

El Alcazar

Paseo de Santo Domingo de Guzmán

Cuesta de las

Church of San Andres

Convent of La Santa Cruz

Cathedral

Church of la Trinidad

Hoyos

Palace of the Condes de Alpuente

Church of San Lorenzo

Carretera a Avila

Paseo de Ezequiel González

Church of San Millan

Avda. Fernandez Ladreda

Carretera de Boceguillas

Church of San Clemente

Alférez Provisional

Avenida del Padre Claret

**Segovia** is an extremely pleasant town, with a well-balanced offering of monuments, vistas, peaceful walking areas and urbanity. By day it is an attractive, vivacious place, without being overrun by tourists whose visits are mainly confined to the west end of the old town between the lofty Gothic Cathedral and the beautiful spired Alcázar. The walled part of town throbs with life – full of schools, with a pedestrian artery of shops running down to the modern centre. Also linking the old town to the new is the dramatic Roman aqueduct whose arches, many-tiered and colossal at their most famous point, penetrate deep into the newer part.

Built up to the crest of a high ridge, the walled town of Segovia is surrounded with fine views southwards to the mountains, northwards to dry desert-like plains. There are glorious churches, most of the Romanesque style, and numerous quiet streets clothed with dignified old houses.

**History** Segovia has a distinguished history. During the Roman occupation it became an important settlement, placed at the intersection of two busy military highways. Under the Visigoths it was elevated to a bishopric. By 1085, when it was taken by the Christian forces from the Moors, the town had a substantial cloth industry.

As a royal residence, the town grew in prestige from the reign of Alfonso El Sabio onwards, reaching a cultural peak under the

**The walled town of Segovia**

patronage of Henry IV Trastamara. Within the Alcázar, Isabel the Catholic was crowned in 1474, and her husband Ferdinand, King of Arágon, swore to observe the Fueros de Castilla here (the existing rights of the Castile kingdom). The fortress was a frequent meeting place of the Cortes, and the town provided the headquarters of the Inquisition under Torquemada.

During the Hapsburg dynasty, a severe breach in trust between the town and the monarchs was formed by the Comuneros Revolt lead by Juan Bravo against Charles V. The town also pitched into economic problems with the general decline of the wool trade after the sixteenth-century, although its huge Cathedral was still being constructed at this time.

Royal patronage only re-emerged during the Bourbon dynasty, whose residences of La Granja and then Riofrío renewed the old Royal relationship. The military importance of the town continued with the successive additions to the Alcázar, and the founding of an Artillery Academy by Charles III.

Segovia was ravaged by Napoleonic troops in the nineteenth century.

### Outstanding Monuments

Aqueduct

Cathedral, Plaza Mayor 9.30–1.00 a.m./3.00–6.00 p.m., Summer 9.00–7.00 p.m.

Alcázar, far western ridge 10.00 a.m.–6/7.00 p.m.

Iglesia de San Esteban, near Plaza Mayor, mass a.m. and p.m.

Iglesia de San Millán, beneath walls near Aqueduct, mass a.m./p.m.

### Notable Monuments

| | |
|---|---|
| Churches: | San Martín, off Calle Juan Bravo, mass 12.30 a.m. |
| | Vera Cruz, north below walls, 10.30 a.m.– 1.30 p.m., 3.30–6/7.00 p.m. closed Monday |
| | La Trinidad, near Plaza Mayor, mass a.m. and p.m. |
| | Corpus Christi, off Calle Isabel la Católica |
| | San Juan de los Caballeros, near Aqueduct at northern side of walled town, closed for repairs. |
| Monasteries: | San Antonio el Real, north-east of new town. 10.00 a.m.–1.00 p.m., 4.00–6.00 p.m. |
| | El Parral, north below walls, closed for repairs |

Civic Buildings:   Museo Provincial de Bellas Artes, Calle
Augustín 6 north of San Martín
10.00 a.m. 2.00 p.m., 4.00–6.00 p.m., closed
Sunday p.m. and Mon.
Casa de los Picos, off Calle Juan Bravo.
Torreón de Loyoza, by San Martín, 12.00–2.00
p.m., 7.00 –9.30 p.m.
Sixteenth century *señorial* houses near Plaza San
Martín, Plaza Conde de Cheste.

**Layout of the Town** A central traffic artery passes beneath
the aqueduct and divides the walled hillside town from the newer
parts of the city. Within the walls, the main street is pedestrian,
leading uphill from the aqueduct (Plaza de Azoguejo) to the Plaza
Mayor beside which is the Cathedral. The street is lined with
shops, several *señorial* palaces and a couple of interesting churches.
Restaurants and bars surround the Plaza Mayor, Plaza Azoguejo
and the linking road between the two.

The western triangle of the walled ridge, from the Plaza Mayor
to the Alcázar, is quiet and pretty, with fine houses, twisting streets
and a number of beautiful churches including San Esteban and La
Trinidad. Beneath the walls to the north are two monasteries and
the twelve-sided church of Vera Cruz. Beneath the walls to the
south-east is a small old district dominated by the important
church of San Millán. The modern town spreads eastwards.

**The Historical City** The whole of the walled town is easily
walkable with few cars to compromise the tranquillity. The
celebrated churches, mostly more interesting to the eye outside
than in, are scattered throughout, and the town respects its fine
architecture with plenty of small squares. There is an
uncommonly generous feeling of space.

**Aqueduct** The aqueduct strikes across the Plaza Azoguejo at
a main entrance to the old town. Built of the local Guadarrama
granite probably in the first century AD, every block free of mortar,
this magnificent Roman construction is one of the landmarks of
the town. Except for the years between 1071 and 1489 when 35
of its arches lay in ruins from an attack by the Moors, it has carried
water continuously from Riofrío to the heart of the city until the
last decade. The tallest piers rise nearly 30m (98ft) as *El Puente* (the
bridge) crosses the Plaza del Azoguejo.

**The magnificent aqueduct is a striking example of Roman construction**

The juxtaposition of the ancient monument and the modern life of the city is striking: quantities of vehicles travelling along the main traffic artery pass through the arches spanning the Plaza; and the repetitive arches become almost monotonous as the aqueduct cuts through the suburbs for over a kilometre ($^1$/2 mile)

It makes an interesting walk to follow the arches from their highest, most impressive point above the Plaza, up the valley side to the Academy del Artillery where the construction sharply changes course by more than 90 degrees and curves towards the water tower on the road to La Granja. Here the arches are reduced to single bows so low that only a small child can walk beneath without stooping. The surprisingly narrow water channel can be seen here.

**Cathedral** The Cathedral, built on high ground by the Plaza Mayor, towers over the town with its glory of pinnacles, battlements and buttresses decorating a pure Gothic outline. Begun in 1525 by when the Renaissance style was prominent, it is the last cathedral of Gothic design in Spain. The main architects were Juan Gil de Hontañón (also working on Salamanca's new cathedral) and his son Rodrigues. It was not consecrated until 1768 although mass was first celebrated here 200 years earlier.

Until the rise of the Comuneros against Charles V, a splendid Romanesque Cathedral stood opposite the Alcázar, but it was destroyed in the fighting and only the cloister, choir and a few features were salvaged for the new building. It is striking how few years passed between the destruction of the old and the beginning of the new – Segovians will relate with pride the tremendous civic effort of the whole town in the main labour of the construction.

From the outside, the mass of the building is imposing with an elaborate curve of the east end exposed to the Plaza Mayor. The dome, and tower – the highest in Spain until damaged by lightning – are both magnificent. Three doors lead into the building: neo-classical at the south, Gothic at the west (the Door of Forgiveness) and Herreriano at the North. The latter granite Puerta de San Frutos, with the patron saint of Segovia standing above, is the main visitors' entrance. On the saint's day, 25 October, San Frutos is said to turn a leaf of the book he holds.

Inside, huge windows of stained glass, some sixteenth-century Flemish, give light to the elegant wide-span arches, beautiful cluster pillars and lace-like vaulting. A flamboyant balustrade traces round the building above the arches.

Beneath the groin vaulting of the Capilla Mayor stands an impressive marble and bronze retable by Sabatini, within which sits an ivory Virgen de la Paz adorned with silver. San Frutos and San Geroteo, first bishop of Segovia, are sculpted here. Opposite is the choir of green marble, brought from the Old Cathedral, with florid carved seats.

Seven polygonal chapels circle the main chapel, and further chapels line the aisles. Of these, the most notable are: Santo Entierro (fifth in north aisle), with a retable of the pietà by Juan de Juni and the Descent by Ambrosio Benson; Chapel of the Conception (last in north aisle), with the sepulchre of the Miñano family, closed by a pure mahogany grill brought from America by the head of the family, and decorated by paintings; San Blas (opposite), with steps to climb the tower; Capilla del Sepulcro (second in south aisle), with one of the many reclining Christs by Gregorio Fernández; Santiago, with a superb retable by Pedro de Bolduque form the 1580s and an outstanding grill. Many chapels have features rescued from the Old Cathedral.

In the elegant Gothic cloister – designed by Juan Guas for the Old Cathedral and finished only twenty years before the building was destroyed – Juan and Rodrigo Gil de Hontañón are buried. The chapel of Santo Catalina contains the tomb of Enrique's infant son who plunged to his death from a window in the Alcázar in 1366. The museum pieces here include a heavy silver monstrance carried by an ostentatious gilt carriage, used in Corpus Christi processions; painting (Pedro Berruguete, Coello, Morales, Van

**Segovia's Gothic Cathedral
dominates the town**

Eyck); ecclesiastical treasures and a lovely thirteenth-century virgin and child. The Sala Capitular, with a white and gold carved ceiling, displays sixteenth-century tapestries and a dominating Valladolid Christ. In one gallery are models of the most famous churches of the town – a useful comparative study.

**Alcázar** At the most western point of the ridge upon which Segovia is built, overlooking the confluence of the Eresma and Clamores rivers, stands this extraordinary fortress. It is reached from the Plaza Mayor along Calle Marqués del Arco, or more spectacularly along Paseo de Ronda which curves towards it along the south walls of the town from beneath the Cathedral. The bastion is graced by slim turrets roofed with slate, and the steep slopes beneath are clad with forest. The feminine silhouette is unique, instantly recognizable, and very beautiful.

The Alcázar served as a royal residence and fortress from the reign of Alfonso VIII onwards, reaching its prime with the Trastamara family (Enrique IV, and Isabella). The failed rising of the Comuneros in Segovia damaged the prominence of the town and of the Alcázar, which only recovered with the interest of Juan II and Philip II who made great additions to the building. In 1862 a fire practically destroyed it. The present building results from the painstaking reconstruction finished in 1882, and houses a military archive and museum. The resulting bright finish and lack of historic atmosphere of the interior can seem disappointing.

The fortified entrance to the Alcázar is from the north through the Torre de Homenaje, a sturdy rectangular tower crowned with twelve defensive turrets built by Juan II. There is little hint, from this side, of the elegance of the other façades. The Torre can be climbed by a narrow spiral stair, passing various ill-lit prison cells leading to the roof from where the views are magnificent.

Through to the right of the granite Herreran-style patio is the main series of rooms open to visitors. Rooms of armour decorated by friezes and nineteenth-century paintings lead to the beautiful Salón del Trono (Throne room). The glorious wood-patterned ceiling surrounded by a gilt frieze is similar to the original design crafted for Enrique IV Trastamara and was brought from a fifteenth-century church in Valladolid after the fire. Much of the intricate stucco work is original. Beneath are reconstructions of the thrones of Ferdinand and Isabella.

The antichamber, Sala de Galera, constructed for Catherine of Lancaster (mother of Juan II) has a fine beamed ceiling different to the oriental original) and stucco frieze. Large windows give an unimpaired view to the countryside north of Segovia. The imposing Coronation of Isabella the Catholic is by Carlos Muñoz de Pablos, of Segovia.

Following is the Sala de las Piñas, constructed for Enrique IV and named after the style of Mudéjar ceiling decoration. Each of the 392 gilded pineapples is distinct. A crossbow of Charles I sits in the centre of the room, which is warmed by a fifteenth-century tapestry.

The tapestried royal bedroom leads to the bright Sala de los Reyes. The geometric ceiling is oddly mismeasured here, and polychrome carvings of royal patronages from Castile, León and Asturias clad the cornice. Sala del Cordón is a delightful small room of tapestries, gilt stucco and a lovely blue coffered ceiling. The continuous rope traced round the walls imitates the Franciscan symbol, apparently placed by Alfonso El Sabio when reprimanded for some arrogantly blasphemous remarks.

Philip II married Ana of Austria in the dark chapel, whose Mudéjar ceiling and fine Castilian retable are recent further importations. The painting The Adoration of the Kings is the prized masterpiece of Bartolomé Carducho and one of the few items to survive the fire.

Finally, a small museum of arms fills a room in the west tower.

**The Alcázar is a dramatic feature of the Segovia skyline**

**One of the spires of the Alcázar**

229

**North of the Plaza Mayor** The Plaza Mayor is pretty, partly arcaded and shaded by acacia trees. The church of San Esteban is reached from here via Calle Escuderos, or Calle Victoria (curving westwards from the Teatro de Juan Bravo).

**San Esteban** the remarkable Romanesque church stands in a square, opposite the stern façade of the Palacio Episcopal. Its glory is the five-storey thirteenth-century tower, named Reina de las Torres Españolas (the Queen of Spanish Towers). The bevelled corners, and clustered pillars between the arched windows make the tower most delicate. An arcaded atrium graces one side. The interior is unremarkable, with a heavy gilt Plateresque retablo, although there is a thirteenth-century Christ.

**La Trinidad** This twelfth-century single-aisled church, is reached via the east extension of Calle Victoria (Valdeaguilla), or through a series of delightful small streets eastwards from San Esteban (Travesía de Capuchinos, Plaza San Quirze, Plaza San Nicolás, etc.). It has been well restored, with blind arches decorating the simple apse. Inside it is quiet, dark and beautifully austere, with important old frescos and barely any sculpture.

### North end of the Aqueduct to the Walls
**San Juan de los Cabelleros** In an almost forgotten part of town at the north-east, within the walls, is the earliest Romanesque church, San Juan de los Caballeros, with magnificent capitals in the arcades. Today it houses a museum of the ceramic artist Daniel Zuloaga. It is approached eastwards from Trinidad (about 5 minutes' walk) or north from the steps behind the aqueduct. This entrance into the old town is not as spectacular as the main pedestrian way, but is pretty and very peaceful.

Between the aqueduct and the old church is a square, Plaza Conde de Cheste, surrounded by fine *señorial* buildings. Along Calle Augustín is the Museo Provincial de Bellas Artes, displaying fifteenth to seventeenth-century paintings and religious sculpture.

### Pedestrian Way from Aqueduct to Plaza Mayor
From the Plaza del Azoguejo, the route curves past the small stairway of Travasera del Carmen, the main meeting place of men before lunchtime during the week. Nearing Plaza San Martín is the palace, Casa de los Picos, which was built by the count of Fuensalida. The building, with an extraordinary façade of diamond-shaped pointed stones, is now the school of Applied Arts

and Crafts. Up the narrow Obispo Gandasequi to the right is an enormous conglomerate seminary.

**Iglesia de San Martín** The twelfth-century church of San Martín dominates the plaza further up the main street. It has beautiful arcades on three sides, with double columns topped with sculptured animal and floral capitals. Inside are three apses with Romanesque decorations, a dusty Gothic retable of paintings and a Gregorio Fernández reclining Christ. The brick tower, three tiered, rises from the centre of the nave where the unusual series of arches give support.

Surrounding the Plaza de San Martín are several fine mansions, with impressive Renaissance doorways, balconies and arcades. The Torreón de Lozoya is particularly attractive, rising high, fortified, and open today as an art gallery.

To the left of Calle Juan Bravo, down steps, are a couple more old palaces, the Casa del Alpuente, clad in the flat geometric design typical of Segovia, and the Alhóndiga, now a exhibition hall.

Further up the road, at the Plaza del Corpus, is an unobtrusive entrance on the left which leads via a patio to an old synagogue, now the church of Corpus Cristi. It is a peaceful building, made unusual by horseshoe arches. In the thirteenth century it was a synagogue of Mudéjar style. Much damaged by fire in 1899, it was rebuilt conserving some of the original features.

## Below the Alcázar and North Walls

**Iglesia de la Vera Cruz** Across the river and through a small village is the church of la Vera Cruz, a unique Romanesque church with twelve sides, modelled on the holy sepulchre of Jerusalem. It was built by the Knights Templar and passed in 1312 to the order of St John of Jerusalem. Today it belongs to the order of St John of Malta. Outside, the sides are punctuated by counterfoil buttresses. Inside, the nave is circular, with a central two-tiered chapel. A sculptured Christ, with articulted hands, and ancient frescos grace one of the chapels. From the Gothic tower are superb views of the walled town.

**Monasterio El Parral** The monastry of El Parral is nearby (east), a pleasant walk from the Alcázar. It is undergoing repairs and may open again within the next decade. Renaissance, Plateresque and Gothic architectural splendours are treasured inside. Jeronimite monks live in this important monastery, which also houses a fine religious museum.

**Convento de los Carmelitas Descalzos** In the Convento de los Carmelitas Descalzoa, just to the west of the church of la Vera Cruz, the body of San Juan de la Cruz is preserved. The saint, confessor to Santa Teresa, lies in a 1920s ostentatious green marble sepulchre, heavily decorated with florid gilt.

**Below the South Walls and across the Valley**

**Iglesia de San Millán** The beautiful church of San Millán stands in a square beneath the walls in the old Moorish quarter of Segovia, just off Avda Fernández Ladreda. It has thirteenth-century arcades with elaborate capitals on the north side, and a tower of oriental influence. The west portal is particularly finely carved. Inside, quiet and somber, the central apse is decorated with carved blind arches. A fourteenth-century Christ on the Cross presides. From the square there is a superb view of the Cathedral rising at the crest of the walled town.

**Iglesia de San Justo** On the far side of the aqueduct, up hill, is the church of San Justo, in which are good Romanesque frescoes. Usually shut, the key may be found with the sacristan of the neighbour church.

**Monasterio de San Antonio el Real** By the source of the aqueduct is the monastery San Antonio el Real. Although quite a distance from the walled centre of the town, it is well worth visiting for the magnificent Mudéjar pannelling in the hall and main chapel, the work of Xadel Alcalde (the Moor who crafted the original ceiling for the Alcázar's throne room), and fine Flemish artistic treasures in the church. The monastery is shut to visitors during the days surrounding religious festivals.

**Shopping** The main pedestrian way up to the Plaza Mayor from the aqueduct (also the *paseo* route) is the main shopping street of the town. It is made of named parts: Calle Cervantes; Calle Juan Brave; Calle Isabela Católica. This long steep street is lined with quality shops selling clothes, shoes and accessories. There are a number of *patisseries*, bookstalls and general shops. (Artes Gráficas, a small book shop in Calle Juan Bravo 31, is attractively set at the back of a delightful small patio of twisting columns clad in dripping ivy within which grows a tall elder tree.)

Just off Plaza Mayor around Calle Cronista Lecea are a small group of local food shops.

Souvenirs are sold around the Plaza Mayor and along the way to the Alcázar, Calle Marqués del Arco.

Below the walls, the major shopping road is the noisy highway, Avda Fernández Ladreda, which cuts between the old town and the new, and its neighbour Gobernador Fernández Jiménez. These are not attractive to the visitor.

There is a very small municipal market next to Plaza de los Huertos (beyond Cronista Lecea off the Plaza Mayor), and a substantial one in the new town off Calle Zorrilla.

Street markets visit the town three times a week. Most attractive is the Thursday morning vegetable market near the Plaza Mayor — up Calle Colón and continuing along Calle Idelfonso Rodrígues. Also, in the new town: Tuesday morning in Zona Mercado San José and Saturday morning in Calle Zorrilla at Plaza de Cascarro.

**The Paseo** The evening stroll moves from the main square beneath the aqueduct (Plaza del Azoguejo) up the thoroughfare to the Plaza Mayor. It is a most pleasant, open walk, passing good views across to the new town, and lined along the way with attractive shop windows. The cluster of bars at the top near the Cathedral provide a popular resting point.

**Parks** Early morning or at dusk, the Paseo Salón is a small quiet garden from which to enjoy the Guadarrama mountains. It is down a flight of steps south of the Plaza San Martín (half-way up the thoroughfare). In the silhouette of the mountain is an outline known as La Mujer Muerte (The Dead Woman) whose resting form, head to the East and feet to the West, is distinct.

A rough park shaded by trees to the south of the town, on the Cuesta de los Hoyos, overlooks the Cathedral, walls and Alcázar. This is a popular weekend picnic spot.

Beneath the Alcázar, a thick wood clothes the steep slopes, and is entered from the north-east side of the fortress.

**Sunday** A quiet day, without any particular attractions. Most restaurants are open at lunchtime.

**Regional Food** All restaurants offering typical regional food offer a similar menu: *Cochinillo* (sometimes called *tostón*) roast suckling pig • *Lechazo* – roast baby lamb (reputedly better eaten in certain towns in the province) • Local trout • *Judiones de la Granje*

**Fiestas**
Semana Santa – colourful processions through the old town.
SS Juan & Pedro , 24 – 29 June, Bullfights and dancing
Romeria de la Cruz, 3 May
Fiesta de las Alcaldesas de Zamarramala: the village of Zamarramala is close to the west end of Segovia. Held on the weekend closest to 5 February, feast of Santa Agueda. A colourful and unique celebration where women wearing traditional sixteenth-century costume take charge of the village.
Chamber music festival, 2nd week of July.

– a huge white bean grown locally • *Sopa Castellana* – a thin broth flavoured with pimento, cayenne and garlic, to which is added bread and an unbeaten egg yolk.

The *patisserie*: particularly sponge cake moistened inside with a paste and iced with marzipan; small almond cakes; *yemas de Segovia* – candied egg yolk similar to the renown Ávilan *yemas de Santa Teresa*.

**Bars and *Tapas*** As well as the front bars of most restaurants (particularly Duque and José María), the Plaza Mayor is surrounded by popular bars which overflow each evening. Most of these are open until late, as are several bars around the Plaza Azoguejo (beneath the Aqueduct).

*La Concepción*, Plaza Mayor 15, In the evening a smart, fashionable café with sophisticated clientelle. In the morning, a gentle breakfast spot from which to contemplate the Cathedral. Outside tables and classical music.

Daytime bars:

*La Tropical*, Calle Carmen, popular morning bar with good *churros* and chocolate. Just up from the aqueduct.

*Cafetaria Korppus*, Plaza del Corpus, on the way from the Acqueduct to the Plaza Mayor, a comfortable bar with good coffee and *patisserie*. Also sells ice-creams and *platos combinados* during the day. Shut Tuesdays.

*Las Tres BBB*, Plaza Mayor 13, excellent coffee and genteel atmosphere. Shut Wednesdays.

Night music and dancing will be found down Calle Escuderos, off Plaza Mayor. Unlike Madrid or Valladolid, however, Segovia generally enjoys an early dinner and sleeps at night.

**Restaurants** Most restaurants here have a *tapa* bar at the front to compliment the main rooms, at which some wait for tables and some take a lighter meal. Dinner is taken relatively early at about 9.30 p.m.

*Mesón de Cándido* – Tapas, – Código Provincial 99, Plaza Azoguejo 5, Tel: 428103. In three storeys of a picturesque fifteenth-century house, decorated in an old Segovian style. A focus of culinary pilgrimage. Cándido is widely reknown for its roast suckling pig. At the foot of the Aqueduct. Booking essential. (AE DC MC V).

*José María* Cronista Lecea II, Tel: 434484 – Tapas – thought by many to be the finest restaurant in Segovia. Near the Plaza Mayor, with two high-ceilinged rooms which fill at lunchtime with Segovians. A casual atmosphere, spacious, serving superb Castilian food. Excellent *tapa* bar in front. (AE DC MC V). Shut November.

*Mesón Duque* Calle Cervantes 12, Tel: 434600 – *Tapas* – on the main pedestrian street form the aqueduct to the Plaza Mayor, with a strong local reputation for traditional cooking. The bar at the front, with its fireplace festooned with garlic and pimentos, is crowded with people taking *tapas*. An alternative entrance from the street below leads into tavern-like rooms beneath the main restaurant (AE DC MC V).

*Casa Amado* Fernández Ladreda 9, Tel: 432077. Near the aqueduct on the main traffic route through. First-floor room, with a bar downstairs. Excellent roast lamb. Very popular locally. Shut Wednesdays and during October (AE V).

*Narizotas* Plaza Medina del Campo 2, Tel: 431806. Little rooms, unsophisticated, lively. Walls decorated with posters. Off San Martín Plaza (AE DC MC V).

*El Hidalgo* Calle José Canalejas 5, Tel: 428190. Just behind San Martín, in a restored thirteenth-century palace, with tables set in a light-filled patio and in surrounding rooms.

*La Cocina de San Millán* Calle de San Millán 3, Tel: 436226. A family restaurant with a garden at the foot of the city walls below Calle Cervantes.

Calle Infante Isabel, off Plaza Mayor, is lined with general restaurants.

Pería Zascandil, Refitolería 1: behind the Cathedral, crêperie that serves until 2 a.m.

## Hotels
## Category 1

*Parador Nacional de Segovia* Ctra de Valladolid. Tel: 430462. A short way out of the town to the north, with an exceptional view of the aqueduct. Very comfortable, with a good restaurant and a swimming-pool. Modern.

80 rooms, d&b 1000–8500 (AE DC MC V).

Well-regarded restaurant.

*Aqueducto* Avda del Padre Claret 10, Tel: 430537. Comfortable, long-established hotel just up from the aqueduct with a good view. Five minutes' walk to the walled town.

78 rooms d&b 6500–5300 (AE DC MC V).

*Los Linajes* Calle Doctor Velasco 9, Tel: 431201. A modern hotel built down a steep ledge hust within the walls close to the Alcázar. The rooms have a clear view across the stark countryside to the north. With a pleasant old entrance-way, although lacking ambience within.

55 rooms, d&b: 7600–5800 (AE DC MC V). Restaurant.

### Category 2

*Las Sirenas* Juan Bravo 30, Tel: 433011. Dignified and simple, on the main thoroughfare within the walls, with limited parking in front.

39 rooms, d&b: 4950–4100 (AE DC MC V).

*Plaza* Calle Cronista Lecea II, Tel: 431228. Plain, adequate, near Plaza Mayor. 28 rooms, d&b 3700–3400.

### Category 3

*Tagore* Calle Isabelle 13, Tel: 420035. Unsophisticated, several minutes' walk from the walls but close to the Monastery San Antonio el Real. Has a swimming-pool, study and garden.

30 rooms, d&b: 2500.

*Victoria* Plaza Mayor 5, Tel: 435711. Very central and plain

30 rooms, d&b: 3000–2650.

*Juan Bravo* Calle Juan Bravo 12, Tel: 431228. Small, well run.

9 rooms, d&b: 2700–2400.

Hostal areas – around Plaza Mayor.

### Camping

*Acueducto* – Carretera de la Granja, Tel: 425000. Cat 2. open 1 June to 30 September. 420 people. 8km (5miles) from the city

### Information

Area Exchange Code 911

| | |
|---|---|
| Tourist Office: | Plaza Mayor 10, Tel: 430328, Open 9 a.m.–2p.m. and 4–6 p.m. Saturday, mornings only. Shut Sundays. |
| Bus station: | Paseo Ezéquiel González 20, Tel: 427725 |
| Renfe station: | Plaza Obispo Quesada, Tel: 420774 |
| Police: | Escuderos 2, Tel: 431212 |
| Taxis: | Plaza Mayor, Tel: 436680 |
| | Plaza Azoguejo, Tel: 436681 |
| | RENFE Station, Tel: 433666 |

Correos
   (Post Office):   Plaza Dr Laguna 5, Tel: 431611
Cruz Roja
   (Red Cross):   Leopoldo Morena 18, Tel: 430311
Municipal
   swimming-
   pools:   Plaza de Toros; Puerta de Segovia
Banking area:   at the foot of Calle Carmen – in the square off
   Plaza del Azoguejo under the Aqueduct.

**Transport**  Cars: Although driving is awkward within the walled part of the town, parking is allowed around the Plaza Mayor and in several small *plazas* (e.g. Plaza San Esteban, Plaza Dr Laguan, or outside the Alcázar) and along a number of streets. Parking is not limited as to time, there is no ticket, and particularly in the Plaza Mayor it is often worth waiting for a space. The traffic is strictly subjected to a single-direction flow whose routes are sometimes surprisingly angular and narrow. Outside the walls parking is fairly easy near the aqueduct.

Urban transport: 4 bus lines running 7.30 a.m.–10.45 p.m. All
   leave from Plaza Mayor: RENFE: line 3 and 4
   Bus Station: 1
   Camping: 2

Inter-city
   transport:
Buses:   Ávila, Coca, Cuéllar, Valladolid (at least three times daily) Madrid (approx. 2 hourly), La Granja (2 hourly) Barcelona (twice daily)
Trains:   Coca, Medina del Campo, Valladolid (twice daily) Madrid and Guadalajara (frequent) Toledo (twice daily)

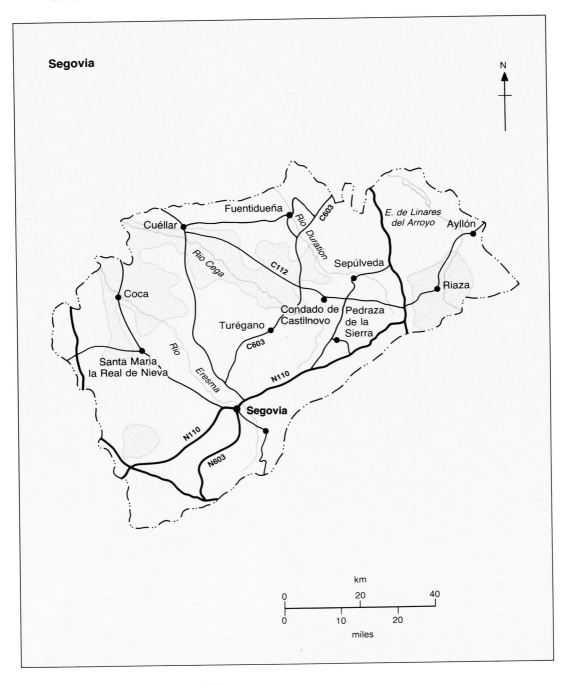

**Segovia** is a relatively small province. Its southern and eastern borders are girded by the sharp curving mass of the Sierras de Guadarrama. The expanse of the foothills to the north, often covered with coarse grass, wild herbs and shrubs, provides the breeding ground for huge flocks of sheep. The central region, hilly and well forested, is veined with river valleys and towards Valladolid the landscape becomes typical of the great cereal plains of the northern Meseta.

Architecturally the attractions of the province are the splendid castles of Coca and Turégano, the old villages of Pedraza and Sepúlveda, and the many lovely Romanesque churches. Two royal palaces, just south of the city, extend the network of opulence built by the Bourbons in the environs of their capital. The countryside attractions are the Guadarrama mountains, which offer skiing, climbing and walking; and, to the north, the deep beautiful gorge of the Rio Duratón.

As with the other provinces which surround Madrid, the province of Segovia is well known and much visited by the people of Madrid. Segovia itself, and the royal sites nearby, are a relatively easy excursion from Madrid, lying fairly close to El Escorial. San Ildefonso de La Granja and Riofrío are both interesting palaces, and both spectacularly situated, although neither have the splendour of the royal palace at Aranjuez (south of Madrid).

## South and South-East

**La Granja** Surrounded by pine forest in the cool Guadarrama foothills, the palace of La Granja, built by order of Philip V (the first Bourbon) is respected more for the fabulous gardens than the monumental house. The landscaping was strongly influenced by French ideas, as was carried out by the formidable skills of Marchand, Carlier and then Boutelou (also responsible for gardens in Aranjuez.

The gardens are vast, over 350 acres in area, and the great elm and chestnut trees, the myriad of paths and quantity of follies were mostly laid out by 1723. The 26 magnificent fountains are fed from the mountain water collected in a huge artificial lake above the house — their extravagance is such that they are only turned on during the summer for two afternoons a week. (Times are variable but usually include Saturdays.) The clusters of sculpture, most worked by Thierry and Fremin, depict mythological tales, and the dramatic effect produced by the multiple basins and water-spouting figures is unparalleled. A tower of water nearly 47m (150ft) high jets from La Fama, while Carrera de Caballos depicts a horse-race bursting with life and energy.

The palace itself, having suffered a bad fire in 1918, has lost much of its original glory. The site was enjoyed as a royal hunting area since Henry IV of Castile built a lodge here. Although gifted to Hieronymite monks by the Catholic Monarchs, it became a summer and retirement residence under Philip V. Theodore Ardemáns, designed and built the Palace (1721–23) but Italian-inspired additions softened the austerity of his main façade (Subisati and Procaccini). The old Hieronymite guest  house is preserved within the four slate-roofed symmetrical wings.

The rooms are beautifully furnished, have elegant patterned marble floors and are lit by great chandeliers from the famous local glassworks. (The factory was built in the village in 1746, and its products furnished royal houses all over Europe.) A collection of Flemish and Spanish tapestries is displayed, and eighteenth and nineteenth-century paintings bedeck the walls. The Italian ceiling frescos of the sculpture gallery and the state gallery are beautiful (Bartolomé Ruscha, the former; Fideli, Sanni and Saxo, the latter). There is an exquisite Japanese room. The *collegiata*, damaged by fire, lost its ceiling frescos, but the splendid marble tomb of Philip V and his Italian wife remain, along with paintings by Maella and Bayeu, and a Salvador Carmona stucco relief.

**Palacio de Riofrío,** a pink palace just south of Segovia, was built by Philip V's widow, the Italian Isabella de Farnese. The section of the Guadarrama known as La Mujer Muerta (The Dead Woman) forms the spectacular backdrop to the palace. The shape of the reclining figure is easy to recognize from here. The palace was designed in Italian baroque style, and its rooms are lavishly decorated with frescos and paintings. Works by Bayeu, Maella, Houasse, Ribera and Velázquez are housed here. The building was ostensibly to be a hunting lodge, and the theme runs through the rooms and museum, which is dedicated to hunting. The park, untended like that of La Granja, is forested with oak and chestnut within which quantities of deer may be seen.

**El Espinar and Navacerrada** The high passes of the Puerta de los Leones and Puerta de Navacerrada link the cities of

Madrid and Segovia. From both of these passes the superb views continue all the way to the valley floor where the city lies. This southern region of Segovia is speckled with holiday resorts. The mountain landscape of Navacerrada is enjoyed by skiers in winter, and in summer climbers challenge the higher peaks. There are a multitude of walking trails.

The main summertime resorts are El Espinar and San Rafael, both of which are surrounded by walking routes. A long but magnificent hike follows a trail across the ridges of the border to the high railway station of Cercedilla (Madrid), with wonderful vistas all along. The mountains here are clothed beautifully: thick forests of Scots pine shelter toadflax, ragwort, valerian and wild herbs, while the higher areas carry rock-roses and broom.

## North-West

**Santa María la Real de Nieva** Between the cities of Segovia and Valladolid lie the small towns of Santa María la Real de Nieva, Coca and Cuéllar.

The convent of Santo Domingo, within the pretty town of Santa María, has a fourteenth-century cloister with remarkable sculptured capitals. The heraldic symbols of its founders, Henry III of Castile and his wife, Catherine of Lancaster (daughter of John of Gaunt) decorate the corners of the cloister. In the Gothic church is a fine retablo with paintings by Antonio Vázquez.

A short distance north from the town, along a delightful quiet road, is the village of Bernados. From here a track leads to the Ermita de la Virgen del Castillo – a lovely walk rewarded by superb views.

**Coca and Cuéllar** Coca and Cuéllar are similar to Medina del Campo (Valladolid) in that their old churches, fortifications and mansions are of brick in Mudéjar style. All three are famed for their fortresses.

**Coca** has a glorious architectural treasure – a most beautiful Gothic Mudéjar castle which stands at the western edge of the town. The severity of the magnificent brick fortress is softened by the brick patterns which decorate the upper walls and battlements. Arab motifs are suffused throughout, both in brick and stucco relief. A deep dry moat surrounds the structure, and a sturdy octagonal keep, penetrated through a pointed arch and a horseshoe arch, guards the entrance. Today the castle serves as the unusual base for an agricultural college, whose pupils will guide visitors round the modernized interior during weekend breaks.

In the Gothic church of Santa María are the magnificent tombs of bishop Don Alonso de Fonseca, for whom the castle was built in the fifteenth century. The marble was worked by Francelli and Bartolomé Ordónez.

Although Emperor Theodosius was apparently born here, little commemorates his birth.

**Cuéllar** The fortress of Cuéllar is totally different. A granite exterior guards a luxurious palace constructed within by the Duke of Albuquerque in the fifteenth century. A Renaissance arched gallery surmounts the castle wall and a further double gallery looks into a large inner courtyard. The rooms built between two of the round towers are decorated with beautiful panelling. Sadly, a superb collection of armour was dispersed when the castle was sacked by Napoleonic troops.

The town of Cuéllar contains a number of Romanesque churches and thirteenth-century monastery. San Esteban, with an apse of patterned brick, has stucco decoration within.

The *encierros* (bull running) of Cuellar, held on the last Sunday in August, is reputedly the oldest in Spain.

From here roads lead towards the province of Valladolid, either to the city, the extraordinary ship-like fortification of Peñafiel on the Duere, or the castle ruin of Iscar.

**The Plaza Mayor in Pedraza**

**North and North-East** Following the valley route that runs parallel with the Guadarrama foothills the first major focus is the ancient walled town of Pedraza. A few kilometres south of it, off the N110, sits Sotosalbos, a small village with the exceptional and very beautiful Romanesque church of San Miguel. The image of the virgin is twelfth century. (The countryside is peppered with these lovely churches: one sits solitary by the main road, and another is found in Santiuste de Pedraza.)

**Pedraza de la Sierra** Pedraza, a walled fortified town perched on a jut of rock, looks marvellous from the approach roads. The climbing road up to the town passes scattered stone ruins and arrives at the only entrance through the massive walls. (There is parking at the far end quite close to the castle.) The town is small within, but surprisingly spacious and extremely pretty. The mansions in the large Plaza Mayor and along the streets are mostly of stone, escutcheoned, and with sturdy wooden doors.

**The imposing stonework of the streets of Pedraza**

The castle, one of the most impregnable, was built to an irregular polygonal plan with a great tower and narrow guarded entrance. As a prison, it housed the sons of Francis I of France for Charles II. Ignacio Zuloaga, celebrated Basque artist, bought the dominating Gothic fortress, restored it with imagination and lived within its mighty tower. A museum here, containing his and other work, is open irregularly.

The other glories of the ancient place are its medieval walls (a pathway circles beneath them), and its colonnaded Plaza Mayor, in which sit some of the restaurants for which the town is famous. Pedraza draws many at the weekends with the same lure as Turégano and Sepúlveda – its superb traditional roasting of lamb. Artesans of the silver and furniture trades work here.

**Turégano** West of Pedraza is the village of Turégano, dominated by an elegant brick and stone castle. Built round a beautiful old Romanesque church, the silhouette of the fortress is complicated by a double wall, a huge keep and the later addition of a Baroque tower to the church within. A major attraction for weekenders, it also has a delightful Plaza Mayor and a scattering of restaurants specializing in the exceptional roasts of the region. From Sotosalbos, a series of pretty, narrow lanes leads here.

**Sepúlveda** Continuing north another centre famous for its chefs is the pretty town of Sepúlveda. Shepherds continually move their flocks through the surrounding countryside of coarse grass and wild herbs. Self-styled *Capital Mundial del Cordero Asado* it is much visited by dedicated connoisseurs, and *figones* surround the pretty Plaza Mayor. The town was important historically – with fine stone mansions as reminders. Again, churches of the Romanesque style are plentiful. The small single-aisled San Bartolomé, just up from the Plaza, is delightful. El Salvador, which is reached through an archway of the walled old town, Arco del Ecce Homo, and up the stepped streets to the top of the hill, dates from 1093, and is one of the oldest examples of the porticoed Segovian style. The sculpture is beautiful, decorating the corbels beneath the roof and the capitals of the porticoed side with animals, faces and tracery. The interior is very simple, only open for mass on the third Sunday morning of each month.

**Duratón Gorge** The town is awkwardly set on the curve of a hillside by the spectacular deep gorge of the Duratón River. The gorge cuts through the countryside for many kilometres, accompanied for only a short distance by roads. From the heights of the town, its route can be seen by the narrow streak of green trees that snake through the grass and cereal undulations.

There are fine walks along the gorge, particularly to the west (the most beautiful season is spring). The most notable in the area leads to the Ermita de San Frutos, a site of pagan worship previous to the 1076 arrival of Benedictines. Looping to the west 17km (10 1/2 miles) away is the village of Villaseca, from where an earth track eventually arrives at the Ermita. The Romanesque chapel, typically porticoed, sits in tranquillity high above the gorge of the dammed Duratón River. From here the views are glorious. (*romería*: 15 October.) The gorge, *Las Hoces del Duratón*, reaches to Peñafiel, in Valladolid.

**Duratón** Further east along the river is the village of Duratón, with a fine Romanesque church, part Visigothic, a short distance away. Its capitals are most delicately carved. South, surrounded by oak woods sits the lovely Moorish castle of Castilnovo, built by Abd ar Rahman I and later extended. It is unusual, built of stripes of brick and stone, with round and square towers at its corners. Today it is privately owned, and in splendid condition.

**Riaza and Ayllón** to enjoy the mountains, the town of Riaza and Ayllón are important, lively bases, They lie in the north of the province on the main N110 route, beneath the rise of the Guadarramas. Thick forests (oak, beech and spruce) and wild flowers cover the mountainside. In both towns the population during the summer months is much greater than the number who live here throughout the cold winter months.

**Riaza,** close to the ski station of La Pinilla, is an attractive stone town built round the circle of its porticoed plaza. The Friday vegetable market spreads beneath the Colonnades. From here a popular excursion reaches to the hermitage of NS de Hontanares. The road ascends steeply through beech, oak and rock-rose to a favourite picnic spot with views right across the Segovian plain. Becoming a foot path, the route continues to the bleak 1,420m (4,659ft) summit from where the surrounding sights are marvellous.

The slopes around La Pinilla and its summit Pico de Lobo (Wolf Peak) at 2,213m (7,269ft) contain many lovely but strenuous walks by the sources of the Duratón and Riaza rivers. Just the other side of the border, in Guadalajara, is the beautiful Reserva Naciónal of the Sierra de Ayllón. The village of Campisábalos is the base for marvellous walks into the beech and meadowed landscape here. South-east along the C114 fall the spectacular winding mountain roads of Guadalajara.

**A panoramic view of the countryside above Riaza**

The pass from Riaza through the mountain range to Cantalojas or Majaelrayo (SG112) is a spectacular narrow route but dangerous at night.

**Ayllón,** the other base, has a handsome Plaza Mayor, and many narrow porticoed streets. The dignified late fifteenth-century Contreras Palace, with heraldic symbols and a splendid portal, is the most important building here. Of the medieval walls, the arched entrance to the town and a solid tower still stand.

The N110 continued northwards towards the delightful Sorian town of El Burgo de Osma, with porticoed streets and a squat Gothic/Renaissance Cathedral. Turning north-west towards Aranda del Duero (C114) the road passes Maderuelo, a proud village on the banks of the Embalse de Linares. It is a pretty place, with a number of stone mansions, a fine Romanesque/Renaissance church and the crumbled remains of old walls.

**Horse Riding** Rutas a Caballo SA, Molino de Río Viejo, Tel: 401159 (or contact via Madrid Juan Bravo 21) Both short and long tours through the Guadarramas.

### Accommodation and Restaurants
### Cuéllar

*San Francisco*, San Francisco 25, Tel: 140009 27 rooms, d&b 3270 (AE DC V). Restaurant recommended.

*Santa Clara*, calle Segovia, Tel: 141178 16 rooms, d&b 2200 Restaurant: *El Rincón Castellano*, Plaza Mayor 13, Tel: 141031. Castillian decor and wood oven for excellent roast lamb. (AE DC).

### El Espinar

La Tipica, Plaza España II, Tel: 181087, 23 rooms, d&b 3800.

### La Granja

*Roman*, Guardas 2, Tel: 470752, 16 rooms, d&b 4800 with good restaurant which shuts part of November/December (V).

*Europeo*, España 9, Tel: 470369, 30 rooms, d&b 4000 (AE).

Restaurant: *El Dolor*, Calle Heroes Alcázar de Toledo, Tel: 470269 Shut Wednesdays in winter, October and November. Excellent local white beans & roasts of lamb and suckling pig.

Restaurant: *El Torreón*, Calle del Puerto de Navacerrada, Tel: 470904 Shut Wednesdays and during October. Pretty garden, wood oven. Near Pradera de Navalhorno. Huge numbers at weekends. (2.5km (1$^1$/2miles) from La Granja).

**Specialized dishes of Segovia** are roast lamb (extremely tender and delicately flavoured from the herbed hillside where the flocks roam); river crabs and trout, from the strong rivers.

## Pedraza

*La Posada de Don Mariano*, Tel: 509886 11 rooms, d&b 10,000.
The town's famed speciality is lamb roasted in wood ovens.
Restaurant: *Hostería Nacional Pintor Zuloaga*, Matadero 1,
Tel: 509835, Shut Tuesdays in winter. In a pretty old *señorial*
house. Run by the Parador chain. (AE DC MC V).
Restaurant: *El Yantar de Pedraza*, Plaza Mayor 1, Tel: 504107.
With first floor balconies out to the square. Shut Mondays in
winter. (AE DC MC V).
Restaurant: *El Jardín*, Calzada 6, Tel: 504130 Shut 1–15 January.
Pretty garden. Open: weekend and festivals.
Restaurant: *Bodegón Manrique*, Calle Provadores 6, Tel: 504079
Open: Tuesday, Saturday, Wednesday, Sunday, Fiestas for lunch only

## Riaza

*La Trucha*, Avda Dr Tapia 17, Tel: 550061 30 rooms, d&b 4900,
pool, garden. Just out of town. The managers are knowledgeable
about the countryside of the region, and are both doctors.
*Los Robles*, Hospital 6, Tel: 550054 – 15 rooms, d&b 1300.
Restaurant: *Casa Quemada*, Isidro Rodríguez 18, Tel: 550051
Regional rustic decor, wood-burning oven and popular. (AE).
Restaurant: *La Taurina*, Plaza Mayor 6, Tel: 550105. Shut
October, serving good kid (*cabrito*) and lamb (V).

## Riofrío

Restaurant: In the Palace, shut Tuesdays and during January, only
lunchtimes.

## Sepúlveda

*Postigo*, Conde de Sepúlveda 22 Tel: 540172, 14 rooms,
d&b 3000.
*Hernanz*, Conde de Sepúlveda 4 Tel: 540378, 12 rooms,
d&b 3000. The roast lamb is outstanding.
Restaurant: *Casa Paulino*, Calvo Sotelo 2, Tel: 540016. Shut
Mondays and during November (AE DC V).
Restaurant: *Cristóbal*, Conde de Sepúlveda 9, Tel: 540100. Shut
Tuesdays and during October. Castilian decor. (AE DC MC V).
Restaurant: *Figón de Zute El Mayor*, Calle Tetuán 6, Tel: 540165,
Only open lunchtimes, no á la carte, only fixed menu of lamb.

## Sotosalbos

Restaurant: Las Carillas, Tel: 401170, (AE V). Open: weekends
and fiestas, some of the best roast lamb in Castile.

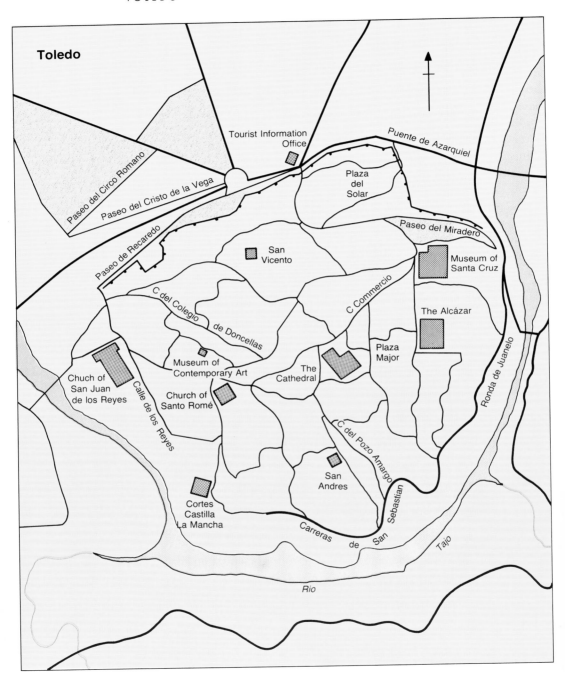

**Toledo** From any angle, the approach to Toledo is spectacular. The city covers the surface of a small hill, its shape and size disciplined by the River Tagus which curves round two-thirds of it. The densely packed roofs, pale brown as the surrounding landscape, are pierced by two famous outlines: the imposing solid square of the Alcázar, and the towering spire of the Cathedral.

**History** Toledo, the Primate See of Spain, lives off the cultural heritage of its great historical prestige. As a capital city, it hosted the governments of Visigoth kings, Muslim leaders and Christian monarchs until Philip II moved his court to Madrid in 1561. Before the late fifteenth-century pogroms, the largest Jewish community in the peninsula thrived here. Unhindered until the era of the Catholic Monarchs, the intellectual synthesis (Hebrew, Muslim and Christian) created a fertile school of sciences, medicine and philosophy, whose powerful centre of translation broke down any barrier of language.

The architectural and artistic legacy is displayed throughout the old city. The museum collections, amongst which are many canvasses of El Greco, are superb. The unique, tangible history of Toledo, from Roman times to the civil war, has established it as a focus of pilgrimage. Its main, thriving industry is tourism.

Within its walls, the city is much as it was several centuries ago. The streets, barely drivable, are narrow, steep and cobbled. The different quarters retain their individuality – some quiet and local, some dominated by commercial tourism. Until mid-morning the ambience is one of local bustle which, as the town fills with tourists, recedes into the less-visited streets. In the early

**The spectacular city of Toledo, the capital city of Spain until 1561**

evening when the wave of visitors departs (most tourists stay only a few hours), the lively normality re-emerges.

## Outstanding Monuments

Cathedral (10.30 a.m.–1.00 p.m. and 3.30–6/7.00 p.m., Sunday 10.30 a.m.–1.30 p.m. and 4.00–6/7.00 p.m.)

Museo de Santa Cruz (10.00 a.m.–6.30 p.m. Tuesday to Saturday 10.00 a.m.–2.00 p.m. Sunday, 10.00 a.m.–2.00 p.m. and 4.30–6.30 p.m. Monday)

Iglesia de San Juan de los Reyes (10.00 a.m.–2.00 p.m. and 3.30–6/7.00 p.m.)

Sinagoga de Santa María la Blanca (10.00 a.m.–2.00 p.m. and 3.30–6/7.00 p.m. shut Sunday p.m. and mon)

Sinagoga del Tránsito y Museo Sefardi (10.00 a.m.–2.00 p.m. and 4.00–6.00 p.m.)

Iglesia de Santo Tomé (El Entierro del Conde de Orgaz, El Greco) (10.00 a.m.–2.00 p.m. and 3.30–6/7.00 p.m.)

**The town houses of Toledo**

## Notable Monuments

Mezquita del Cristo de la Luz

Iglesia de San Román (Museum of Visigothic art – 10.00 a.m.–2.00 p.m. and 4.00–6.30 p.m., shut Sunday p.m. and Monday)

Alcázar (10.00 a.m.–1.30 p.m. and 4.00–6.30 p.m., Shut Monday)

Casa y Museo de El Greco (10.00 a.m.–2.00 p.m. and 4.00–6.00 p.m. shut Sunday p.m. and Monday)

Hospital Tavera (10.30 a.m.–13.30 p.m. and 3.30–6.00 p.m.)

Museo de Victorio Macho (10.30 a.m.–1.30 p.m. and 4.00–6.00 p.m.)

Taller de Moro (mudéjar art and ceramic museum: 10.00 a.m.–2.00 p.m. and 4.00–6.30 p.m. – shut Sunday p.m. and Monday)

Museo de Arte Contemporaneo (10.00 a.m.–2.00 p.m. and 4.00–6.30 p.m., shut Sunday p.m. and Monday)

Monasterio de Santa Domingo el Antiguo (11.00 a.m.–1.30 p.m. and 4.00–7.00 p.m., shut Sunday a.m. Winter: Open only Saturday)

**Ancient and modern meet in the narrow streets of Toledo**

**Plaza de Zocodover**

251

**Layout of the town** Orientation is notoriously difficult inside the walls. The main entrance through the walls of the old city is the Puerta de Bisagra, just outside which is the Tourist Office. The main square is the angular Plaza de la Zocodover, situated at the top of the hill far over to the north-east near the Alcázar. Cars and buses headed for 'Centro Urbano' will arrive here. The Cathedral is more central, joined to Plaza de Zocodover by the main commercial thoroughfare – Calle Comercio.

The most notable monumental sites are situated in two areas: the triangle formed by the Alcázar, Plaza de Zocodover and the Cathedral; the triangle fanning westwards from Santo Tomé to the two ends of Calle de los Reyes Católicos in the old Jewish quarter. The link between these two areas is Calle Trinidad. Restaurants and bars cluster round the north side of the cathedral, and around Santo Tomé.

**The Historic City** Plaza de Zocodover, the heart of the city, is an irregular triangle full of cafés with two arcaded sides. Beneath the east arcades on the far side of the road, an arched stair leads to the Museo de Santa Cruz via Calle Cervantes. The Alcázar is uphill from the Plaza, built at the highest point of the city. The Cathedral is reached via the main commercial street – Calle Comercio.

**Cathedral** Although the tourist entrance and ticket office for the Cathedral are at the west cloister door (Puerte del Mollete), there is a quieter, less crowded entrance via the Puerta de Reloj. This is reached by leaving Calle Comercio at the pedestrian junction Cuatro Calles and walking down Calle Chapinería.

**The Lion Gate of the cathedral**

The Puerto de Leones, Gothic and plateresque, designed by Francisco de Villalpando, to the south, is guarded by shield-bearing lions. Its inside is a lovely door panelled with sculptured walnut above which a tympanum enclosed the geanological tree of Mary. Mass is celebrated somewhere in the Cathedral every hour.

The Gothic cathedral is massive and of a height which can be appreciated only from outside the city. The north tower, of lead-covered wood, with the spire, reaches to 100metres (328ft). The bell, 'la Gorda', weighs 17.5 tonnes (17$^1$/2 tons). The nave is the longest in Spain after that of Seville Cathedral. The great Gothic vaults, elegant and plain, are supported by 88 clustered piers. The beautiful sixteenth-century stained glass, best with the morning sun, lights the dark, somber, grandior of the interior. The cloister, entered by the Puerte del Mollete, is frescoed by Bayeu and Maella, and decorated with Plateresque sculpture.

The retable of the High Altar, late Gothic, is magnificent: sculptured in larchwood, clothed with gold leaf and polychromes, the images are hooded with dripping Gothic canopies. International masters worked on the scenes of the Passion, coming from Holland, Antwerp, Spain, France and Italy to work under Enrique de Egas. The gilded filigree enclosing the chapel is carved with four layers of saintly figures, each individual surrounded with other smaller images, and surmounted by misericords. The tombs within are: south – Alfonso VIII, Sancho III; north – Sancho IV and Cardinal Mendoza, whose ostentatious Renaissance sepulchre (Covarrubias) necessitated partial destruction of the chapel surround in 1495. His tomb, amongst the kings, was requested by the Catholic Queen, Isabella. The High Altar is enclosed by a railing surmounted by Charles V's escutcheon. It was worked for seven years and designed by Villalpando. Behind, the pair of gilt metal bronze pulpits were worked from the extravagant tomb of Álvaro de Luna after his fall from grace. Behind the High Altar is a double ambulatory.

**The Choir** The fifteenth-century choir has exceptional walnut stalls. To the south are carvings of remarkable flowing beauty by Alonso Berruguete, outstanding among which are the panels of St Jerome with the lion, and Abraham with his son. To the south are works of Rodrigo Alemán, whose 54 detailed reliefs depict the battle for Granada. At the back is a life-size Transfiguration by

253

Berruguete carved from a single piece of alabaster. He also worked the Transcoro medallion of God the Father. The carved animals — foxes, lions and elephants — are beautiful. Above the seats, the figures are worked in jasper. The filigree is most delicate.

**The Transparente** This is an extraordinary addition to the Cathedral, a rococo masterpiece that is almost shocking in its contrary style. Built by Narciso Tomé and his family in the mid-eighteenth century, by order of Cardinal Astorga, its purpose is to allow natural light to enter the chamber of the Holy Scarament which is housed above the High Altar, and which is in the centre of the golden sun-burst. The florid sculptures are of coloured marbles, alabaster and bronze relief, with the monumental Last Supper figures carved of white Carrara marble around an alabaster table. Angels tumble from the great hole cut in the roof, some painted, some carved. The stream of light is most powerful with the high late-morning sun.

**The Chapels** At the West end, to the left of the door, is the Mozarbic Chapel — in which the rite, of Visigothic origin, is celebrated at 9 a.m. daily. (The rite is simple, long and punctuated by many hymns.) It has a beautiful dome, and the walls are frescoes by Juan Borgoña depicting the battle of Orán (1509). The Chapel of Santiago is opposite the Transparente, flamboyant Gothic in style and constructed by Álvaro de Luna for his family. The scollop shell and moon are symbols of his coat-of-arms. The Chapel of San Idelfonso houses the tombs of Cardinal Gil de Albornoz and family. The Kings Chapel, usually closed, to the north side of the Transparente, houses the sarcophagi of Castilian royalty including Eurique II, Eurique III and Juan II.

To the north of the High Altar is the Capilla del Sagrario, dedicated to the Virgin of the Tabernacle, patron of Toledo, where the silver throne of the Virgin weighs 590kg (1,300lb). The marble, jasper and jewelled retable is sumptuous. Here mass is celebrated daily.

Near the treasury, placed in the nave, is the Chapel of the Descension, where the Virgin is said to have appeared to Saint Idelfonso, Bishop of Toledo, in the seventh-century. A grating at the back of the chapel guards the stone that she touched.

**The Treasury** An immensely heavy door, near the main entrance, guards the magnificent great processional monstrance. A

The dusty hats, one hanging in front here, and several more strategically placed on chapel railings or hung from the vaults, celebrate the last wishes of their cardinals, each of whom had the right to be buried where he wished in the Cathedral. The hats stay undisturbed until they disintegrate.

gold crucifix within, encrusted with jewels, belonged to Isabella I, and the monumental silver outer monstrance was crafted by Enrique de Arfe. Three gilded volumes of the bible of St Luis (thirteenth century), a pearl-encrusted crown and the sword of Alfonso VI are also kept here.

**The Chapter House** Carved pear-wood cupboards balance the lavish stucco relief, glorious Plateresque doorway and gilded ceiling. Beyond is a stunning artesanal ceiling of gold, blue and red below which are frescos by Juan de Borgoña. Around the walls are portraits of the different bishops of Toledo. The panel of Cardinal Lorenzana, 1804, is by Goya.

**The Sacristy** The gallery of paintings is a Renaissance room decorated in black marble and gilt, with baroque ceiling frescoes by Luca Giordano, creating a totally different atmosphere to the dark Gothic Cathedral. The great treasures here are the series of paintings by El Greco: 'The Twelve Apostles' and 'Jesus' (particularly 'St Peter in Tears'). The end wall displays his 'Expolio' in magnificence, with the glow of the bright-red cloth projecting through the entire gallery. Other paintings and painters include a Van Dyck 'Holy Family', Bassano's The Deluge, Velázquez, Goya, Titian, Rubens and others.

Continuing through the rooms – very peaceful – ecclesiastical robes, tapestries, sixteenth- and seventeenth-century embroidered gowns, and caskets of gold and silver are displayed. Upstairs, twin pictures by Morales and works by Caravaggio stand out.

**Museo de Santa Cruz** This dignified museum, usually excluded from tour-group itineraries, is one of the greatest assets of the city. The Renaissance building, with a fine Plateresque facade, was designed by Enrique Egaz and endowed by Cardinal Mendoza (whose extravagant tomb sits prominently in the Cathedral). In the shape of a greek cross, the two floors are lit from the centre by a simple cupola. The galleries are open and spacious, with fine artesanal ceilings of Mudéjar inspiration above and Renaissance design below.

Within the museum, the treasures are displayed uncrowded. Flemish tapestries and carpets, lovely examples of sixteenth- and seventeenth-century furniture, chests, inlaid caskets and paintings are beautifully laid out. The whisper of polyphonic music enhances the tranquillity.

Above, the galleries are hung with paintings. Twenty works of El Greco surround his 'Assumption of the Virgin Mary'. From the upper ceiling to ground level is draped the banner flown by Juan of Austria at the 1571 Battle of Lepanto. Strikingly arranged and lit, gold embroidery glistens against the rich blue damask.

The provinical archaeological museum, housed in the basement, is reached through a fine cloister.

**Alcázar** A fortress has been here since Roman times, playing a vital role in the successive waves of power governing this key city. The present design, enhanced by Charles V's architect Juan de Herrera, suffered severely in the Napoleonic wars and was all but destroyed in the civil war (as photographs within illustrate).

The pristine reconstruction houses a garrison, and a museum dedicated to war, with rooms exhibiting the historical development of weaponry, and others dedicated to the memory of the Toledan Francoist heroes of the civil war. The evocative chronicle of the 10-month seige withstood by Colonel Moscardo and those with him in 1936 is the main focus of the museum: a war-scarred room recalls the famous episode during which the Colonel sacrificed his son to the opposition rather than hand over the fortress; a gallery of photographs remembers those who perished; and empty vaults illustrates the living quarters. With the rescue of the survivors by Franco's troops, the beseiging force was totally annihilated.. In the context of the pre-seventeenth-century historic buildings in Toledo, the reminder of such recent traumas suffered here makes a sharp contrast.

The church of San Juan and the two synagogues are all in the Calle de los Reyes Católicos, which leads up from the second gate into the city – Puerta del Cambrón..

**Monasterio de San Juan de los Reyes** Juan Guas designed the great church to be the pantheon for the Catholic Monarchs, Ferdinand and Isabella, in acknowledgement of their triumph at Toro (1476). The outcome of that battle gave Isabella clear title to the Castilian throne against a strong claim by Juana de la Beltraneja, supported by the Portuguese. The Monarchs actually lie entombed in Granada, the last stronghold of Moorish rule until their victory entry in 1492. Their initials and arms (a yoke and seven arrows) decorate the ceiling and walls of the interior.

The church, single aisled with lofty vaults, is decorated in high Gothic and Mudéjar style. The Gothic cloisters are very beautiful, with delicately carved lacework of Isabelline filigree. The upper storey has a splendid Mudéjar ceiling, the corners of which are arched with escutcheon-bearing lions. The majestic late Gothic exterior, with a polygonal tower graced with pinnacles, is spectacular when seen in silhouette at night.

**Synagoga de Santa María la Blanca** This tranquil building was probably constructed in the late twelfth century. Of the twelve synagogues in the Jewish community, only this and El Tránsito survived. With the violent preachings of St Vincent Ferrer (1411), tolerance of the community began to disintegrate and within a century it was dispersed and the synagogues destroyed. This temple was converted to a church in the sixteenth century.

Within the rough brick exterior is a delight of graceful arches which take on a golden hue with the sunlight that filters in. Above the arches are friezes of geometrical designs worked in stucco. The octagonal columns are topped with capitals carved from plaster of Paris, and each design is distinct. Of the original floor (tiled with *azulejos*) a small part remains.

*Awe-inspiring and tranquil – the Synagoga de Santa Maria la Blanca*

This building illustrates beautifully the interdependence of the Jewish and Moorish communities in Toledo previous to the collapse of religious tolerance. At a time when Christian rulers dominated the city, Moorish builders constructed the temple for their Jewish neighbours, and the building materials (brick and stucco rather than stone), the ground plan (five aisles) and the geometric decorative motifs are all entirely Moorish in style and motif. Only one small panel betrays the religious beliefs of its users: the first panel above the arch immediately to the left of the main entrance is carved with a Star of David, the single tribute to the Jewish faith.

**Synagoga del Tránsito** The sumptuous interior of El Tránsito contrasts greatly with the intimacy of Santa María. It was constructed in the 1350s for the treasurer of Pedro I of Castile, Samuel Levi. Beneath a cedar *artesanado* ceiling, the walls are decorated with elaborate stucco friezes of interlacing foliage. Rose and grey marble double columns complement the polychromed filigree of the latticed windows. Surrounding the upper walls are Hebrew inscriptions of Psalms, and praises dedicated to Pedro I.

The history of the temple is eventful. It was used by the Knights of Calatrava after 1492, then taken over by the Alcántara military order, and finally used as a barracks in the eighteenth century. In 1877 the building was listed as a National Monument in an attempt to stem the damage.

The Sephardic museum, in the adjoining rooms, adds perspective to both this and the earlier synagogue.

**Iglesia de Santo Tomé** The annexe to this church, which is up the hill from Synagoga del Tránsito, is entered from the tree-lined south side and houses one of the most famous of El Greco's works: 'El Entierro del Conde de Orgaz' ('The Burial of Count Orgaz'). The painting is superbly lit, hung alone without any superfluous distraction, and the visitor is provided with comfortable seating from which to contemplate the masterpiece. The work, of the burial of the Chancellor of Castile (Don Gonzalo Ruiz de Toledo) by St Stephen and St Augustine, was painted expressly for this room. A self-portrait of the artist is amongst the line of distinguished faces, seventh from the left. The city is endowed with a large number of El Greco's paintings, being his chosen home after 1577, and this is the finest single display to be seen.

Behind the church is the museum Taller de Moro and the sixteenth-century Palacio de Fuensalida, today the seat of the government of Castilla-La Mancha. The Taller de Moro, once a Moorish workshop, is lavishly stuccoed within and its museum displays Mudéjar artefacts and ceramics.

**Casa del Greco** is behind El Tránsito, and can also be reached down the souvenir shopping street of Calle de San Juan de Dios which runs down from Santo Tomé. One of the most visited of Toledo's monuments, this quaint house and museum does little justice to the master. The house was part of the original Abulafia estate of Samuel Levi, the powerful Jewish advisor to Pedro I. The picturesque interior is furnished with pieces of the time of El Greco, and displays a number of copies of his works, and some unfinished paintings. The Museum, although it contains an important set of his 'Twelve Apostles' – an interesting comparison with the earlier set displayed in the Cathedral – is poorly lit.

**The Museo de Arte Contemporaneo** is close to Santo Tomé, in Calle de Las Bulas, and the house of the distinguished sculptor Victor Macho is south off the Calle de los Reyes Católicos, displaying some of his notable work. At the end of the street is the pretty Paseo del Transito, a green shady garden from which there are views of the Toledan countryside.

**Puertas de Bisagra** The Old and New Puerta de Bisagra are next to each other at the base of the hill. The Tourist Office is opposite. Puerta Vieja, a Moorish fortification, was used by Alfonso VI when he retook the city from Muslim occupation in 1085.

The Renaissance Puerta Nueva, built by Alonso de Covarrubias, dates from the reign of Emperor Charles V (Charles I of Spain) whose heraldic eagles decorate the tower roofs. Today, this is the main entrance to the walled city.

**Iglesia de Santiago** The Mudéjar church of Santiago sits to the right of the gates. Along the main route towards the Plaza de Zocodover, a diversion under the beautiful fourteenth-century Puerta del Sol leads past the Mezquita del Cristo de la Luz. This delightful mosque of the tenth century was built on Visigothic foundations and extended into a church in the twelfth century. A legend tells of a lamp, hidden here with a crucifix at the arrival of the Moors in 712AD, which was discovered miraculously still burning when Toledo was retaken by Christians in 1085. The little building has a lovely façade of interlacing arches and portals surmounted by a long Arabic inscription in intricate brickwork. It sits proudly within a small garden, whose attendant can show visitors inside to see the distinctive vaults, nine cupolas and horseshoe arches of the aisles.

A pretty cluster of narrow streets leads west from here through ancient buildings to the fine Diputación from where Calle Real leads to the Puerta del Cambrón (near the synagogues and Iglesia de San Juan de los Reyes). The Monasterio de Santo Domingo el Antiguo is south across a wide square from the Diputación. The ancient eleventh-century foundation has a church notable for the paintings in its retables – all by El Greco. Several are original, and some are copies. The choir and rooms within the cloistered monastery display a large quantity of religious artefacts.

**Iglesia de San Román** The Church of San Román stands near the monastery, across the 'Plaza de Padilla'. (It is also reached from the Cathedral by walking up Calle Nuncio Viejo, left along Calle Alfonso X, and up past the imposing church of San Idelfonso; or from Iglesia de Santo Tomé via the uphill Calle de Alfonso XII.) The church is a fascinating mixture of architectural styles and decoration. Romanesque murals (some in a poor state) decorate Cordoban-style horseshoe arches. Beneath these are capitals of Visigothic, Mozarabic and Byzantine design. The church, mostly in Mudéjar style, is irregularly shaped. A fine museum of Visigothic artefacts is displayed within. A stone fragment of the Apostles Creed gives archaeological proof of the existence of Visigothic Christianity, and various jewels and royal treasures illustrate the superb craftsmanship of the time.

### Outside the Walls

**Hospital Tavera** At the foot of the Paseo de Merchán, outside the main Bisagra gates, stands the sixteenth-century Hospital Tavera. A dignified Renaissance building with a beautiful twin patio and a lofty church, it is the home of the Duchess of Lerma, whose private quarters are open to the public. The visit feels pleasantly amateur in style, and the rooms, decked with fine furniture, tapestries and portraits, are without explanatory notes. The library houses the complete bound hospital archives. Paintings by Tintoretto, Zurbarán, El Greco and Ribera are displayed. Particularly notable are José Ribera's 'Bearded Lady', recording the seventeenth-century woman, infant at breast, and a 'Holy Family' and 'Baptism of Christ' by El Greco.

The church, with a retable by El Greco, houses the tomb of the Cardinal Juan de Tavera – an alabaster masterpiece of Alonso

**The Castillo de San Servano**

Berruguete, who died while working here. The crypt, for the Dukes of Lerma and Medinaceli, has an extraordinary resonance

**Castillo de San Serrano** The Castillo de San Sevano is picturesquely placed on a hill beyond the east walls of the city. Built by Alfonso VI, it was reconstructed in the fourteenth-cenutry and is, today, part of a school.

**Shopping** The main shopping street in Toldeo runs from Plaza de Zocodover down towards the Cathedral. Calle Comercio (which becomes Calle Hombre de Palo) is lined with shoe and clothes boutiques, paper shops and bars. Around Santo Tomé, further down, cluster the souvenir shops.

Calle Comercio is a busy street, mostly pedestrian and quite steep. Falling south are streets of pleasant food shops and quality boutiques. This network of narrow lanes, small but lively, leads, via fish, bread and butcher shops to the modern municipal market (open: morning only).

The artesan skills for which Toledo is renown are the forging of sword blades and the working of Damascene decoration. Souvenir shops selling these goods are scattered liberally through the streets, particularly south beyond Calle Santo Tomé (into San Juan de Dios) and beside the Alcázar in the Plaza de Capuchinos.

Damascene is the technique where a blackened steel surface is inlaid with fine silver and gold wire to form intricate patterns. The skill can be watched in a number of shops, or in the artesan workshop in Calle Madalena in the new town (opposite the Hotel Cristina). This decorative technique is extremely expensive – and there are imitations for sale cheaply, that compromise the artisan method. Juan Morales Galán, Plaza de Conde 4, Tel: 223586 (by Santo Tomé church) has some excellent examples of the craft.

Toledo has had a tradition of sword making since it was a Moorish capital; its success is rumoured to be due to the particular quality of sand or water in the Tagus River. Production can be watched at Casa Zamorano, Calle de la Cuidad 19, Tel: 222634. (The workshop is close to the Cathedral – across Plaza del Ayuntamiento and up the narrow stepped alley beyond.)

Marzipan is the city's sweet speciality, bought by weight in a variety of shapes and recipes. Santo Tomé 5 (almost opposite the restaurant Placido) produces a spectacular example of the marzipan and dried fruit *pesca* (fish) – a dragon-like creature curled solidly in a box.

A small antiquarian bookshop is tucked behind the Cathedral along Calle Cardinal de Cisneros. Kept in chaotic disarray, it sells remnants of poorly kept vellum hymnals and old maps.

**The *Paseo*** The evening walk has an unusually long route which incorporates the commercial high street. From Puerta de Bisagra, the route wends up along Calle Real del Arrabal, past Puerta del Sol, following the curve of Cuesta de las Armas (from which there are lovely views) and arrives in Plaza de Zocodover. From here it continues along Calle Comercio to the Cathedral. Plaza de Zocodover, with its many cafés, is essentially the main meeting area.

**Parks** There are few patches of green in the walled city. From two there are marvellous views across the Toledan countryside: the Paseo del Tránsito, beside the synagogue, in which is a children's playground; and Paseo del Miradero, off the main curving street leading up from the main Bisagra gates to the Plaza de Zocodover.

Outside the main gate is the Paseo de Merchán, where boule is played and ice-cream sellers walk. Up beside the walls along the Paseo de Recaredo to the Puerta de Cambrón is a beautiful shady strip of trees and flower beds from which the views are fine. Below and beside the new town developments is a small well-kept field in which Roman ruins are preserved.

**Sunday** Toledo is full every day with tourists, and changes little at weekends. Many souvenir shops stay open, as do the important museums. A market and stamp fair is held in the Plaza de Zocodover during the morning. The Cathedral services are very well attended, and are frequent throughout the morning.

**Regional Food** The food here is unrefined with strong flavours. The following dishes are typical of the area: stewed partridge (*perdiz estofada*) – beware of the time of year when ordering (best served in the hunting season). Slowly cooked and served with boiled potatoes • Soused partridge (*perdiz escabechadas*) Roasts of lamb • Stew of lamb, tomato, saffron and spices (*Cuchifrito*) • *Gazpacho Manchego* – a stew of rabbit, pork, chicken and lamb • *Carcamusas* • *Tortilla a la magra* • Marzipan – sweets of various shapes to be bought in the *patisséries*. Almond soup, spiced

**Fiestas**
Semana Santa: notably solemn 'Procesion de Silencio'. Several very formal processions and haunting music through the streets.
Corpus Cristi: renowned in Castile for the colourful spectacle of the processions. Balconies hung with embroidered shawls, and streets strewn with herbs. Celebrations continue for several days, with bullfights, and music. Summer fiesta, late August: Fiesta Grande – the city is alive night and day, with dancing, corridas, music and fireworks. Semana de Música: Early October, and May: with a variety of concerts. Some are performed in the beautiful Museo de Santa Cruz amongst the tapestries and old furniture.

with cinnamon, is an unusual but superb dish. Excellent Manchego cheese.

**Bars and *Tapas*** There are quantities of bars in Toledo. They cluster in several areas: round the Cathedral; in the Plaza de Zocodover; to the back of the Plaza in the Calle de Santa Fé; and along the Paseo route. These, and most of the restaurants, serve *tapas*. The Plaza de Zocodover has, of course, many popular cafés.

**Restaurants** At lunchtime the restaurants cater mostly for the visitors. The menus are relatively expensive here.

*Cardenal* (*see:* Hotel Cardenal, Tel: 220862) A very elegant restaurant, well patronized, where Toledan fare is mixed with sophisticated cuisine. Well away from the packed city streets in a quiet garden beside Puerta Vieja de Bisagra. Highly recommended (AE V MC DC).

*El Abside* (*see:* Hotel Maria Cristina.) An excellent businessman's restaurant (AE V MC DC).

*Adolfo* Calle Hombre de Palo 7, Tel: 227321. Exemplary Toledan cooking presented well. A quiet, intimate restaurant with a coffered ceiling, duck-egg blue tables and candles. Close to the Cathedral (AE V MC DC).

*Casa Aurelio* Plaza del Ayuntamiento 8, Tel: 227716. *Tapas*. A lively ham-decorated bar upstairs, with good tapas; a small, quiet but pretty restaurant downstairs — wood-beamed ceiling and flowers. Good cooking. Close to the Cathedral.

*Placido* Calle Santo Tomé 4, Tel: 212603. Delightful in summertime when tables are set in the small square outside and in the open patio within. Near the Cathedral. Shut October to March.

*La Botica* Calle Plaza de Zocodover 13, Tel: 225557. *Tapas*. A big restaurant — two floors inside and rows of tables in the square. An entertaining position from which to watch the life in the square. Very popular with foreign tourists — the Spanish eat inside (AE V MC DC).

*Palacios* Calle Alfonso x El Sabio 3, Tel: 215972. Good fish and shellfish, small rooms, comfortable. Close to the Cathedral. Shut Sunday evenings and Mondays.

*Chirón* Paseo de Recaredo 1, Tel: 220150. Just outside the Puerta del Cambrón, near the Iglesia de San Juan de los Reyes. Built on several floors down the hillside, the views of the Toledan countryside are superb. A huge restaurant.

*La Tarasca* Calle Hombre de Palo 8, Tel: 224342. *Tapas*. A light, marble-floored restaurant, with a smart bar next door which serves excellent *tapas* and a good breakfast in a café ambience. Refined dishes of the region (AE V MC).

**Hotels** There are few hotels inside the old walls – several within comfortable walking distance, and two with fine views of the city from afar.

### Category 1

*Cardenal* Paseo de Recaredo 24, Tel: 224900. Housed in a sixteenth-century palace at the foot of the old town, just inside the walls. Pretty, peaceful gardens, and an exceptional restaurant. A very elegant hotel.
27 rooms d&b 6900. Parking (AE V MC DC).

*Almazara* Carretera de Piedrabuena 47, Tel: 223866. 3.5 km (2miles) from Toledo, in the quiet Cigarrales landscape dotted with trees, with a lovely view of the city. Some rooms have private terraces overlooking Toledo. No dining-room, but breakfast is served.
21 rooms d&b 4900. Parking (AE V MC DC).

*Parador Conde de Orgaz* Paseo de los Cigarrales, Tel: 221850. Modern but as with all Paradors, tastefully decorated and furnished. A taxi ride or 20 minutes' walk from the city walls. Situated high up in the hills across the river, very peaceful, with superb unimpaired views of Toledo. Restaurant.
77 rooms d&b 11000–10500. Parking (AE V MC DC).

*María Cristina* Marqués de Mendigorría 1, Tel: 213202. In the new part of the city, more tailored for the businessman than the holiday traveller, but extremely comfortable. An excellent restaurant, El Abside.
65 rooms d&b 6250 – 5800. Parking (AE V MC DC).

### Category 2

In this category, the situation of the hotels – close to the centre of the old city – compensates for lack of character and a quantity of tour groups.

*Alfonso VI* Calle General Moscardó 2, Tel: 222600. Next to the Alcázar, thus close to the Plaza de Zocodover. Huge dining-room.
88 rooms d&b 6150. Separate Parking (AE V MC DC).

*Carlos V* Plaza Horno Magdalena 3, Tel: 222100. Between Alcázar and Plaza de Zocodover. Big arched dining-room.

55 rooms d&b 6000 – 3180. Separate Parking (AE V MC DC).
*Maravilla* Calle Barrio Rey 7, Tel: 223304. Smaller, simple, just off Plaza de Zocodover. Good lunch menus in restaurant.
18 rooms d&b 4590 – 3295. Separate Parking.

## Category 3

*Labrador* Calle Juan Labrador 16, Tel: 222620. Close to Alcázar. Rather cramped but adequate.
40 rooms d&b 2625.
*Las Armas* Calle Armas 7, Tel: 221668
19 rooms d&b 2600.
*Santa Bárbara* Avda Santa Bárbara 8, Tel: 220298
14 rooms d&b 2700.

## Information

Area Exchange Code 925
World Heritage List 1986

| | |
|---|---|
| Tourist Office: | Puerta de Bisagra, Tel: 220843 |
| | 9.00a.m.–1.00 and 4.00–6.00p.m. Mon/Fri, 9.00a.m.–3.00p.m. Sat. 10.00a.m.– 3.00p.m. Sun. |
| Police: | Tel: 223407 |
| Cruz Roja (Red Cross): | Tel: 222900 |
| Banking area: | Around a plaza up Calle Mola – a right turn at the top of Calle Comercio as it leads off Plaza Zocodover. |

## Transport

| | |
|---|---|
| Taxis: | Cuesta Carlos V (behind Alcázar) Tel: 222396 |
| *Ambulatorio* | Tel: 221698 |
| Buses: | Transport from New town to beside Alcázar via Plaza de Zocodover |
| Cars: | Few cars negotiate the streets within the walls – many of which are so narrow that wing-mirrors have to be closed. |
| Parking: | Plaza de Capuchinos, beyond the Alcázar; cars are directed here via the Centro Urbano signs which take them through Plaza de Zocodover to the Alcázar. Unless very early morning or late evening, the Plaza is likely to be full. Small alternatives are found within the old town – |

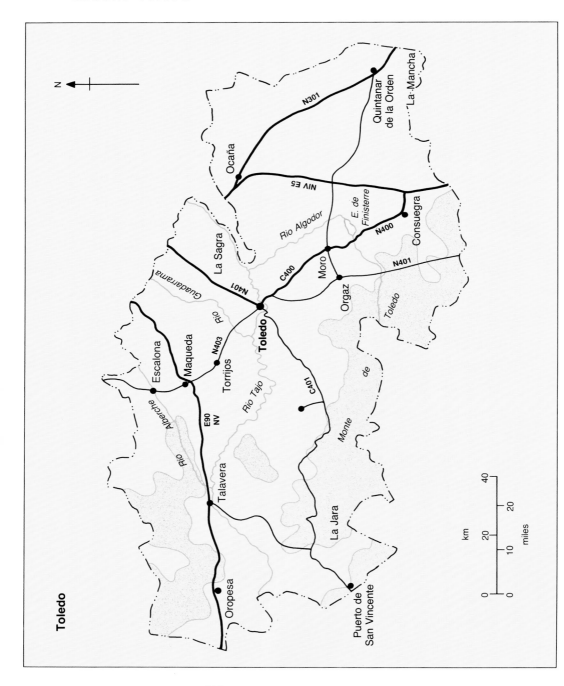

but navigation is uncomfortable. A better alternative is to park in the new town or along the walls towards Puerta de Cambrón, to the north-west of the city.

Inter-city travel:  RENFE Tel: 221272 – across the river via the Puente de Azarquiel (traffic road) or via the pedestrian Puente de Alcántara.

Bus Station:  Tel: 215850, in Plaza Honda, beneath Hospital de Tavera.

Connections with Madrid by bus and train at least hourly.

Connections south to Cuidad Real by train.

Frequent bus routes to Extremadura, and Castile-León cities.

Talavera de la Reina – central junction terminal for buses north and south of Gredos.

**Around Toledo** The province of Toledo is huge, expansive and sparsely inhabited. The countryside is spectacular. To the south-east are great hazy brown plains of cereal, long sweeping vistas ended by sharp hill rises, and striped fields of olive trees and vines dotted with crisp white huts. To the south-west are the Montes de Toledo – unexploited cool hills whose coarse cover provides superb hunting ground. Westwards run the river valleys of the Alberche and the Tajo which are cultivated, forested and excellent for fishing.

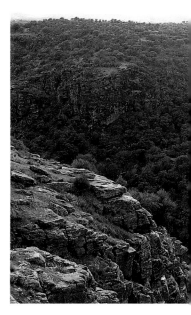

**The rugged landscape of Toledo province**

Castles abound, both in good and ruinous condition, often atop ridges. The small towns are rarely picuresque, most being agricultural centres, although many have a Mudéjar architectural dignity. The villages are often barely drivable, and seldom penetrated by tourists. There are treasures to be found, but these are well spaced through great tracts of land.

The monumental city of Toledo, carrying a great weight of visitors every day, passes very few of its travellers on to its province. Most return directly to Madrid; take an excursion to the green oasis of the Aranjuez Royal Palace; or travel on either south to Andalucía or west to the Extremaduran treasures – the glorious monastic shrine of Guadalupe, and the historic towns of Trujillo and Cáceres.

**East** of the capital are the dusty plains of cereal, interrupted by jutting hills and vine fields. Just above the river border with Madrid, sits the Bourbon residence of Aranjuez and the pretty villages of

Chinchón and Colmenar de Oreja, the latter with wonderful views stretching far over the plain. (See pages 112 – 118).

South of the River Tajo the area produces wine, its main centres being Ocaña, Yepes and Noblejas.

**Ocaña** is notable for its dignified eighteenth-century Plaza Mayor, fifteenth-century ducal palace, and the Monastery of Santo Domingo (whose baroque church has fine walnut choir stalls).

**Yepes** is similar to many country villages in this area – alone in the expanse of radiating fields and still carrying much of the great thirteenth and fourteenth-century fortification wall which protected it centuries ago. Within there is the bustle and liveliness of modernity. The church in the centre is another village characteristic, being a Gothic/Renaissance building guarding a fine retable with paintings of Luis Tristán (1616).

South from Ocaña, the fast NIV cuts through the plains passing two interesting places – the old village of La Guardia and the town of Tembleque – before it arrives at Madridejos near Consuegra. In La Guardia is a fine parish church decorated with Italian frescos. Tembleque has a large and charming Plaza Mayor, entirely surrounded by multi-tiered, wood-balconied houses. (Like so many Toledan towns, it does not provide for tourists – few bars open on to the delightful square.)

The sparse network of straight roads criss-crossing the landscape provide an entirely different perspective from the main routes, with almost no travellers save a farm tractor to interrupt the timeless vistas.

**South** The gravitating point at the south of the province is Consuegra, past which, in the province of Ciudad Real, is the famous bird sanctuary of Las Tablas de Daimiel. Near these marshes are various scenic reminders of the adventures of Don Quixote (Puerto Lápice, the windmills of Campo Criptana).

**Consuegra** is dedicated to the production of wine, and during the harvest the entire population from the children upwards work to collect the fruit. The backdrop to the working town is an extraordinary sight when approached from the south or west.

On a sharp ridge above the town sit several white windmills, and the splendid ruin of a castle of Roman foundation, later owned by the Knights of Malta. The castle shell, still with three of its round towers and infrastructure, commands a breath-taking

**Consuegra, with its castle and windmills**

view in every direction. The windmills, usually closed and inoperable, were the flour-grinders of the town until twenty years ago, and some are still set in motion once a year during the town's late October fiesta. Like others of the region, they were introduced here from the Netherlands in the 1570's, only a few years before the literary hero imagined them as giants. The town, like many others in this border area, takes pride in these images reminiscent of Don Quixote.

**El Toboso,** a beautiful little village east of Consuegra, also retains a tangible connection with Cervantes' hero. Here sits the house of Don Quixote's lady-love, Dulcinea; it is open for visitors to see its traditional inner courtyard and its beautifully furnished rooms. The town hall keeps a collection of editions of the novel.

From Toledo, various landmarks dot the way to Consuegra. Above Almonacid a dominating Torre de Homenaje sits within crumbling walls. In Mora, the flying centre of the region, is a twelfth-century castle ruin and Gothic parish church. The shell of a square fortress dominates the entrance to Orgaz, and from its side protrudes a dignified baroque church designed by Alberto Churriguera, housing a copy of El Greco's 'El Expolio'. The towns themselves are unexceptional.

Further south is Los Yébenes, across a short range of scrub-covered hills. The community, again guarded by a castle ruin, is an important hunting centre in which skilled leather workers and gunsmiths are established. Every bar exudes interest in the sport.

From here runs a straight road to Consuegra, clothed with extensive wine and almond groves in which sit small white houses. The view of the Consuegra ridge is marvellous.

**South-West** Guadamur is a short distance from Toledo city to the west and there are several exceptional monuments. By the village of Guadamur stands a splendid fifteenth-century fortress, lovingly restored in the last century. It is open only on the mornings of the tenth, twentieth and thirtieth day of each month. The beautiful castle has a square ground-plan with round towers at the sharp angles of the walls. The rooms within the graceful keep have been furnished with period items, and until the last few years the castle was a residence of the private owners. The turret rooms are delightful. There are very few castles in Spain where such a style of living has been retained.

**La Puebla de Montalbán** is a small town with a pleasant Plaza Mayor. The grandiose church of Nuestra Señora de la Concepción has a most unusual interior for this area, with obvious Italian influence shown by its Corinthian pilasters and sculptured busts. The hermitage of Nuestra Señora de la Soledad has an important interior, eighteenth-century frescos and a 'Tears of St Peter' by José de Ribera. Its pretty castle, has a fine sixteenth-century Plateresque portal, and within, a splendid wood-panelled ceiling decorated in Mudéjar and Plateresque style.

**Nuestra Señora de Melque** South from here along the C403, through the beautiful rolling olive groves and cultivated fields, two ruins stand alone in the midst of the countryside. About 15km (8 miles) from la Puebla, a track leads east across the hillside to arrive at a desolate forested ridge. Here are the wind-battered remains of the ninth-century Mozarabic hermitage Nuestra Señora de Melque. It still has a few horseshoe arches, and is protected by an uninhabited farm shack.

**Castillo de Montalbán** A rough earth track running west from the same point on the road twists through fields for a few kilometres to lead to the Castillo de Montalbán. This magnificent ruin was rebuilt in the twelfth century by the Knights Templar, and its walls extend round a small field overlooking a spectacular, deep shrub-clad gorge. It is entirely out of sight of settlements,

**Visigothic window of the Mozarabic hermitage Nuestra Señora de Melque**

**The magnificent ruin of the Castillo de Montalbán**

271

utterly peaceful, and likely to be deserted. With its proximity to the steep gorge, the site is not safe for children.

**Montes de Toledo** The Montes de Toledo rise just south of these two ruins. The routes twisting along the foothills are quiet and fragrant. The villages are agricultural and all have a strong interest in hunting. Cereal fields and groves of olives and almonds surround the villages. The Montes, covered with holm oak, pine, eucalyptus and thickets, are the home of a third of Spain's roe and fallow deer population. Partridge, quail and ring doves are abundant in the less forested areas.

Like Los Yébenes, Las Ventas con Peña Aguilera, in the harsh beauty of the east foothills, is a major hunting centre. The hermitage here, Nuestra Señora del Aguila, has a lovely twelfth-century tin and silver image within. Further west is the small village of Hontanar, near Navahermosa. Spectacular remains lie just outside: a twelfth-century fortress stands several hundred metres

**The Montes de Toledo**

away from a sturdy fourteenth-century tower, and nearby is a field of ancient rectangular sepulchres carved into the granite slope.

Just south of here the road passes spectacularly through the winding heights of the Montes. Further along the foothills is the substantial pale town of Navalmorales, near which are the rambling ruins of a possibly Roman fortress known as the 'Cuidad de Vascos'.

These lovely routes continue through the scented countryside over the border of Extremadura to the beautiful monastery of Guadalupe, or the watered forested summits of the Reserva Naciónal de Cijara.

**West** The Tajo valley spreads west from the City of Toledo towards the Parque Natural de Monfragüe and Plasencia.

**Talavera de la Reina,** the major town; is the second largest in the province and the main industrial centre with communication links in all directions. Since the Middle Ages its

commercial base has been the manufacture of ceramics – its tiles and artefacts decorate monuments throughout Castile. The town is surrounded by wheat fields dotted with great oak trees, and the hills to the north are thickly forested with pine and oak. The long winding approach through the hills from the north is extremely pretty.

Talavera expects few visitors. It is busy, noisy, thriving, and its main shopping streets throng with people. The town is shaped like a half moon on the north bank of the wide River Tajo. The oldest part, twice walled, is in the centre, and the newer streets radiate from it.

The main town gardens of the Ermita de Nuestra Señora del Prado are to the east of the old town, through which the Madrid NIV road penetrates Talavera. The park of palms, shrubs and flowers surrounds the colossal Ermita de la Virgen del Prado and the bullring, with fountains at the east end and tiled benches throughout. The west end, in which sits the hut of the Tourist Office, is the preserve of the older men of the town, who meet here throughout the day. The *paseo* route also takes in this park and the main commercial circuit. (The bus station stands to the side of the park, and street parking for cars is fairly easy to find nearby. The RENFE station is further away to the north.)

The red-brick *Ermita* gives an introduction to the industrial town history. Its porticoed façade carries religious scenes in blue tiles of the sixteenth to eighteenth-centuries. Inside, the walls (particularly the sacristy) are clad with older tiles from the fourteenth and fifteenth centuries. As with all buildings of this type, grilles allow the devout to see the image within throughout the day.

The older part of the town is approached through the main shopping streets at the west end of the park, where there are a number of solid brick Mudéjar churches.

The Plaza del Pan is an unusual square, with the town hall on one side and the Romanesque/Gothic parochial church of Santa María on the other. The square is light and pretty, entirely decorated with Talavera tiles, and shaded by palm trees. In the streets behind the church is the delapidated collegiate of San Jerónimo.

Throughout the town, signs and notices are attractively written on tile and some façades are beautifully decorated with ceramic designs. The town museum stands beside a remnant of the old wall

**Pottery for sale in Talavera de la Reina**

**The ceramic decoration of the red-brick Ermita**

near the gardens of Santa Clara. Within is an excellent exhibition of the development of technique and fashion in ceramics.

A less formal small collection of ceramics can be seen in the Fábrica de Cerámica Artística, Avda Portugal 32 (the western main entrance) Tel: 802909. Beautiful ware is produced here and visitors are welcome to watch the entire production process. The skills of intricate decoration are impressive. (The shops open 9 a.m. to 6 p.m. Monday–Saturday, and production stops 1–3 p.m.)

During the town fiesta of Las Mondas, traditional songs with ancient gypsy roots are performed. The fiesta, on Easter Tuesday, is renowned throughout the region.

**El Puente del Arzobispo,** on the Tajo border with Extremadura, is another important ceramic centre. It is a small, dusty village, not pretty, lining the wide but little-travelled main road. Dozens of artesans work here, and many invite visitors to watch them at work. A church with a superb sectioned alabaster retable stands near the Plaza Mayor.

The villages nearby are ancient settlements, set in the coarse landscape of shrubs, cereal fields and holm oaks. The communities are tightly packed within the surrounding walls, and the traditional way of life is firmly entrenched. The narrow streets are extremely awkward for cars.

**Lagartera** welcomes visitors, but it is awkward to venture far into the hilly village with a car. The village is famous for the artesanal embroidery which is worked in many households here; the skilled work is most beautiful. The tiny centre of lace work, Navalcán, is less easily visited, far off any main routes, hidden in the foothills of the Gredos behind the Embalse de Navalcán.

**Oropesa,** the main town by Lagartera, rises spectacularly to the side of the busy NIV road which runs from Madrid to Cáceres via Talavera. Publicized by its Parador, which occupies the main castle, Oropesa is a pretty stop with marvellous views across the valley sweep to the abrupt rise of the Gredos mountains. Two castles sit aside here, the older dating from the twelfth-century. The town also has two fine churches, one by Juan de Herrera, and the steep high street has several wood-framed old buildings. In the open square through which the road bearing south passes, is a pretty Ayuntamiento displaying tiles from El Puente del Arzobispo.

**North-West** The arc from the city of Toledo to Talavera contains several impressive castles, and some exceptionally pretty roads. Torrijos is a commercial centre north of Toledo city (carrying several conference hotels). A rather eccentric church sits in the main village with an imposing Plateresque façade.

The walled village of Maqueda has a pretty square fifteenth-century castle on the rise behind. The home of the local Guardia Civil, it is well kept but closed to the public.

**Escalona** Approached from the south, through the vineyards of the Mentrida region, the fortress of Escalona is most impressive. A sheer wall and great tower rise above the wide clean waters of the Alberche. The walled town sits beside, with an attractive Plaza Mayor and several *señorial* buildings. The castle became the property of Don Álvaro de Luna when commander to the King Juan II. Within the Mudéjar double fortifications he had a palace built, of which remain only ruins of the round tower, with its decorated vaults, and various columns. The red fortress is only open on the afternoons of the 2nd and 4th Saturday in the month and 1st and 3rd Wednesday (all day).

Surrounding Escalona for several kilometres, intermittently interrupted by vines, are great pine forests. The deep green velvet quilt spreads over the hills between the Alberche and the Tiétar valleys. The routes through the forests from Piedralaves (Ávila) to Talavera or to Escalona are very lovely.

**North** There is little of note north of the city of Toledo. Illescas, a small industrial town has a fine church, El Hospital de la Caridad, in which are treasured a number of paintings by El Greco. The gallery is no match or substitute for the superb collections in Toledo.

**Hunting** of big and small game takes place in the south of the region and amongst the Montes de Toledo.

**Fishing** Trillo, on the Tajo river, is an exceptional fishing area.

**Local Specialities** The fare is pastoral and spices are frequently used • stewed partridge (*perdiz estofada*) is a speciality, cooked slowly and served with potatoes. • *Cuchifrito* is a stew of lamb with tomato, egg, saffron and white wine. • marzipan, particularly in the city of Toledo but also in various country towns, is delicious. • Manchego is a cheese produced throughout the region of La Mancha. There is a huge variety of preservation, curing and ingredients – some made from sheep milk, or a mixture of sheep and dairy milk.

## Accommodation and Restaurants

### Consuegra

*Las Provincias*, Ctra Toledo, Tel: 480300.

34 rooms, d&b 3500.

### Oropesa

*Parado Virrey de Toledo*, Plaza de Palacio 1, Tel: 430000.

44 rooms, d&b 8000. Fine hotel in the less old of the two castles. Marvellous views.

### Talavera de la Reina

*Beatriz*, Avda Madrid 1, Tel: 807600.

160 rooms, d&b 5400 (AE DC MC V), good restaurant: Anticuario

*Perales*, Avda Pio XII 3, Tel: 803900.

65 rooms, d&b 3500.

*Auto-Estación*, Avda de Toledo 1, Tel: 800300.

40 rooms, d&b 3200. Above the bus station beside the main Parque. Restaurant: *El Arcipreste*, Calle Banderas de Castilla 14, Tel: 804092. Rustic and animated with a big *tapa* area in front (V).

### Las Ventas Con Peña Aguilera

*Hostal Joaquín*, Calle Victoria 45, Tel: 418023.

27 rooms, d&b 3650. Restaurant serves good game.

### Los Yébenes

*Montes de Toledo*, Ctra Nal 401, Tel: 321100.

39 rooms d&b 6700, restaurant. Views over Los Yébenes towards Consuegra.

*Hostal Casa Apelio*, Real Arabia 1, Tel: 320005.

Restaurant: *El Puerto*, Ctra Madrid/Cuidad Real, Tel: 320405. Above the town with views across. Home cooking, unrefined and very popular.

**Camping** Near Toledo city:

| | |
|---|---|
| El Greco: | Ctra Toledo–Puebla Montalbán, Cigarral El Angel, Tel: 220090. Open all year, 450 People. Category 1 |
| Toledo: | Ctra de Madrid Toledo, Tel: 358013. Open 1 April to 1 September. 350 people. Category 1 |
| Circo Romano: | Avda Carlos III 19, Tel: 220442. Open 1 March to 30 September. 240 people. Category 2. |
| Casalegas: | Ctra de la Presa, Tel: 869102. Open 1 April to |

Escalona:

Sesena:

30 September. 320 people. Category 2
Camping Municipal, Ctra Toledo-Ávila: Tel:
781034. Open all year. 500 people. Category 3.
El 36, Ctra de Andalucia, Tel: 895 7035.
Category 3. Open all year. 544 people.

**Square in Talavera de la Reina**

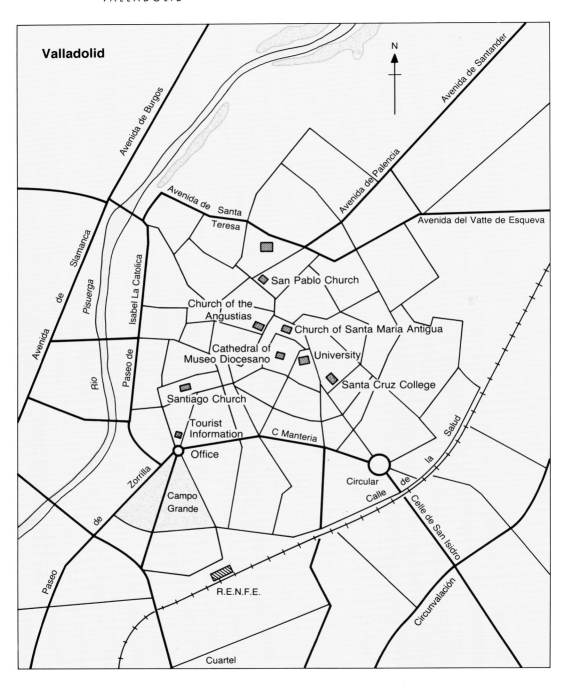

Valladolid

N

Avenida de Burgos

Avenida de Santander

Avenida del Palencia

Avenida de Santa Teresa

Avenida del Vatte de Esqueva

Slamanca

de

Avenida

Pisuerga

Isabel La Catolica

Rio

Paseo de

San Pablo Church

Church of the Angustias

Church of Santa Maria Antigua

Cathedral of Museo Diocesano

University

Santiago Church

Santa Cruz College

Tourist Information Office

Zorrilla

de

C Manteria

Salud

Campo Grande

Circular

Calle

de

la

Celle de San Isidro

Paseo

R.E.N.F.E.

Circunvalación

Cuartel

**Valladolid** is the splendid capital city of the regional autonomy of Castile and León. Big, industrial, noisy and traffic-bound, it has little obvious attraction to a tourist. However, for the traveller interested in more than the purely monument-based towns, its rich cultural offering combined with its modernity and vivacity can act as a magnet. It is a wealthy, dignified city, and has an intensity of life to compare with that of Madrid. The city is endowed with many fine religious buildings, impressive civic architecture, and a superb museum of religious sculpture whose celebrated collection is without equal in Europe. The historical legacy is formidable.

Unlike Salamanca, Ávila or Segovia, Valladolid does not dwell on its powerful historical prominence, and shows little sympathy for the relaxed visitor who may well find it irritatingly exhausting. The city is a demanding energetic centre. Its deep historical roots combined with its commercial stature, and the civic pride of its people (Madrid is not rated here either for its social or commercial prominence) make it a unique city to be approached with respect.

**History** The town, 'Belad Walid', was captured from Moorish power by Alfonso VI in 1074, a decade before the major part of Castile was conquered. The town grew in prestige, becoming a powerful archbishopric. Here St Ferdinand III was crowned, the Catholic Monarchs were wed, Philip II and IV were born, and Maria Molina passed her regency. For a short while, during Philip III's reign as the Americas were opening (Peru and Mexico), the town replaced Madrid as the seat of government for Spain. Napoleon's devastating campaign in 1809 was commanded from headquarters in Valladolid.

Today the wealth of the city is continually ensured by the agricultural riches of the Castilian corn trade, and by its prominence as an industrial centre.

### Outstanding Monuments
Museo Naciónal de Escultura, 10.00 a.m.–2.00 p.m., 4.00–
    6.00 p.m. Shut Sunday p.m. and Monday, festivals (in College
    of San Gregorio, 10 minutes walk NE of Plaza Mayor)

### Notable Monuments
Churches:
Cathedral, 9.15 a.m.–1.00 p.m., 5.00–7.00 p.m. (by Plaza Libertad).
San Pablo, mass a.m., p.m. (by San Gregorio).

Santa María la Antigua, mass a.m., p.m. (near Cathedral).

Las Angustias, mass a.m., p.m. (near Cathedral).

Convento de Las Huelgas, mass a.m. (5 minutes walk east of Cathedral).

University, (just east of Cathedral).

Museo Arquelógico, Palacio de Fabio Nelli, 10.00 a.m.–2.00 p.m., 4.00–7.00 p.m. Shut Saturday p.m., Sunday p.m., Monday festivals (east of Sand Gregorio, and 5 minutes walk north of Plaza Mayor).

Museo Oriental, 4.00–7.00 p.m., Festivals: 10.00 a.m.–2.00 p.m. (in Convento Augustinos Filipinos, at foot of Camp Grande).

Museo de San Joaquín y Santa Ana, 10.30 a.m.–1.00 p.m., 4.30–7.00 p.m., shut Monday, Festivals. (West of Plaza Mayor).

Casa de Cervantes, 10.00 a.m.–3.30 p.m., shut Monday, Festivals (near Plaza Zorilla, off Calle Miguel Iscar).

Casa de Colón, 11.00 a.m.–2.00 p.m., 5.00–7.00 p.m., shut Sunday p.m., Monday. Festivals (by Las Huelgas Reales, east of Cathedral).

**Layout of the City** The city is large and sprawling, and requires a significant amount of walking. There are three focal points:

The fountain-adorned Plaza de Zorilla, at the apex of the triangular park Campo Grande. (At the foot of the park are the rail and bus stations.) A main traffic route, Paseo de Zorilla, courses up its east side to the city centre.

Plaza Mayor, 5 minutes walk north of Plaza de Zorilla along the pedestrian Calle Santiago. Between these two Plazas are a net of shopping streets. Ten minutes walk north of Plaza Mayor, past the local colour of Plaza de Val, spread in an arc, are some of the most notable buildings, including the National Museum of Sculpture.

Plaza de la Libertad, 5 minutes west of Plaza Mayor along the arcades of the triangular Plaza de Fuente. The Cathedral, and churches of Las Angustias and Santa María la Antigua are here. East is the University and a number of churches. Calle Angustias curves north-west to Plaza San Pablo and the National Museum of Sculpture.

**The Historic City** Museo Naciónal de Escultura. Housed in the Colegio San Gregorio is a magnificent museum of religious sculpture (and paintings), beautifully displayed to powerful effect. It is a unique and breath-taking collection. Although pieces date from the thirteenth to the eighteenth centuries, the museum concentrates on the early Renaissance Valladolid school of religious imagery. The main quartet are Alonso de Berruguete (1480–1561), Diego de Silöe (1495–1565), Juan de Juni (1507–77) and Gregorio Fernández (1556–1636).

Three rooms are devoted to Berruguete's dismantled masterpiece, the monumental retable of 'San Benito el Real', of polychrome sculpture and paintings. Diego de Silöe's skills, are partly responsible for the beautiful choir stalls of San Benito (Room 10). The delightful sculptured group of the Holy Family is his work. Sculpture by Juan de Juni includes the powerful composite work of the Burial of Christ, and the very beautiful head of Santa Ana. Gregorio Fernández, a master of extraordinary realism, is represented by several forceful groups, including a Pietá and one of his many agonized reclining Christs (Christo Yacente). In this same Room 5 is a painting of Francisco de Zurbáran, the 'Santa Faz'. Other notable pieces are the head of San Pablo (Alonso de Villaabrille) and La Magdalena Penitente (Pedro de Meña).

The building is itself notable. The façade of the college, late fifteenth-century, is a masterpiece of Isabelline decoration, designed by Gil de Silöe and Simon de Colonia. The interior has several very beautiful Mudéjar ceilings, and a magnificent lace-carved Plateresque gallery from which leads a splendid Gothic staircase.

**Iglesia de San Pablo** The church of San Pablo, beside the Colegio, has a façade even more flamboyantly carved than that of the San Gregorio. Designed again by Simon de Colonia, its Isabelline richness is in great contrast to the lofty plain interior, which is decorated by a marble retable, and a small number of sculptures including one by Gregorio Fernández.

Opposite the square is the palace from where Philip III reigned.

**Cathedral** The massive Cathedral was originally commissioned by Charles I of the architects Francisco de Colonia and Rodrigo Gil de Hontañón. Its monumentalism was subsequently designed by Herrera (architect of the monastery of San Lorenzo El Escorial) for Philip II. The existing building

**Iglesia de San Puebla**

shows only the lower part of the west front and one of the towers of that design, far from complete at Herrera's death in 1597. Deformed by the resulting imbalance of proportion, the great Doric pillars and enormous apse give some idea of the planned scale. Alberto Churriguera finished the façade over a century later. From outside, the untidy mass, solid, heavy and without elegance, sadly lacks the majestic impact that the design deserved.

Inside is a magnificent retable carved by Juan de Juni 1572. In the adjoining Gothic church – which would have been built over if the original plans had been fulfilled – is a Diocesan Museum, displaying sculptures, gold treasures, a silver monstrance by Juan de Arfe and a thirteenth-century Christ.

**Iglesia de Santa Mariá La Antigua** Behind the Cathedral is the church of Santa María la Antigua, with a beautiful Romanesque tower and portal. Inside are Gothic groin vaults.

**Nuestra Señora de las Angustias** The church of las Angustias is across the Plaza de la Libertad. Treasured within are a number of fine sculptures: a retable by Cristobal Velázquez, bas-reliefs by Francisco del Rincón, and a masterpiece by Juan de Juni: the Virgen de Los Cuchillos (in the sumptuous south chapel).

**Pasaje Gutiérrez** is a delightful, old-fashioned arcade just south of the Cathedral (along Calle Cascajares and off Fray Luis de León). Somewhat decayed, its ceilings are frescoed and lit by a splendid dome of stained glass.

**The University,** guarded by small sitting lions, is east of the Cathedral, across the Plaza de Cervantes and along Calle Librería. The Churrigueresque baroque façade was designed by Narciso and Antonio Tomé, pupils of Alberto Churriguera. (These masters also crafted the extraordinary baroque Transparente in Toledo Cathedral.) It is a splendid building, with Corinthian columns, Italianate ornamentation and a flamboyant Gothic courtyard.

**Colegio de Santa Cruz** Next to it is the Renaissance Colegio de Santa Cruz, founded by Cardinal Mendoza (who was subsequently buried in Toledo Cathedral).

**Iglesias de la Magdelena and las Huelgas, Casa de Colón** Beyond the University, along Calle Cardenal Mendoza, the three buildings are close together. La Magdelena, a vast church, was built by Gil de Hontañón in the sixteenth century, and carries the magnificent escutcheon of the Bishop

Don Pedro de Lasgasca (Viceroy of Peru), whose tomb is kept within. The church of Convento de las Huelgas is behind, housing important sculptures of Gregorio Fernández and Juan de Juni. The small Casa de Colón celebrates the life of the discoverer, who died in Valladolid.

West of the Plaza Mayor, parallel with the river, are a number of convents and find old buildings.

**Palacio de Fabio Nelli** The sixteenth-century Palace of Fabio Nelli is north-west of the Plaza. Within is the provincial archeological museum, displaying amongst the artefacts some well-preserved Roman mosaics.

**The Convento de San Benito,** south of the museum and beside the Mercado Val, has a massive church whose monumental Herreran double portico, by Juan Gil de Hontañón, dwarfs all surrounding buildings.

**Convento de Santa Ana** Just south-west of the Plaza Mayor is the Convento de Santa Ana. The circular chapel houses a museum of religious treasures, including works by Sabatini, Goya, Gregorio Fernández and Pedro de Meña.

**Iglesia de Santiago** Towards Plaza de Zorilla from the Plaza Mayor (Calle Santiago) is the Church of Santiago, with a Berruguete, Adoration of the Magi. The baroque reredos of Alonso Manzano and Juan Åvila dominates the nave.

**Casa de Cervantes** At the top of Campo Grande, is the Casa de Cervantes. The literary figure lived here for the years between 1603 and 1606. The museum is prettily laid out, with period furniture and a collection of relevant editions and material.

**Convento Agustino Filipinos** At the other end of the park is the imposing block of the Convento Agustinos Filipinos, where a superb collection of Chinese and Philippine artefacts, brought back by missionaries, is displayed.

**Shopping** Valladolid is a strong commercial city and has a superb selection of boutique-lined shopping streets fanning from the Plaza Mayor to beyond the Plaza Zorilla. For food and general things, the north of Plaza Mayor is well stocked. To the south-east of the main square, towards Plaza de España is another shopping area of a cheaper quality.

**Boutiques** The main network of streets carrying boutiques and *pastelerías* include: • Calle Ferrar, which flows from Bajada de la Libertad across the Plaza Mayor, well stocked with *pastelerías*. Calle Cebadería, the arcaded street on the other side of the Plaza Mayor, also offering excellent sweets. • Calle Theresa Gil, partly pedestrian, left off Calle Ferrar, for fashion. • Calle Duque de Victoria, leading up to Plaza de España. • Calle Santiago, a substantial pedestrian street full of quality shops running from the Plaza Mayor to Plaza Zorilla. An arcade here, Las Francesas, includes a supermarket, cafés and a good ice-cream shop, *Kuwait*. Calle María de Molina, north off Plaza de Zorilla to Plaza Santa Ana, with some of the finest shoe shops. Note the pretty façade of the Lopez de Vega Theatre on the right towards the Plaza de Zorrilla. • Calle Zúñiga, off Plaza Santa Ana, with excellent young fashion. • Paseo Zorilla, which flows down one side of the Campo Grande, is a one-sided thoroughfare of shops, but noisy.

**Food** For food shopping, the most entertaining place is the Mercado Val. Just north of the Plaza Mayor, it is a huge oval covered market whose roof was constructed last century. The abundance is staggering, and the stalls open both morning and afternoon. The streets surrounding offer many small grocery shops and bakeries. The bread of Valladolid is renowned, and there are excellent *chorizo* (spiced sausage) pasties.

**Markets** Street markets selling books and artisan goods are held frequently in the Campo Grande. A Saturday market is held beside El Corte Inglés (far down Paseo Zorilla) and behind San Gregorio, – but neither of these are as entertaining as that held by the Cathedral on Sundays.

**The Paseo** Very vigorous here, the *paseo* route is extremely long and well attended. *Pastelería* shops are open during the early evening. The route follows one of the main shopping routes of the city, much of which is pedestrian.

Flowing from the Cathedral up Bajada de Libertad, under the arcades of Calle Ferrar past the Plaza Mayor, the route turns left along the pedestrian Calle Santiago which it follows to the fountains of Plaza Zorilla. It then pours down the Paseo Zorilla beside the Campo Grande. The wave peters out before arriving at the bullring, turns, and its strollers walk gently back to the centre of town to begin the nomadic evening of the tapa rounds. The *paseo* route, lined all the way with shops, is just as lively on Sundays.

**Parks** Valladolid has very lovely gardens, which are most alive on a Sunday before lunch or late afternoon. Beside the river lies a beautifully tended rose garden (with a welcome small bar-restaurant *La Roseleda*) which gives way to a small shady park of trees as it nears Zorilla.

The favourite park is the Campo Grande, with its romantic winding paths, thick wild ground-cover and trees hanging with ivy. The landscaping and generosity of greenery is such that it is easy to distance the city outside. Peacocks and ducks (from the small lake) wander through the undergrowth to the delight of many a child.

**Sunday** Like Madrid, this city changes greatly on Sundays. Unlike many of the famous Castilian cities, Valladolid does not host many visitors on Sundays, and can appear unattractively quiet. However, most museums are open from 10 a.m. until 2 p.m. and the day is full of traditions that are entertaining to join.

The city starts late and gently. Breakfast is pleasant taken in the Plaza Mayor at the old-style café Lyon D'Or or in the quiet morning cafés of Plaza de la Libertad. *Patisséries* are open until 3 pm.

In the Plaza de la Libertad a colourful market sells old records, clothes, stamps and a variety of bric-a-brac. The quality is poor, but the ambience is very lively. On a small triangular corner of the Plaza, men and boys huddle in concentrated discussion – they are bargaining over football cards.

**Going out in Valladolid** It is vital to have an idea of the social geography of Valladolid in order to make the most of the vivacious city. Particularly in the evening, the two main areas, both of which are magnets for throngs of people, become very distinct in character. Apart from these, there is a wide sprinkling of lively pockets.

**Centre Plaza: Plaza de la Libertad** The centre of this area in the curve behind the church Santa María la Antigua (off Plaza de la Libertad) and flows into Calle Angustias, Calle Esgueva, Calle Marqués de Duero and Calle Paraiso. By day its bars and cafés are pleasant, and quietly popular for *tapa* lunches.

From 8 p.m. onwards, the area fills with people, the noise and clientele varying from street to street. The night-time atmosphere can be a little daunting, especially at weekends when the crowds are thickest and the volume loudest, but there are a few bars and

**Fiestas** Semana Santa: devotional processions of great solemnity and formality. Slow drum beats provide the only music and many brotherhoods, each with different garb, accompany images of the passion. The images themselves, some from the Sculpture Museum, are magnificent.
Summer Fiesta, St Matthew. September, bullfighting.

**Festivals** International Film Festival – one week in October.
Choral festival – one week in November.
Theatre Festival – two weeks in May.
Horse jumping – International Grand Prix, early June.
Regional Trade Fair of Castile and León – September.

taverns that combine vivacity, welcome and quality very successfully.

By 10 p.m. the crowd begins to drift up Calle Leopoldo, Calle María Picavea and Calle Platerías in which are many of the fashionable music-bars (e.g. Picaria, El Minuto, Nivel). These streets throb with life deep into the night. The flowing social pattern is so well established that it is almost impossible to walk against the great tide of people moving 'up' the way towards the 'next' fashionable area. A midnight stroll from Iglesia Vera Cruz down towards Las Augustias will be a battle.

**Centre Plaza: Plaza Mayor** This area to the left of the Plaza Mayor, stretching from Plaza Santa Ana down to Plaza la Rinconada, has a totally different character from Plaza de la Libertad at night. Full of people until the early hours, its energy is more refined without the throngs of lively young (under twenties). It is a tremendous place to spend an evening amongst the electricity of the party spirit, sustained by the many excellent *tapa* bars and restaurants.

High fashion night-bars are, again, just up the road, around Calle San Lorenzo. The movement to these is subtle throughout the evening. In a mews close to the Plaza de Poniente, up Calle San Lorenzo, is a rather exclusive pocket, refreshing in the summer, where two music bars (one: *Congreso*) overflow with well-dressed young people.

**Cafés** Valladolid is blessed with many good cafés, usually open all day, quietly fashionable and closing relatively early at night:

*Café de la Antigua*, Paraiso 1, Good breakfasts, and comfortable even when the locality is exhaustingly crowded.

*Café Magnolia*, Calle Augustias, opposite the Calderón Theatre. Red plush and quiet.

*Café Lyon D'or,* Plaza Mayor, a Victorian café with tables outside. Very pleasant on a Sunday morning.

*Café Norte*, Calle San Francisco 12, on the plaza Mayor, for those who enjoy an old-fashioned *pantalla* afternoon. (Shows old Spanish musicals on a big screen throughout the afternoons – patronized by a nostalgic older generation.)

*Chocolatería Toledo*, on the corner of the plaza de la Cruz (by the University) and Núñez de Arce, Patronized by students.

*Cartablanca Bar*, on the corner of Valandes and Colón, nearby the

University, with a refined atmosphere and good cocktails. Open Sundays.

*Café Pagiama*, in the delightful old shopping arcade of Passaje Gutiérrez.

**Tapa Bars** Calle Correos is one of the best streets in the town for good bars. Each bar has a different character, but most are excellent. Particularly recommended are:

*La Mina*, Calle Correos 7, Tel: 352443, Sister restaurant to La Croilla with a similar tavern ambience.

*La Tasca*, Calle Correos 5, *tapas* and roasts from the oven.

*El Cocho*.

*Taberna El Pozo*, big and lively with a restaurant.

*Castél del Parrillado*, a hall of a bar with refined *tapas* and food of high quality.

*Pan Con Tomate*, 18 Plaza Mayor, lively and fun *tapa* bar.

Calle Pasión is also full of bars.

**Restaurants** There are fairly few restaurants in Valladolid as most people go out for *tapas* rather than meals. The *tapas* are excellent.

*Taberna del Hidalgo* Paraiso 4, Tel: 295525 Good quality *tapas*. with a restaurant behind. Bursting with life. Open every day.

*Taberna Carralito* Calle La Antigua 6, Tel: 204716 Tapas Festooned with garlic and popular especially at lunchtime, with only a few tables. Open every day.

*Santi* Plaza Correos 1, Tel: 339355 A sophisticated but lively restaurant in a patio off Calle Correos with the welcoming surroundings of beamed ceiling and stone walls. A good exponent of the local cuisine.

*La Parilla de San Lorenzo* Calle Pedro Niño 1 (Esquina San Lorenzo), Tel: 335088. This is an entertaining restaurant, whose oven and wood grill glow between the *tapa* bar and the dining-room. Both rooms are stone walled, one barrel-vaulted and one beamed. The roasts – lamb, suckling pig and kid – are superb (AE DC MC V).

*Machaquito* Calle Caridad 2, Tel: 351351 A dignified quiet international restaurant, good for roasting and game. Shut Sundays and 1–15 August (AE DC MC V).

*La Criolla* Calle Calixro Fernández de la Torre, Tel: 330370 Tapas. A terrific *tapa* bar and an informal and spirited restaurant which serves great wooden platters of grills (or fish) and salad which are presented to the centre of the table to be shared by all. Very popular for all meals and for Sunday lunch (AE DC MC V). Shut Mondays.

*Mesón La Fragua* Paseo de Zorrilla 10, Tel: 337102. An exceptional restaurant, with an international reputation. Excellent, Castilian food, good wine list and a very pleasant ambience. On the main *paseo* route. Shut Sunday evenings.

*Mesón Panero* Marina Escobar 1, Tel: 301673. Between Plaza España and Plaza Zorrilla.
Superb uncompromised traditional fare – stews, pulses, roasts.
Shut Sunday evenings and July and August (AE DC MC V).

*La Goya* Puente Colgante 79, Tel: 355724. Out of the centre across the Pisuegra from Paseo Zorrilla. A popular favourite, with a pretty terrace and traditional cooking. Shut Sunday evenings and during August (V).

*El Lugar* Mantilla 1, Tel: 398504 Excellent Atlantic fish, refined ambience. classical dishes. Off Plaza Zorrilla. Shut Sunday evenings (AE V).

*Mesón Cervantes* El Rastro 6, Tel: 306138 Refined, tucked into the quiet corner behind the Museo Cervantes. Fine Castilian cooking. Shut Mondays and during November (AE DC V).

**Hotels** Being the political and commercial capital of Castile and León, the hotels of Valladolid cater well for the business traveller but not for the casual visitor, whose choice is mainly between the impersonal luxuries of the big hotels, or the characterless comforts of the smaller ones.

### Category 1

*Hotel Felipe IV* Gamazo 16, Tel: 307000 Smart with every comfort. Peacefully placed beside the Campo Grande, away from the main Zorilla road.
130 rooms d&b: 8190 (AE DC V). Parking. Restaurant.

*Hotel Olid Melía* Plaza San Miguel 10, Tel: 357200 An excellent, luxurious hotel, central, north of the Plaza Mayor and near to San Pablo and San Gregorio.
234 room d&b: 9420 (AE DC MC V). Parking. Restaurant.

*Hotel Meliá Parque* Joaquín García Morato 17, Tel: 470100. Modern without character, but very comfortable, close to the railway station and easy to find. The other side of the Campo

Grande from the centre of town (15 minutes to Plaza Mayor).
306 rooms, d&b: 8000 (AE DC V).

*Hotel Lasa* Acera Recoletos 21, Tel: 390255. Suave and elegant, on the quiet side of Campo Grande.
60 rooms d&b: 8100 (DC V).

## Category 2

*Hotel Mozart* Menéndez Pelayo 7, Tel: 297777. A pretty, pleasant hotel close to the centre, less commercially based than the bigger hotels. A little difficult to drive to, but worth it.
38 rooms, d&b: 6800 (AE DC MC V).

*Roma* Heroes Alcázar de Toledo 8, Tel: 354666. Near the Plaza Mayor. 38 rooms, d&b: 3225.

*Hotel Imperial* Peso 4, Tel: 330300 Straightforward and very central (off Plaza Mayor).
81 rooms d&b: 5200.

## Category 3

*Hotel Lima* Tudela 4, Tel: 202240. Simple, central.
21 rooms d&b 3100.

*Enara* Plaza de España 5, Tel: 300311.
26 rooms, d&b 4250.

*Greco* Plaza Val 2, Tel: 356152.
21 rooms, d&b 3100.

Cheap hostals around Plaza Val and Plaza Santa Ana.

## Information

Area Exchange Code: 983

Tourist Office:   Plaza Zorilla 3, although obscured by trees.
                  Tel: 351801

Correos
(Post Office):    Plaza de la Rinconada, Tel: 330660

Renfe:            Estación del Norte, (across Campo Grande)
                  Tel: 303518

Bus Station:      Puente Colgante 2, (across Campo Grande)
                  Tel: 236308

Airport de
Villanubla:       Tel: 259220

Police:           Tel: 357066

Cruz Roja
(Red Cross):      López Gómez 2, Tel: 302439

Banking area:     between Plaza de Zorilla and Plaza de España.

### Transport

| | |
|---|---|
| Taxi: Radio: | Tel: 291411 |
| Buses: | Good services from near the RENFE station – for the centre take buses headed for Plaza Mayor, Plaza de la Libertad. For the Tourist Office (a few minutes from the centre) Plaza Zorilla, at the apex of Campo Grande. |
| Inter-city Travel: | |
| By air: | connections to Madrid and to Barcelona, Balearics and Canaries during the summer season. |
| By Bus: | connections to all major cities of Castile and León |
| | Frequent connections with Madrid |
| | Barcelona and Seville (three times daily) |
| By Train: | Frequent connections to Madrid. |
| Cars: | Valladolid is a major town, and street parking is extremely limited. There is a big underground car-park beneath the Plaza Mayor, to which traffic is directed by Centro Urbano signs. Others are scattered throughout. The city is prone to traffic jams in the centre, and the streets carry a heavy weight of vehicles. |

**The rolling autumn fields of Valladolid**

292

**Around Valladolid** With vast rolling plains of cereal, vineyard-lined rivers, and fields of sugar beet, the province of Valladolid has an affluent agricultural base. It is the heart of the vast autonomous region of Castilla-León, whose government sits in the capital city. The towns, castles and religious buildings illustrate the formidable power of the area historically, and the commercial base of even the small hamlets is very apparent. There are few pretty winding roads, and few places that exploit their historical treasures. The four main towns, each of which are endowed with spectacular monuments, attract a substantial number of visitors: Medina de Rioseco (north), Tordesillas (west), Medina del Campo (south), and Peñafiel (east). The rest of the province, dignified and proud, remains little known.

Valladolid can be divided into three. The area north-west of the city is an extensive rolling plain of cereals, punctuated by thin holm oak forests, with smooth hills clad by strategic lines of fortified churches or castles. The villages are solidly built of white stone.

To the east the terrain is harsher, with smaller agricultural fields, and irrigated land taking advantage of the two rivers, the Pisuegra and the Duero. Vines line the Duero to east and west, and fill the valley south of the capital.

South of the city, the landscape varies from grain plains near Salamanca, to the thick pine forests and jutting ridges towards Segovia in the east. The villages, increasingly commercial, are generally not pretty, and the older buildings, many Mudéjar in style, are mainly of brick.

### North-east towards León

**Medina del Rioseco** The main route between León and Valladolid, the N601, passes through the old market town of Medina del Rioseca, distinguished by massive churches and a delightful porticoed main street. (The town is awkward to drive in. Except for the main road entrances, there is no obvious place to park.) In the sixteenth and seventeenth centuries the town prospered as an important trade centre, and still retains importance in its region as a livestock market (weekly on Tuesdays).

The main shopping street, running from the north entrance to the town through to the Plaza Mayor, is lined with ancient heavy timber trunks supporting the deep upper floor projections of the houses. In the shadow of these porticoes stretched the old market

293

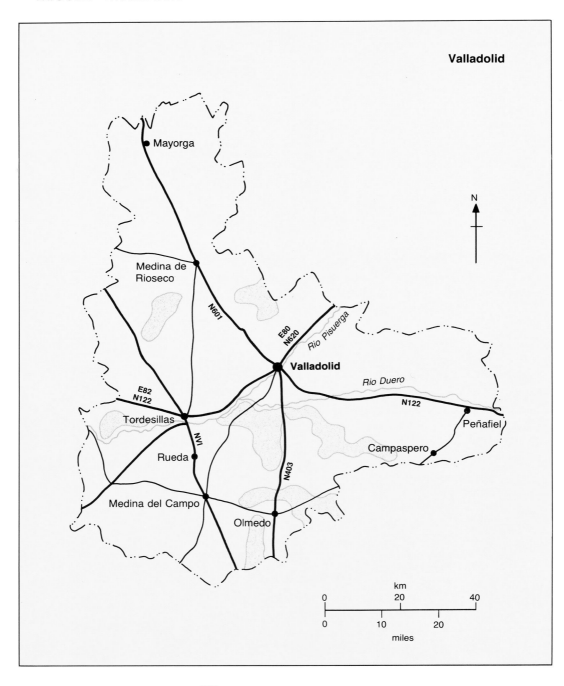

**Valladolid**

stalls. This street, the Calle de la Rua, contains the liveliness of the town – elsewhere it is quiet and sprawled.

The churches, vast white temples with monumental facades and rich interiors, illustrate the erstwhile wealth of the town. Santa María de Mediavilla, the most important of these, stands close to the Calle de la Rua with a splendid baroque tower. Displayed within are various valuable polychrome sculptures. The main reredos is worked by Juan de Juni and Esteban Jordan. The museum, displaying religious artefacts and paintings, guards a monstrance of Antonio de Arfe, and various Phillipino treasures. The Benavente Chapel is outstanding with its elaborate decoration: set behind a beautiful sixteenth-century grille crowded with stucco reliefs and cherubs; entirely frescoed; and crowned with another Juan de Juni reredos. The church is open during the morning and for mass at 7.30 a.m.

Santiago is another massive building, designed by Rodrigo Gil de Hontañón (of Salamanca, Plasencia and Ciudad Rodrigo fame) and supporting a façade by Alonso de Tolosa. While repairs are carried out, its fine (Joaquín) Churrigueresque altarpiece is in Santa María. The churches of San Francisco and Santa Cruz are also considerable buildings.

Further north through the grain fields towards León the agricultural villages are small and hard-working without specific impact. The N601 passes Mayorga, a small quiet town notable for its Mudéjar brick seminaries, and amongst its churches is the pretty Santa María de Arbas. A little east of Medina de Rioseca are two splendid castles.

**Montealegre,** a colossal square white fortress (nothing remains within), sits at the crown of a plateau overlooking an infinite plain of wheat within which Rioseco can be seen. The village is pleasant to wander around, its stone and adobe houses displaying various traditional features (old threshing boards used as doors, bee entrances in the walls of houses).

**Ampudia** Just over the border of Palencia is Ampudia, a pretty spacious village with many streets arcaded by porticoed houses. The baroque church here is fine, and the castle, well renovated, is palatial. Privately owned and furnished, it is open only on Saturday mornings to display a few rooms and a museum. At weekends many families from Palencia and Valladolid visit here.

**Villalba de los Alcores** A little south is Villalba de los Alcores, retaining ruins of a castle and monastery. It is a solid agricultural village reminiscent of a cotswold hamlet. The triangle within Medina de Rioseco, the capital and the western border point on the N122 (towards Toro) contains a number of castles and some important ecclesiastical buildings.

**Villagarcía de Campos** On the C519 is Villagarcía de Campos, in which stands the first model for the Castilian Jesuit church. The collegiate, built to the lofty classical design of Juan de Herrera, serves the village as a parish church but is attached to the active Jesuit seminary. The museum, only open on festival days (10 a.m.–1 p.m. and 4–6 p.m.) is entered from the seminary entrance behind the church building. It has an unusual collection of seventeenth-century reliquaries and a number of less interesting paintings.

**Ureña,** with a great circle of white walls on the crest of a hill, is exciting to approach from here. The village is small, but the fortifications are magnificent, high and almost complete. Walking within them, the views from the various openings are marvellous. Just below is a lovely Romanesque hermitage.

**Real Monasterio de la Santa Espina** Across from Ureña is the beautiful Monasterio de la Santa Espina, part of which has been, for 100 years, a highly respected agricultural college. The Cistercian monastery itself was founded in 1104 and enjoyed strong royal support until the crisis years of Mendízabal which left it abandoned. The oldest part lines one side of the cloister leading to the church: the twelfth-century chapter room, sacristy and library. The low, robust vaulting is austere and dignified, and great clustered pillars surround the entrances.

The church, with early Gothic pointed arches, and a Renaissance main apse, is of majestic proportions, and of great height. The lack of decoration, excepting the church capitals facing the outer aisles (away from congregational distraction), is characteristic of the Cistercian style. The baroque twin-towered façade of the church was added in the seventeenth century. As with most monasteries, the attack of Mendízabal resulted in the disemination of the monastic treasures.

Part of the original reredos is in the Mares Museum of Barcelona, and the centrepiece is in the nearby church of San

Cebrián. A small number of monks reside here, and will gladly show visitors around. The splendid church is the parish church of the village of Castromonte. On the outside of the entrance archway is carved a clock, signifying that the order within were no longer distracted by worldly time-keeping. (A comparative visit to the Romanesque Cistercian monastery of San Bernardo, to the east of the capital on the Duero, is interesting.)

In two villages close to the monastery, Wamba and San Cebrián (owner of the Monastery's main reredos panel) are important parish churches of the rare Mozarabic style – tenth-century building of stone and brick with Arabic motifs of horseshoe arches and decorous brick design.

## Tiedra, Mora del Marqués and Torrelobatón

Horizontally north of the Duero sits another spectacular line of castles: Tiedra, Mora del Marqués and Torrelobatón. The latter is one of the best preserved castles in Valladolid – a solid square moated tower without merlons. It was here that the only successful battle was fought by the Comuneros, led by Juan de Padilla, against Charles V.

## Fuensaldaña

Further east at Fuensaldaña, the pretty castle is now home to the Junta of Castilla y León – a slender tower, carefully restored, giving the fortress a uniquely graceful appearance. Cigales is to the east. Approached along the VA901, the great white twin tower dominates the countryside from many kilometres away. This is a small, popular weekend village. Nearby, Trigueros is a pretty tumbling village with a castle ruin.

## West

**Tordesillas,** on the N122 west of Valladolid, is reached via Simancas. This castle, a formidable fortress, guards a vast archive of documents dating from the time of Charles V until recent years – a function (along with that of a prison) assigned to it by the Catholic Monarchs. Inside, efficiency has replaced the old rooms with modern linings. The slate roofs are an unusual addition of the seventeenth century.

Tordesillas, on a busy route junction, is renowned for the Treaty of 1494 signed here by the Catholic Monarchs and Portugal, attempting unsuccessfully to divide the world (discovered and yet to be discovered) into equal shares. The

**Above**
**The twin-towers, added in the seventeenth century**

**Real Monasterio de la Santa Espina**
(taken by Antonio Sigüenza Molina)

Portuguese, winning Brazil, fared well. The town contains a extraordinary treasure of Mudéjar art within its Real Monasterio de Santa Clara, a palace of Alfonso XI that became a convent upon the death of another royal resident, Pedro I the Cruel. The sad Queen Juana la Loca (the Mad), daughter of Isabel I and mother of Charles V, lived here for 40 years until her death in 1555. Its prominence continues, receiving royal and state persons frequently and being a major host to high ecclesiastical meetings.

The convent, still home to cloistered nuns, sits overlooking the river a short walk from the extremely pretty porticoed Plaza Mayor. A visit starts with the miniature Arabic Courtyard, a delightful patio of lobed horseshoe arches and ceramic decoration. A small room decorated with pure Arabic designs is nearby. The stucco work and flowing Arabic script is beautiful. (Clearly the aesthetic qualities of the script was more important to the Christian king than its meaning.) The ceiling of the Salón Dorado is a spectacular golden puzzle of coffered shapes, beneath which the walls are decorated with blind horseshoe arches.

The church and its anterooms display oriental motifs. The main apse has a most beautiful artesanal ceiling, and the vaults are strangely decorated with non-symetrical writhing dragons. The chapel of Contador Saldaña is notable for its Gothic flamboyance. At the west end a splendid grille separates the nuns from the congregation. The Arabic baths, under repair, remain with fine wall decorations.

Run by the Patrimony National, and shown by guided tour, 9.30 a.m.–1 p.m. and 3.30–6.00 p.m. and 3.30–6.00 p.m. Shut Mondays.

An important Mudéjar church stands nearby, that of San Antolín, in which is a good museum of painting (including the

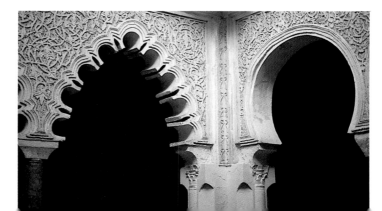

**The Arabic courtyard of the Covento de Santa Clara, Tordesillas**

'Immaculada' of Pedro de Meña) and sculpture (Alonso de Berruguete, Gregorio Fernández, Juan de Juni, etc.). Note also the opulent sixteenth-century Chapel of the Alderete family.

Cars can be parked in the pretty Plaza Mayor.

**South** South of the Duero from Toro to the banks of the Eresma is an area dedicated to viniculture, and speckled with pine forest and grain fields. The main villages are Nava del Rey, producing a rich sherry-like wine; Rueda, famous for its lighter white wines; Serrada; La Seca and Pozáldez. The villages are not particularly attractive, but a visit to the *bodegas* beneath the soil is interesting. Their air vents can be seen poking through amongst the vines. Producing huge quantities of wine, the winemakers have unostentatious front offices from which they frequently sell the wine, co-operative style, by bottle or litre.

If travelling from Toro to this area, there is a very pretty view of Castronuño (C112) from where there is also a river swimming area.

**Medina del Campo** is the main commercial centre with a railway junction of great importance. Its historical eminence was in the sixteenth and seventeenth centuries, when it was one of the primary market places of Europe, and indeed produced the first bill of exchange in the world. Today its commerce is based on the local industry of high-quality furniture making, and the surrounding agricultural wealth. Apart from enjoying the fresh vivacity of the town, particularly lively at weekend evenings, there are a number of monuments that reflect the historical impact of the town.

The castle, La Mota, is one of the most recognizable in Castile and is paired frequently with Coca because of its Mudéjar design and build (although lacking the finesse of the Coca brickwork decoration). A protecting fortress for the trade centre, its grand shape grew in the fifteenth and sixteenth centuries from an earlier foundation, with a great towering keep projecting at one end, crusted around its parapet with corbelled parapets and battlements. Built for war, but also used as a prison and a palace, it has a well-protected entrance and extensive inner rooms. Queen Isabella I lived here, and died in a palace in the town centre. (The market used in her time, sitting near the centre on the river, still trades every day.) The castle is open to the public, but, apart from the fine vaults, is more impressive outside than in. It has been

301

rebuilt many times, suffering ravages during the Comuneros revolt, during the nineteenth century and the civil war.

The unique country residence, the Casa Blanca, Dueña's Palace, makes an attractive visit, with a Renaissance and Plateresque patio, a hall handsomely clad in Mudéjar panelling, and medallions and escutcheons dignifying the walls. The town has a pleasant, spacious Plaza Mayor, without homogenity but with pretty gardens. The streets contain a number of fine *señorial* houses, typically of brick with stone corners. The churches, massive and again of brick, lack elegance but have a certain majesty.

**Olmedo** Nearby is Olmedo, an open wealthy town, quietly growing industrially while basking in the fame handed to it by Lope de Vega's *A gentleman of Olmedo*. Its sturdy town walls, fine old houses, and great church towers are impressive. The Mudéjar influence here, flourishing in he thirteenth century, is seen in the churches of San Juan and San Andrés, whose Romanesque ruins still show the Mudéjar apse. San Miguel is another attractive example. Pine woods and sugar beet fields surround the town.

Between Valladolid and Olmedo is the extensive area of Matapozuelos zoo, the main zoo of Castilla y León.

**Portillo Ridge** Eastwards towards Cuéllar (Segovia), above the pine woods, are two spectacular castle ruins of Iscar and Portillo. From the crest of the Portillo ridge fabulous views stretch across the provinces of Valladolid and Segovia. The economy of

**The splendid interior of the Monasterio de San Bernardo**

the area is based on lumber and resin, and the proud, hard working villages are not pretty.

**East** This fertile area is watered by the river Pisuegra which curves from Palencia, the rivero Esgueva, and the great river Duero. The countryside is splashed with meadows, pine woods, cereal fields and on the Duero vines.

**Tudela** is a few kilometres outside the city. A noble town surrounded by asparagus and strawberry fields, it has a fine parish church guarding a Virgin and Child by Juan de Juni. Two small pilgrimage chapels stand just outside.

**Olivares de Duero** Further along is Olivares de Duero, whose parish church is sumptuously decorated with Italianate frescoes.

**Valbuena de Duero** is known for its superb vineyards from which are made one of the finest wines in Spain, the Vega Sicilia wine. Before the nineteenth-century traumas of Mendízabal led to the abandoning of monasteries, the twelfth-century Cistercian monastery of San Bernardo made the great wine for the monarchs of Europe. Today it is a magnificent shell, housing some reliefs by Gregorio Fernández and some elaborate baroque altarpieces. The pale church, with early Gothic vaulting, is robust and beautiful. In the chapter, stone sepulchres sit in niches with old Romanesque frescoes. Although the cloister is in a ruinous state, it retains much of its former majesty.

Open: 10 a.m.–1 p.m. and 3.30–6 p.m. – if the doors are locked, the bar in the small village may find the key.

**The remarkable castle above Peñafiel**

**Peñafiel** One of the most remarkable castles in Valladolid stands above Peñafiel. The walled town, spread below a sharp, narrow ridge of hill, thrives today, from the production of sugar. The extraordinary castle, built to the contours of the ridge, is shaped like a ship: 210 metres (230yds) long and only 24 metres (26yds) wide, with a great *Torre de Homenaje* standing proudly in the middle. Twelve cylindrical buttresses defend each side. From the top of the tower the exceptional form can be appreciated.

Although a castle has stood on this rock at least since 943AD, the present one was constructed in 1456 by Don Pedro Girón, under Enrique IV after Juan II destroyed the last to control the rebelling Juan of Aragón.

Open: 9 a.m.–1 p.m. and 3.30–6 p.m.

303

Below in the town are several imposing religious buildings. The Dominican Convent of San Pablo was built 1324 by Infant Juan Manuel using a fortress originally built by Alfonso X. The Gothic-Mudéjar church has blind arcades outside and a most beautiful Plateresque chapel within. Much of its treasure has been dispersed.

Plaza del Coso is an extremely pretty square, recognizable from several films where the quaint houses backed by the magnificent fortress made a perfect set.

Arriving from Valladolid, pass round across the river towards the castle. A route passes Santa Clara (before the river), then San Pablo, then the Plaza Coso and finally the pretty Parque de San Vicente from which the road leads to the castle.

The chefs of Peñafiel are some of the most famous in the region – roast lamb is superb here.

### Local Specialities

Bread, particularly the *lechuguino* loaf • salt cod (*bacaloa*) is cooked well. • roast baby lamb (and to a lesser extent roast suckling pig) is best eaten in Peñafiel and Tordesillas. • lamb trotters (*Manitas de cordero rebozados* ) • from Villalón comes the delicious cheese, *pata de Mulo*. • game is cooked with marinades flavoured with rosemary and thyme.

**Fiestas:** Easter Sunday morning: the "Angel de Peñafiel" processions 14–17 August, Fiestas of San Roque. August fairs.
The Torre de la Vega fiesta, held in September, involves the energetic chase of an angry bull through the countryside by the local people, some mounted. The danger used to be accentuated by the placing of fire-bearing darts in the back of the bull.

June is the prime month for fairs and festivals, and the Maundy Thursday religious processions are notable.

The people of Valladolid boast that their bread is the finest in Castile (explained by the superb flour they produce in the extensive northern plains) and that their wine is unrivalled. The wine of the Duero and Eresma is excellent. The red wines of Peñafiel and Valbuena, the white Ruedas and the heavy perfumed wines of Nava del Rey enjoy a high reputation. Vega Sicilia, from Valbuena, is an exceptional wine, regarded as one of the finest in Europe.

### Accommodation and Restaurants

Medina del Campo
*La Mota*. Fernando el Católico 4, Tel: 800450.
40 rooms, d&b 2700. No restaurant (v).
*El Orensano*, Claudio Moyano 20, Tel: 800341.
24 rooms, d&b 3000 (v).
Restaurant: *El Paso*, Claudio Moyano 1, Tel: 801895, good fish and roasts. (Both this and its neighbour are highly regarded.)
Restaurant: *Madrid*, Claudio Moyano 2, Tel: 800693, roasts.

### Medina del Rioseco

*Almirantes*, Pso San Francisco 2, Tel: 700125.

30 rooms, d&b 6100, (AE DC MC V), quiet and very comfortable.
*Castilla,* Juan Carlos 10, Tel: 700078.

17 rooms, d&b 2500.

Restaurant: *Mesón de la Rua,* San Juan 25, Tel: 700519, Shut Thursdays and part of September and October. Home cooking.

Restaurant: *La Era,* Plaza Mayor 9, Tel: 700959, wood-oven roasts.

## Olmedo

*Piedras Blancas,* Ctra Madrid, Tel: 600100.

24 rooms, d&b 3600, just out of town.

## Peñafiel

*Infante Don Juan Manuel,* Ctra Valladolid-Soria, Tel: 880361 30 rooms, d&b 3400, 5km (3miles) out of town.

Many restaurants here serving a menu of roast lamb. The town is famous for its cooking.

Restaurant: *Asador Mauro,* Calle Atarazanas, Tel: 880816 (v).

## Tordesillas

*Parador Naciónal,* Ctra Nal. Tel: 770051, 73 rooms, d&b 8000 2km (1mile) outside town, in the midst of a pine forest. Restaurant. (AE DC MC V).

*El Montico,* Ctra Valladolid, Tel: 770751.

34 rooms, d&b 7000 in pine woods, with tennis courts and pool 5km (3ml.) from town. (AE DC MC V).

*Juan Manuel,* Ctra Burgos/Portugal, Tel: 770911.

24 rooms d&b 3100, Just outside town. Good restaurant.

Restaurant: *Mesón Valderrey,* Ctr NVI, Tel: 771172. (AE DC MC V). Roasts of suckling pig and lamb.

## Camping

Simancas:

El Plantio, Tel: 590082. Open 15 June to 15 September, Category 1, 100 people.

Tordesillas:

El Astral, Tel: 770953, Open 1 April to 30 September, Category 1, 800 people.

Cubillas de Santa Marta, Tel: 500087. Open all year, Category 2, 280 people.

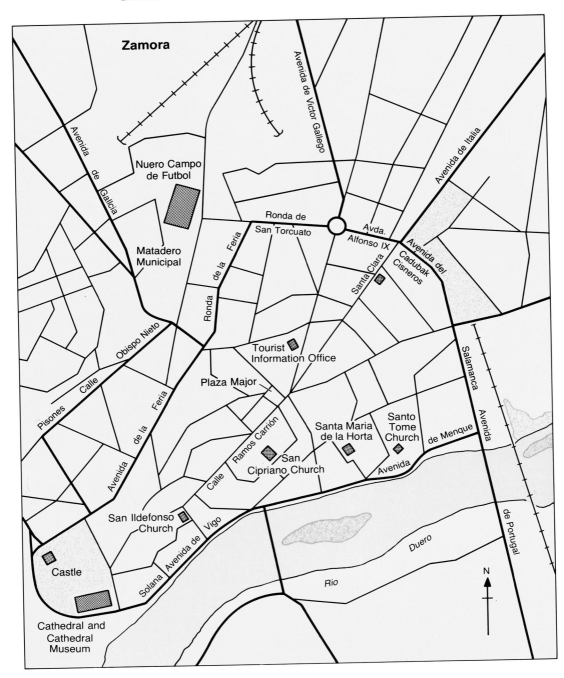

Zamora

Nuero Campo
de Futbol

Matadero
Municipal

Avenida de Galicia

Avenida de Victor Gallego

Avenida de Italia

Ronda de
San Torcuato

Ronda de la Feria

Avda.
Alfonso IX

Santa Clara

Avenida del Cadubak Cisneros

Ronda

Obispo Nieto

Calle

Pisones

Tourist
Information Office

Plaza Major

Avenida de la Feria

Ramos Carrión

Calle

San
Cipriano Church

Santa Maria
de la Horta

Santo
Tome
Church

de Menque

Avenida

Salamanca

Avenida

Avenida

San Ildefonso
Church

Vigo

Avenida de

Solana

Castle

Duero

Rio

de Portugal

N

Cathedral and
Cathedral
Museum

**Zamora** is a quiet unflustered town of pale yellow stone rising above the great river Duero. With an important Cathedral, castle remains, numerous superbly kept Romanesque churches, and some attractive civic buildings, the town displays its early historical prominence well. The freshness and tranquillity is delightful.

**History** Zamora was renowned in the Middle Ages for its boundary of impregnable walls, and its spirited fight in the frequent battles against Visigoths and then Moors. It was a stoic defender of the Castillian kings. For Doña Urraca, to whom the city was given by her father Fernando I, Zamora withstood a harsh seige imposed by her treacherous brother Sancho II. The city stood firmly behind Isabella la Católica against Juana la Beltranja during the vital battle of Toro. At the height of strategic importance, the city was defended by three castles, of which only one fort remains. Its prosperity in the Middle Ages is illustrated by the marvellous collection of Romanesque churches, and, similarly, its gradual decline after the sixteenth century may be seen by the marked lack of later ecclesiastical architecture.

Today it is a small city, whose wealth is based on the agricultural produce of the province. Its reputation is one of quietness and relative commercial insignificance. Its historical collective energy is no longer as evident as it was.

**Outstanding Monuments** the Cathedral, its museum is open 11.00 a.m.–2.00 p.m. and 4.00–6.00 p.m. (far west end).

**The tranquil streets of Zamora**

307

Iglesia Santiago del Burgo, mass 1.00 p.m. (centre of Calle Santa Clara, close to Plaza Mayor).

Iglesia La Magdalena, mass 9.00 a.m. (Calle Carrión, near the Cathedral).

**Notable Monuments** Churches (all Romanesque except San Idelfonso): Santa María de la Horta, mass 9.00 a.m., 8.00 p.m. (Near the river, down Calle Balborraz beneath Plaza Mayor).

Santa Tomé (closed, key from caretaker of Santa María de la Horta, beside).

San Cipriano mass 9.00 a.m., 8.00 p.m. (south-west of Plaza Mayor).

Santa María la Nueva (closed) and Museo de Semana Santa 10.00 a.m.–2.00 p.m. and 4.00–6.00 p.m. (north of Plaza Mayor, by the north walls and Plaza Puentica

San Juan de la Puerta, mass a.m. p.m. (in Plaza Mayor).

San Idelfonso, closed for restoration, (off Calle Ramos Carrión), near the Cathedral).

Secular buildings: Palacio de los Momos – now the Palace of Justice, east of Plaza Mayor, on Calle de San Torcuato).

Casa del Cordón, below San Cipriano.

Palacio de los Condes de Alba y Aliste, – now the Parador hotel, on Calle Ramos Carrión, just east of Plaza Mayor.

**Layout of the Town** The town is shaped like a cone above the river Duero. The Cathedral, placed at the far western promontory, is linked to the far eastern edge of the modern town by an artery that cuts through the middle of the cone. This runs from the Calle Tordesillas, outside the walls, via the pedestrian Calle Santa Clara to Plaza Mayor, from where it continues as Calle Ramos to the Cathedral. Santa Clara is the main commercial street.

Inside the walls are several areas of different character. To the South of San Juan de las Monjas is a quiet but old, poor area which reaches down to the river with plain streets and humble housing. North of Calle San Torcuato the area is distinctive for a definite local feel, spiced by a few very pretty streets. There are several *barrios*, each dominated by its church. Outside the walls, the new urban areas are unremarkable.

**The Historic Town** The walls, where visible, are attractive – pale yellow and formidable. the surviving gates are Doña Urraca Gateway, Traitors Gate (beside the castle – where King Sancho II

**Zamora Cathedral**

was murdered) and the Puerta de Olivares to which is adjoined the house in which El Cid apparently lived.

The Cathedral, several Romanesque churches and a couple of Renaissance palace façades should be seen here. Of the churches, many are no longer in use and are therefore awkward to see inside (frequently the inside is of less importance than the exterior). The Cathedral and the remains of the castle are situated at the fat western edge of the old town high above the River Duero, on the gold stone rise of Santa Marta hill. The churches are scattered throughout, and a visit to the major ones involves a walk that touches much of the town.

**Cathedral** The Cathedral stands at the far west end of the limestone ridge, high above the Río Duero. Beside are tailored gardens and the remaining castle, now a school of art.

The Cathedral, mostly constructed between 1135 and 1171, is of distinguished appearance, a solid pale golden building with a dome tiled with fish-scale shaped stone, and a mighty Romanesque tower. Approached from the centre of town, it is a formidable building, with Renaissance cloisters clothing one side, and a colossal Herreran Portico with great Corinthian capitals dominating its façade. The Bishop's Portal, facing the Duero, is more characteristic of the building – a beautiful Romanesque arch carved delicately.

Inside, the Cathedral is dark and surprisingly lacking in spaciousness, Its most remarkable feature is the dome, modelled on that of San Sophia is Constantinople, and one of the outstanding trio of Byzantine/Romanesque lanterns of Castile, (the others are Salamanca Old Cathedral; Collegiata of Toro.) The cupola is supported on pointed arches, and lit by 16 slim Romanesque windows.

Beneath the early Gothic vaulting of the nave, is the choir. The walnut stalls are lively and carved in the style of Rodrigo Alemán, with profane burlesques decorating the seat. In front is the High Altar between two chapels of very different style. To the left is a famous thirteenth-century Virgin, (Virgen de la Majestad) polychromed in the sixteenth-century. The High Altar displayed a retable by Fernando Gallego until this was replaced by the monumental jasper and marble Renaissance altarpiece.

At the west of the Cathedral are three chapels. That of San Idelfonso (north) and San Juan Evangelista (south) flank the bigger centre chapel. They are both remarkable: San Idelfonso has a beautiful retable by Fernando Gallego; San Juan Evangelista has a Flamenco-Gothic carved tomb by Dr Juan de Grado, above which is a flamboyant genealogical tree.

Through the cloister, by Juan de Mora, is the museum. Treasured within are magnificent fifteenth and sixteenth century French and Flemish tapestries, given to the Cathedral by the Counts of Alba and Aliste in 1608. The depiction of the Death of Achilles is wonderful, with vivid blues and superb detail. Other fine pieces include a splendid gold and silver custodia (school of Enrique de arfe), and a very lovely statue of the Virgin by Ordónez. The historic archives were destroyed by fire in 1591, and remaining documents are kept in a library by the Cathedral.

The surroundings of the cathedral are most peaceful. Two old gates lead out through walls, one to the north, beyond a small old church, and the other by the Bishops Portal to the Cathedral. A walkway just within the walls to the south leads to a tranquil bay overlooking the river.

**Iglesia de la Magdalena** Towards the Plaza Mayor, past the big church of San Idelfonso is the delightful small church of La Magdelena, open only early morning and evening. The south façade is particularly fine, with a portal carved with floral motifs, heads and twisted cord. Within is a splendid twelfth-century tomb supported by twisted pedestals, surmounted by reliefs and guarded by angels. The building is long and narrow.

**Palacio de los Condes de Alba y Aliste** Further along the street is the Palacio de los Condes de Alba y Aliste. Now a Parador hotel, it is worthwhile taking a drink within to see the patio and staircase.

Beside a wide street the south walls leads to the small San Cipriano (built 1025) beyond which are steps leading down to the Plaza Lucio. Here is the fine façade of Casa del Cordón decorated with conch shell corbels, escutcheons and twisted cord. In the *barrio* by the river are the beautiful twelfth-century Santa María de la Horta, and Santo Tomé (both single aisled). Within Santa María is a thirteenth-century statue and old Romanesque capitals. Santo Tomé is very simple and almost totally unadorned.

On the other side of the central street of the old town, to the north, is the quiet church of Santa María la Nueva, of Visigothic origin.

**Museo de la Semana Santa** Beside is the Museo de la Semana Santa in which are displayed most of the sculptures processed during the holy week. The quantity and size of the floats is remarkable. The distinct costumes worn by the brotherhoods, with pointed hoods and coloured cloaks, are also displayed.

**Plaza Mayor** The Plaza Mayor is rather unbalanced, with the pretty arched police building on one side, and the big church of San Juan sitting askew in the middle.

**Palacio de los Mamos** Down the tangent to Calle Santa Clara, Calle de San Torcuato, is the dignified Palacio de los Momos, with a fine Renaissance façade decorated with Isabelline window surrounds and carved chain links running the width of the building. It is now the Palace of Justice.

**Iglesia de Santiago del Burgo** On the pedestrian street of Calle Santa Clara is Santiago del Burgo, a lovely church built at the same time as the Cathedral. Within, it is three-aisled, with sturdy columns and intricate capitals supporting early Gothic vaults. A heavy gilt retable dominates the High Altar. It is a beautifully balanced building.

There is a profusion of old churches, each of pale stone. Two outside the walls are Santiago de los Caballeros, beneath the Castle, in which El Cid is reputed to have been knighted; and San Claudio de Olivares, on the banks of the river beneath the Cathedral, with beautiful Romanesque capitals and a fine north portal. The great walls may be walked both on the north side of the town, entered through the colossal gate of Urraca, and on the south side, from which the views are of the wide river.

**Shopping** Zamora is not a notable shopping town. Without a strong commercial wealth, and with few visitors, it satisfies its local customers sufficiently and economically. There are very few souvenir shops.

The municipal market is worth visiting – a two-level building covered by a rectangular iron and glass structure in the Plaza Fray Diego de Dezo. Beneath the eaves are the vegetable stalls of small local growers.

Santa Clara is the main shopping street. At plaza Constitución are the main banks (shut on Saturdays), the Tourist Office and the Post Office.

A market is held by Santa María de la Horta on Tuesday morning.

**The *Paseo*** Santa Clara, the main pedestrian social route through the old town, hosts the *paseo* to the Plaza Mayor. On Friday lunchtimes and at weekends the stroll extends beyond the ring road (Avda de Portugal) along the gardened side of the Avenida Requejo. Daily at midday the small part around the

**The lunchtime *paseo* in Zamora**

church San Juan becomes a crowded mingling of men, which dissolves gradually as the 1 p.m. mass begins.

**Parks** Beside the castle is a well-kept garden of shrubs and rosebeds. Views from here are lovely. There is a small strip of garden just beyond Calle Santa Clara, on its busy extension in the new town (Avda Requejo). The main park is Campos de Valorio, beneath the north-east walls. This opens along a stream tributary of the Duero, with trees and picnic tables, and extends into forest. There are playing fields here.

**Fiestas** Semana Santa is the most important festival here, and one for which Zamora is renowned. The processions begin on Palm Sunday and floats accompanied by hooded penitents pass through the streets each day of the week. There are 14 different brotherhoods and many sculptures. The evenings of Maundy Thursday and Holy Friday are the most important, but all prosessions are of the utmost solemnity, with little sound save the mournful beat of drums. The occasion is profoundly austere.

**Bars and *Tapas*** The main tapa street in Zamora is Calle Herreros, just down off the Plaza Mayor. It is not particularly welcoming to visitors, but is lined with small smokey bars and is very lively at weekends. There are a couple of good bars amongst the local haunts:

*Bodega El Chorizo* – excellent *chuleta a la Braza*.
*Mesón la Pieddra* – welcoming, with good grills.
Elsewhere:
*El Figón*, Avda Portugal Tel: 533159. The most fashionable *tapa* bar, and highly recommended – always full with a very comfortable ambience and good t*apas*. Just outside the old town with its own regular clientele. There are a few tables for meals. Shut Mondays.
*Mesón D'Angelo*, Calle Alfonso de Castro, Tel: 534954. Quiet and social, in a less-frequented part of the walled town, with a restaurant downstairs. The onion tart is highly recommended,

### Cafés

*Café Cariatide*, Benavente 5. An old style cafe, smokey, popular and always full of people.
*Café Michelos*, Calle Toro/Diego de la Sada. Open until late, behind the area of discos: Parque de los Marinos, south of Avda Roquejo, east of the walls.

**Restaurants** There are plenty of restaurants here – a couple of very high quality.

*Paris* Avda de Portugal 14, Tel: 514325. Highly regarded. Excellent Castilian cooking in a smart, refined restaurant. On the main road dividing the new town from the old. Intimate ambience (AE DC MC V).

*Parador* Plaza Viriato 5 (*see* hotels). A good restaurant in tasteful surroundings (AE DC MC V).

*Serafín* Plaza de Maestro Haedo 2, Tel: 531422. With a popular café in front. The restaurant is well regarded locally. 'Moderno' decor. Good fish and roast kid. (AE DC MC V).

*Valderrey* Calle Benavente 7–9, Tel: 514189. A smart restaurant with popular café beside. The menu changes daily and the food is honest. Expects foreign clients.

*El Cordón* Plaza Santa Lucia 5, Tel: 534220. Beside the Palacio de Cordón, in the quiet plaza, a restaurant of several rooms decorated in traditional style. Good Castilian roasts, delicious tapas.

*El Pozo* Ramón Álvarez 3, Tel: 533710. A big family restaurant, simple and honest. (V) (Similar in size but with an Art Nouveau style, is the next door restaurant to *Español*.)

**Hotels** There is a fairly small choice.

### Category 1

*Parador Nacional Condes de Alba y Aliste* Plaza de Viriato 5, Tel: 514497. A lovely place to stay, between the Cathedral and the Plaza Mayor. In an old palace built in 1459 with a fine Renaissance cloister and magnificent staircase, furnished with old pieces and tapestries.

27 rooms d&b 9000 – 7500. Restaurant: recommended (AE DC MC V). Parking and swimming-pool.

### Category 2

*Dos Infantas* Cortinas de San Miguel 3, Tel: 532875 Close to the central area, comfortable and unremarkable. No restaurant, but breakfast is served.

68 rooms d&b: 5750 – 5150 (AE DC MC V).

*El Sayagues* Plaza Puentica 2, Tel: 525511 Modern but comfortable, off the Avda de la Feria beneath the NW walls of the town.

56 rooms d&b 4600–4000. Restaurant.

### Category 3

*Hostal Trefacio* Alfonso de Castre 9, Tel: 513189.

36 rooms d&b 2500.

*Hostal Sanabria* Plaza de la Puebla 8, Tel: 526672.
10 rooms d&b: 2315–1900.

*Calle Benavente* – 3 hostals above each other:

*Luz* Tel: 513152. 14 rooms d&b 2100.

*Chiqui* Tel: 531480. 10 rooms d&b 2500.

*Sol* Tel: 533152. 12 rooms d&b 2100.

## Information

| | |
|---|---|
| Area Exchange Code | 988 |
| Tourist Office: | Calle Santa Clara 20 531845 |
| | 8.00 –3.00 /9.00 –2.00 sa. |
| Correo (Post Office): | Santa Clara 15, 513371 |
| Renfe: | Information: 521456 |
| | Station 10 minutes walk from Santa Clara north – bus no 3) |
| Estación Autobuses: | Condes de Alba y Aliste 3, 521281 |
| | (by the bull ring 5 minutes northwest of Santa Clara) |
| Police: | San Vicente 1 512393 |

**Transport** Cars: The town is quite easy to drive through. Parking is allowed in nearly every plaza, and few roads have the awkward, narrow, twisted shape so redolent of walled city streets. To visit the old town in comfort, it is worth parking near the Parador and circling the town by foot. The old town is not very large.

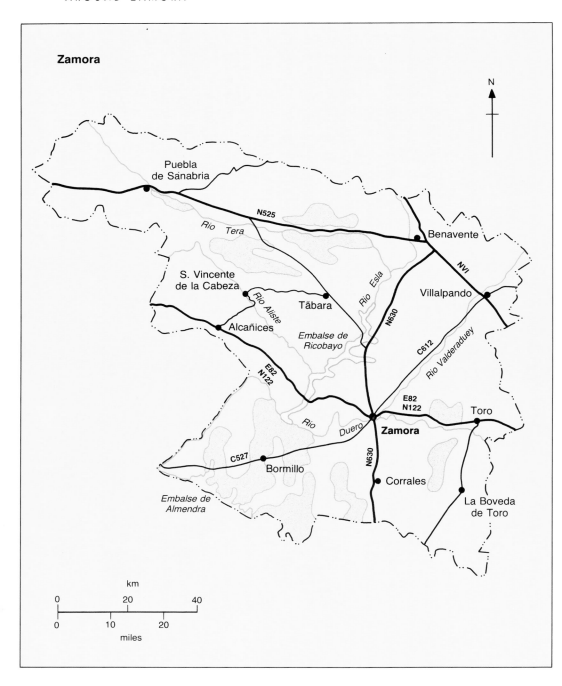

Zamora

N

Puebla
de Sánabria

N525

Rio Tera

Benavente

NVI

S. Vincente
de la Cabeza

Rio Esla

Villalpando

Rio Alisle

Tãbara

N630

Alcañices

Embalse de
Ricobayo

C612

Rio Valderaduey

E82
N122

E82
N122

Toro

Rio

Duero

Zamora

C527

N630

Bormillo

Corrales

Embalse de
Almendra

La Boveda
de Toro

km

0          20          40

0     10     20

miles

**Around Zamora** Zamora is a province that is usually passed through rather than visited. Its main roads connect Galicia and Asturias with the centre and south of Spain, and neither the city nor its province hold a prominent position in travellers' itineraries. Apart from the Lago de Sanabria – a beautiful glacial lake high in the mountains near Galacia – and Toro – a historic town to the east – the province is mostly undisturbed by travellers.

The landscape is varied. To the west rolls the characteristic bolder-strewn terrain, softening a little with olive and vine groves close to Portugal, and bordered by the majestic rocky wildness of Arribes del Duero which cuts the two countries apart. The Sierra of la Culebra rises north-west of the city, thickly forested and abundant with wildlife. The fertile valley of the Tera River flows across the northern block of Zamora. At its source near Galacia is the Lago de Sanabria, and at its conjunction with the River Esla sits the second city of the province, Benavente.

The generous waters of the Esla feed the region between Benevente and the provincial capital, and run into the Duero. The route of the Duero east from the capital divides the smooth terrain in two: the Tierra del Pan (bread) above; the Tierra del Vino (wine) below.

**South-West** The area between the Duero and the Tormés to the west of the Salamanca/Zamora road is populated by humble farming settlements, dominated by the unsophisticated village of Bermillo de Sayago. Both rivers are dammed, with the Duero creating three long reservoirs, and the Tormés filling the huge basin of the Almendra, 7km (4miles) across. This reservoir is excellent for fishing and water sports.

**The fertile plains of Zamora. Note the pigeon house**

The scenery of the area is dry and rugged, alternating between patches of grain and pasture with fine cork oaks; localized market gardens; and granite hillsides of rock-rose, gorse and holm oaks. The roads are lonely and desolate. Close to Ledesma (on the Tormés in Salamanca) are Almeida, blessed with sulphureous spring waters; Peñausende, a settlement built upon a surprising rock projection by which are ruins of a castle, and Alfaraz de Sayago, which treasures another castle ruin.

**Fermoselle**  At the end of the Embalse de Almendra is Fermoselle, an attractive town, long and narrow, perched on a stretch of escarpment surrounded by olive, vine and fruit groves. It makes a pretty visit, with a fine twelfth-century church, castle ruins and a handful of welcoming restaurants. The wine is good.

**Arribes del Duero**  The entrance into Portugal is lined with superb views of the pitched gorges of the Arribes del Duero. which continue along the dramatic banks of the Duero along the Salamancan/Portuguese border. The area is spectacular, generally harsh and, where there is earth, tightly terraced. Here, particularly in the steep cliff edges of the Tormés and Duero near the border, is a haven for birds of prey (particularly eagles) and black storks. Wolves are also to be found.

**North-East**  North of the river Duero lies a valley watered by the Aliste and the Esla rivers. There are two dramatic crossings over the gorge of the Duero from the south: the fine iron Puente de Pino by the Arribes del Duero, and the Villalcampo dam. This leads to the Ricobayo reservoir into which flow the Aliste and the Esla.

The N122 runs from Zamora to the beautiful surrounds of the Portuguese city of Bragança. There are very few cars that leave this road to visit the Aliste villages. They are tiny, often consisting of little more than a farmstead. The network of roads is frequently unlinked, and within the wild hilly landscape are some architectural delights, like the Alba castle perched on a perfect conical hill above the river. It is, however, awkward to travel around.

**Campillo**  The village of Campillo treasures an ecclesiastical gem. On a plateau by the eastern bank of the Ricobayo reservoir, at the end of a 10km (6miles) limb from the N122, the small community tends the seventh-century Visigothic church of San Pedro de la Nave. The little church, prim and perfect, was moved in 1930 to save it from the rising reservoir waters. Visitors are

welcome and, as a service is held only on Sunday mornings at
10 a.m., the key is kept in the café nearby for any visitor who
makes the journey. Inside, the frieze decorations carved in the
golden stone are beautifully preserved. This building has barely a
single rival in the peninsula.

**Alcañices** On the road itself there are few notable towns.
Alañices is a pleasant town, with remains of defensive walls, the
sixteenth-century palace of the Marqueses del Alcañices, and two
fine churches. It is a wealthy market centre for the surrounding
region (including the nearby villages of Portugal). With several
hotels and restaurants it is an attractive and popular town to stop in.

The ZA913 north from Alcañices is a pretty route crossing
through the pine forests of the Culebra Sierras. Closer to Zamora,
the twin towns of Ricobayo and Muelas del Pan sit by the

**The Visigothic church of San
Pedro de la Nave**

**Goats near the Embalse de
Almendra**

Ricobayo dam and are popular bases for the sports enjoyed by the reservoir.

**North** The Esla valley is served by the N630 artery which runs from the north of the peninsula (Oviedo and León) down to Andalucía. It links Zamora with Benavente. The treeless landscape to the east is characteristic of the grain plains – a continuous sea of flat fields, green in winter and gold in summer, occasionally punctuated by round adobe pigeon houses. The vistas are long and undulating and the roads straight, often with a lone majestic church standing on the curve of a hill in the distance. These fine buildings sometimes stand a little apart from the agricultural villages, taking advantage of the vistas.

**Villalpando and the Reserva Natural** Villalpando, a commercial centre with ruined walls, fine old houses, and a number of Mudéjar churches, was a central focus of the Comuneros Revolt against Charles V. Nearby is a series of lakes known as the Lagunas de Villafalila. Here is a Reserva Natural in which quantities of birds, both migratory and native, are protected. Several species of duck, geese, lapwings, purple herons and even flamingoes can be seen here.

**Castrotarafe** Grain is also produced between the Esla and the main road. Two superb ruins sit by the river banks, each easily missed. The site of Castrotarafe, approached along an earth track, fills a field with its crumbled walls, the side of a church and the ruins of its castle. Surrounded by agricultural land, the remains of this settlement, a prominent centre of the Order of Santiago in the twelfth century and abandoned 200 years ago, lie peacefully undisturbed.

**Monasterio de Moreruela** Further along the main road, an abrupt turning west just before the village of Granja leads through fields to the shell of the Cistercian monastery of Moreruela. Seven-apsed, Romanesque and abandoned, this is a truly magnificent ruin. There remains, apart from the roofless, bramble-filled church, the outer walls of the eighteenth-century seminary and other parts. It is easy to explore the site, which, like Castrotarafe, is unencumbered by visiting hours or guardians.

**Benavente** This industrial and commercial centre second to Zamora, is a lively but relatively unattractive town placed at a busy crossing point of the Via Plata route and that running from

Galacia to Castilla and Zaragoza. There are good public transport communications here, and street parking is awkward but not prohibitive. (The Parador, at the top of the town, may have easier spaces.)

Its strategic position has given it an active trading history. Much damaged during the Peninsular Wars, its sloping streets are a mixture of old and new, and within these stand two fine Romanesque churches. Santa María de Azogue, in the centre was originally constructed in the late twelfth century by order of Ferdinand II (also builder of the walls of Ciudad Rodriogo). Much restored since, it displays a mixture of styles, including a badly cracked classical west portal, although the south door remains Romanesque. The interior is most unusual, with five apses whose arches are decorated with zigzag motifs and whose capitals bear foliage sculptures.

**The ruin of the Cistercian monastery of Moreruela**

San Juan del Mercado, in the Plaza España, was built at the same time as Santa María but has survived with less outstanding features; its glory is the south door, intricately carved with figures. The north door is simple.

All that remains of the castle is a stocky octagonal sixteenth-century tower, El Caracol (the Snail), on the ridge of the town, and now incorporated into the Parador hotel. Around it are delightful rose gardens which hold a fine view over the surrounding agriculture. These gardens are much frequented at the weekends. The street that runs from here into the town arrives at the central plaza in which Santa María stands. The town has good shops, excellent *pastelerías* and abounds with children.

**West** form Benavente, the glacial lake of Sanabria lies along the straight C620 close to the border of Galicia. The road accompanies the River Tera, whose valley is lush and green with fertility. The Valverde is a soft fertile triangle between the river and the Sierra de Culebra, with many clay-coloured villages and a patchwork of small fields. The *bodegas* here, seen also in Valladolid, are characteristic of every village. Dug into the

**Below**
**The *bodegas* are characteristic of every village in the Valverde**

**Right**
**The twelfth-century church at Mombuey**

322

ground, with round doorway entrances and clay or brick chimney vents, these cellars store the produce of the fields. The cellars of Santa María de Tera (which also has a fine Romanesque church) are driven into the hillside, their entrance porches prettily grassed. On the main road, the orange casts of Camarzana look extraordinary.

Further on, the road passes through increasingly forested terrain. At Mombuey there an old part to the south of the road which guards a twelfth-century church with a most unusual slate-roofed tower.

To the north of the road rises the Sierra of La Cabrera, clothed with oak and spruce, populated with little slate-roofed stone villages.

**La Puebla de Sanabria** Its pretty castle can be easily seen from the main road, is the central town of the area, and its popularity with weekenders and holiday-makers can be sensed immediately. The town is extremely pretty, steep and sloping, with slate-roofed houses with extending balconies. At the top of the town the small Plaza Mayor (in which there are a few parking places) is surrounded by the old Ayuntamiento, old houses, and

**La Puebla de Sanabria**

the walls of the square fifteenth-century castle built by the Duque de Pimental, one of the Benavente dynasty. Part of the castle is now a library. Within the Plaza is the twelfth-century parish church whose round-arched portal, decorated with figures, is beautiful. The town thrives on its visitors, who fill the many restaurants and bars with good humour. Across the river extends a limb of the town.

The *fulpo sanabrese* (octopus) is delicious.

**Parque Natural del Lago de Sanabria** The route to the Parque Natural del Lago de Sanabria passes towns similarly inundated with visitors during the summer. Mercado del Puente, which holds a market weekly on Mondays has grown around the huge area reserved of the visiting stalls.

The lake itself lies spectacularly in a basin of forested hills. Two villages look over it. San Martín de Castañeda, a village of villas, sits nestled in the hills above, its road continuing up to the magnificent Benedictine (subsequently Cistercian) monastery of San Martín, which now serves as an information centre. The religious sanctuary has a long history, being originally a Visigothic temple. On the lakeside is Ribadelago, the ugly new white houses built to replace the dwellings of the old village devastated by floods from a burst dam in 1959. The water is much used for water sports.

**Parque Natural del Lago de Sanabria**

The surrounds of the lake, with height ranging from 800m (2,600ft) to 2,124m (7,000ft) above the sea, contain a great variety of flora, and remarkable pockets where the microclimate is unique. Snow falls in the peaks from November to May. Forests of Pyrenean oak, chestnut, holly, yew and hazel clothe the hills. Willow and ash grow by the streams. Depending on altitude, the ground is carpeted with medicinal herbs and exquisite bulb flowers, ferns, heather and gorse.

There are many walks around the area. Ribadelago Viejo, at the far side of the lake, is a good starting point from where four separate tracks lead through the hills. A lovely walk of about 10km (6miles) follows a path accompanying the young Tera up to the tiny lake of Cueva de San Martín from where it turns to return to base via the spectacular slopes near San Martín de Castañeda.

A shorter, steep path winds up to Pico del Fraile (with fantastic views over the lake) and joins the long forest track that visits the collection of small mountain lakes, at a height of around 1,600m (5,250ft) and continues across the Sierra de Segundera from the mountain village of Porto, at the Galician border, to beyond the highest reservoir of the Tera.

Another walk passes from the village of Vigo de Sanabria (below San Martín de Casteñeda) to Laguna de los Peces. A road visits the Laguna travelling on beyond San Martín. This village can also be reached by a path up the hillside from the hostal base at the eastern tip of the lake. The wildlife here includes snakes, roe deer, Royal and Culebrera eagles, red-legged partridge and a variety of snakes.

## North-west

**Sierra de la Culebra** There are two ranges of mountains that rise in Zamora. The sharp rise of the high Sierra de la Cabrera forms the boundary between the province and León. Parque Natural del Lago de Sanabria lies in its west summits.

Sierra de la Culebra, striking diagonally through the province above the Aliste, is less formidable, with peaks attaining only around 1,200m (3,940ft). Within the area of the whole range is a National Reserve of hunting, thus protecting the great quantity of wildlife. Roe and fallow deer and wild boar roam the coniferous forests. The prize of the reserve is the wolf – which lives here in greater numbers than anywhere else in Spain.

Few roads pass through this Sierra. The main route, running North of Alcañices, (ZA913), travels via the attractive stone and slate town of Villadeciervos which sits in the heart of the reserve. The abrupt rise of the mountains is spectacular from the rural areas to the south. At the western end is the village of Calabar, which has sulphureous springs from the mountainside. The reservoir of Cernadilla collects water to the north.

### East

**Toro** with an undulating sea of cereal to the north, and vineyards to either side, Toro sits directly east of Zamora. It is a quiet town whose streets retain much of its wealthy, distinguished history. It sits on a plateau above the Duero, which is crossed by a sturdy 22-arched thirteenth-century bridge. The wonderful Romanesque/Gothic Collegiata de Santa María and the castle overlook the valley while in the streets behind are several important Romanesque churches and fine *señorial* houses. A walk around the town is rewarding.

Toro was a royal seat and provincial capital. In its castle Fernando II was proclaimed king, Henry II held Cortes, and Juan I lived with his wife Beatriz of Portugal. The decisive fight between Isabella of Castille (supported by Ferdinand of Aragón) and Juana la Beltraneja (supported by the Portuguese) was fought here at the Battle of Toro.

The entrance to the town from the main road is graced by an archway. The street leads beneath the baroque Torre de Reloj to the Plaza de España, where the Ayuntamiento (in which is the Tourist Office) is surrounded by tiered wood-framed brick houses, and reaches on to the Collegiata. The church is graceful, and stands alone.

The pale Romanesque building, founded by Alfonso VII, was built between 1160 and 1240. The different periods of building are recognizable by the stone, the earlier being calcite stone, the later more rosy. Nave and transepts are barrel vaulted, the aisles groin vaulted. Over the crossing the dome's lantern is like that of the Cathedrals of Zamora and Salamanca (Old Cathedral), with Byzantine influence and two tiers of Romanesque windows.

The north portal, late twelfth century, is lavishly carved. The sculpture depicts Christ between John and the Virgin, with 24 Elders of the Apocalypse, and 14 musician angels. The south portal is less fine. The west portal, thirteenth century, is the most important, named the Puerta de la Majestad. Its superb carvings were painted in 1774 and survive in excellent condition, sheltered from the weather. The middle-column sculpture is of the Virgin and child, the tympanum is carved with the Coronation of Virgin, and the outer archivolt carries the Last Judgement. A guide from the Ayuntamiento will take visitors round the Collegiata, San Lorenzo and San Sebastián at 11 a.m. and 12 p.m.

**The north portal of the thirteenth-centuary church of Toro**

San Lorenzo is east of the Plaza de España, close to the Collegiata. Built in the twelfth and thirteenth ceturies in Mudéjar/Romanesque style, it is the best preserved in Toro. Inside, it is single aisled, with blind arcades friezed at the base with saw-tooth decoration. A florid Gothic sepulchre inside is the tomb of Pedro of Castille and his wife, and the imposing retabledisplays paintings probably by Fernando Gallego.

San Sebastián (1294) is of brick Mudéjar style, away to the west of Plaza Generalísimo (in which the town food shops are).

To the left of the main thoroughfare are streets of stone houses and churches, amoungst which is El Salvador, early thirteenth-century, with a fine fifteenth-century Virgin and child. Of the Palacio de las Leyes here, only a door remains, but it is extraordinary decorated in German Gothic style (1440).

Covento de Sancti Spiritus, is out on a limb to the West of the town. Founded 1303, it has a Mudéjar/Romanesque church within which is the alabaster tomb of Queen Beatrice of Portugal, wife of John I of Castile. The museum houses religious sculpture and painting, and the sacristy is filled with silver treasure and reliquaries (mostly sixteenth to eighteenth centuries). A Mudéjar ceiling graces the High Altar of the Church of the Catholic Kings. Open: 10.30 a.m.–12.30 p.m. and 4.30–6.30 p.m. (erratic).

The wine of Toro is dark, fruity, and fullbodied, about 13/15 degrees proof. Bodega Cooperative Nuestra Señora de las Viñas, Morales de Toro, Tel: 998 698023, or Luis Mateos SA, Eras de Santa Catalina, Toro, Tel: 988 690890, will welcome visitors.

**Fiestas** Carnival Toro: Semana Santa – Cheese and olives are eaten on Wednesday. *Hojaldre* and *Bollos* of oil are sold throughout the week. The *romería* of Cristo de las Batallas on the first Monday of Pentecost in May (a Romanesque church 14km (8 1/2 miles) away along the Duero) 18 August: San Agustín, bullfighting.

## Accommodation and Restaurants
### Alcañices
*Argentino*, Ctra de Zamora 11, Tel: 680160.
20 rooms, d&b 3600.

**Bermillo de Sayago** Restaurant: *La Torre*, calle Iglesia, Tel: 610250, big and unsophisticated

**Benavente** *Parador Nacional Rey Fernando II de León*, Paseo Ramón y Cajál, Tel: 630300.
30 rooms, d&b 8000–7000. (AE DC MC V). Mostly modern but incorporating the old castle tower. Views.
*Raúl*, Ronda Rancha 15, Tel: 631042.
23 rooms, d&b 2800. Good restaurant.
Restaurant: *Avenida*, Acd G Primo de Rivera 19, Tel: 631031.

### Fermoselle
Restaurant: *La Colomba*, Sanjurjo 124, Tel: 613291.

**La Puebla de Sanabria** *Parador Nacional*, Ctra Zamora, Tel: 620001.
44 rooms, d&b 8000–7000. Outside the town with good views.
*Los Perales*, Ctra de Villacastín, Tel: 620025.
38 rooms, d&b 4000, very comfortable below the town. Good restaurant.
*La Trucha*, Padre Vicente Salgado 10, Tel: 620062.
27 rooms, d&b 3500, restaurant.
Restaurant: *Peamar*, Plaza Arrabal 10, Tel: 620136, Popular.

### Toro
*Juan II*, Paseo del Espolón 1, Tel: 690300.
42 rooms, d&b 4100, by the Colegiata, a terrace over the river, pool, good restaurant.
*Dona Elvira*, Antonio Miguélez 47, Tel: 690062.
19 rooms, d&b 3500, Restaurant. on the main road.
Restaurant: *Catayo*, José María Cid 7, Tel: 690060, just off Plaza España, good roast kid.

### Camping
*Lago de Sanabria*, Galende, Peña Gullón, Tel: 620938, Cat 2, 600 people, 11km (7miles) from the lake, March to September (excluding 10–15 April).
*El Folgoso, Vigo*, Tel: 620194, Cat 2 800 people, next to the lake.
*Los Robles*, Ribadelago de Franco, Tel: 620076, Cat 1, 120 people, on the lake, open: 1 July to 31 August.

**The view west to Portugal**

Part Four: **Useful Information**

**Ávila mountainscape**

**Sports** The variety of countryside in central Spain allows for almost every type of sport to be enjoyed.

**Spectator Sports** The main spectator sports are football and basketball. Football, played usually on Sunday afternoons, attracts great public attention and bars will be crowded with people watching television. Real Madrid is the main club, and the most politically important matches are those against their great rival Barcelona.

**Jai-alai** This is a spectacular sport that is much played in the Basque country but little seen outside. There are various forms, the main being played in a long three-sided court. Two or four players sling a ball against the end wall either by hand or with a wicker 'claw' attached to an arm. The game is reputed to be the fastest ball game of all. There is a great deal of betting throughout the games. The game may be seen in Madrid. Information from the Federación Española de Pelota, Los Madrazo 11, 28014 Madrid, Tel: 221 4299.

**Motor-cycling and Motor-racing** are both raced at the Jarama race-track just north of Madrid.

### Active Sports

**Aerial Sports** Flying and gliding are enjoyed particularly over the plains of Toledo (Mora 30 0194) and in Segovia (Fuentemilanos 48 5172). Information from the Real Aero Club de España, Carrera San Jerónimo 15, 28014 Madrid, Tel: 429 8534 (p.m. only).

**Canoeing** There are abundant good rivers in the region. Information from the National Federation, Calle de Cea Bermúdez 14, 28003 Madrid, Tel: 253 0604.

**Cycling** Not a popular sport in central Spain. There are relatively few repair shops. The roads are generally in poor repair for cycles. In the less populated areas villages are often many kilometres apart with little traffic, but there are plenty of drinking-water fountains in the hillsides. The mountain areas are hard but beautiful, with lovely herb fragrances, while the flat areas tend to be unending. There is usually little wind, but the heat can be relentless in the flat areas. Information from the National Federation, Calle de Ferraz 16, 28008 Madrid, Tel: 242 0434.

**Golf** One of the most prestigious pastimes in Spain, with many beautiful courses. One of the finest is a few kilometres from Madrid – Real Club de Puerta de Hierro (36-hole). There are 11 around Madrid and a few more in the region. Most are privately owned with admission to non-members on payment of a fee for temporary membership. The majority belong to the Real Federación Española de Golf which requires a licence including sports insurance for play (this is easily acquired for a small cost). Information from Capitán Haya 9, 28020 Madrid, Tel: 455 2682.

**Mountain Climbing** The peaks of the Gredos, especially around Béjar and Arenas de San Pedro; and the peaks of the Guadarrama, especially Peñalara and La Pedriza, are popular climbing areas. Information from the National Federation, Calle de Alberto Aguilera 3, 28015 Madrid, Tel: 455 1381.

**Sailing** Sailing and windsurfing may be enjoyed in every province, each of which have substantial reservoirs in which water sports are very popular.

**Skiing** There is skiing with good facilities in the Guadarramas – La Pinilla, Valdesqui and Navacerrada; and skiing in the Gredos near Béjar (a lesser quality). Material from ATEDUM (Associacion Turistica de Estaciones de Esqui y Montaña) which will give information on snow and the resorts. Contact Juan Ramón Jiménez 8, Edif. Eurobuilding 28036 Madrid, Tel: 458 1557. For general information on tuition, facilities and snow contact Federación Española Deportes de Invierno, (Winter Sports Federation) Calle de Claudio Coello, 32, 28001 Madrid, Tel: 275 8943. A map 'Mapa de Estaciones de Esqui' is available from the Tourist Office.

**Sports for the Handicapped –** Information is available from the National Federation, Calle de Ferraz 16, 28008 Madrid, Tel: 247 1718.

**Swimming** Swimming-pools will be found in substantial villages and all towns. It is a custom for town families to spend weekends by the municipal pools, many of which have gardens, social areas and bars.

**Tennis –** most towns have a few courts, although these are often within a club for which temporary membership is necessary. The sport is booming and facilities are growing. Information from Real Federación Española de Tenis, Avda Diagonal 618, 08028 Barcelona, Tel: 201 0844.

**Horses** Racing: Madrid has a racecourse 7km (4miles) from the city (towards La Coruña, bus from Moncloa) which has two seasons – spring: February to June, autumn: mid-September to early December. Racing is held on Sundays and sometimes on Thursdays, Saturdays and fiestas. This is one of the three courses in the country. Information: Real Sociedad de Fomento de la Cria Caballar, Madrid, Tel: 207 0141.

Jumping is held in the grounds of Club de Campo where there are a number of annual events. Polo is played throughout the year at two Madrid clubs. Real Club de la Puerta de Hierro, Avda de Miraflores Tel: 216 1745 is a private club for members only. For the public there is Club de Campo Villa de Madrid, Ctra Castilla, Tel 207 0395. There are several organizations that take groups into the heart of the countryside on horseback. These often take the ancient transhumant shepherd paths to cross the hills. Trips last from a day to three weeks. Addresses are given in the information sections of provincial areas, particularly Madrid, Ávila, Salamanca and Segovia.

**Fishing and Hunting** Both these sports are energetically pursued by the people of central Spain. The main guadian body is ICONA, the national institute of nature conservation. Their main address is Avda Gran Via de San Francisco 35–41, Madrid, Tel: 266 8200. For information about provincial head offices call 435 5121.

The head offices of the Autonomous Communities are:
Madrid: Consejería de Agricultura y Cooperación de la Comunidad Autónoma de Madrid: Calle Orense 60, 28020 Madrid, Tel: 455 7703.
Castilla y León: Consejería de Agricultura, Ganadería, y Montes de la Junta de Castilla y León: Calle Muro 4, 47001 Valladolid, Tel: 305055.

Castilla-La Mancha: Consejería de Agricultura de la Junta de Comunidades de Castilla-La Mancha: Calle Duque de Lerma 3, 45004 Toledo, Tel: 210316.

**Fishing** The main fish to be caught are: trout, barbel, carp, bream, tench, black bass, perch, boga and pike. River crab are to be found in few areas, and may only be fished during the day on Thursdays and Saturdays and fiestas. To fish, a licence may be applied for from the provincial ICONA office, giving information about the areas where fishing is permitted. A map 'Mapa de Pesca Fluvial' is available from Tourist Offices, showing the species of particular rivers and giving guide-lines for fishing seasons.

**Hunting** There is abundant hunting, both of small game and big game. The best area for small game is south of Madrid in the plains of Toledo, where the red partridge is plentiful. There are big game reserves in all the Sierras, the most remarkable being that of the Gredos reserve of Ávila. Here the prized *Capra Hispanica* may be hunted.

The season for small game in general, runs from mid–October to early February. Animals include rabbit, hare, partridge, quail, turtle dove. Big game consists of wild boar, roe deer, buck, fallow deer, Capra Hispanica and *moufflon* (wild sheep).

There are several types of hunting land, ranging from free zones where only a licence is necessary, to municipal-owned local reserves, private zones and national reserves of various levels. Locally owned zones (*cotos*) are often hunted on Thursdays and Sundays, and parties may welcome a travelling extra who wishes to participate – they will usually be found in the local hunting bar.

A foreigner is required to hold a licence from ICONA (provincial offices can supply licences) which may be obtained with a passport, a licence from home and a customs permit for the import of a weapon. Insurance cover is compulsory.

There are various organizations who take groups hunting for both small and large game for the duration of a week or more: Viajes Conde, Calle de la Princesa 7 28008 Madrid, Tel: 247 1804 (big). Ibercaza, Calle de Carranza 12, 28004 Madrid, Tel: 448 6541 (big/small). Caza en España, Apdo 57 Majadahonda Madrid, Tel: 637 5029. Espacaza, (specializing for European hunters). Calle de Nuñez de Balboa 31–4, Madrid Tel: 275 7622. A map 'Mapa de Caza' is available from Tourist Offices.

**Monfragüe National Park**

**Things of Special Interest to Children** The Spanish people love children, and above all those under 18 months old. Young people, from the age of one onwards, will often be seen out with the family until after midnight. They will be displayed beautifully dressed during the *paseo* time at weekends, when families meet socially in the town squares.

The traveller with a baby will be well looked after. Bars are happy to sterilize bottles and many restaurants will prepare special food. Breast feeding is not considered unsightly – it is unnecessary to breast feed in privacy. Pharmacists can advise on general problems, and baby food and nappies will be found here and in supermarkets. The baby clothes in Spain are delightful.

Hotels will be helpful with children, and it is nearly always possible to have an extra bed in the room, at an additional cost of no more than 30 per cent. Many restaurants will prepare small portions for children. It is quite usual for children to accompany parents and parties of friends for the late evening meal. There is cheaper travel for children.

There are few things of specific interest to children in central Spain. In general, cultural things are not adapted for children at all. Apart from municipal swimming-pools, and the small playgrounds that exist in every town (swings and climbing frames) there is very little entertainment on offer.

Zoos – one in Madrid (see listing, page 72) and one in the province of Valladolid (Matazopuelos)

Aquariums – one in Madrid (see listing, page 72)

Safari – near Madrid (see listing, page 74)

Horses – most major towns have horse stables close by which welcome children.

The feast of the Three Kings – the vesper of the 6 January – is a procession specifically for children, when sweets are hurled from the passing floats to yells of '*caremelos – aqui, aqui*' from the young crowd. Sweets are for the good children, coal is for those who have been bad (a coal lorry follows each king's entourage). It is customary for children to receive their Christmas presents on 6 January.

There are many castle ruins in the region – these may be exciting to explore but unsafe for children. Great care should be taken.

**The landscape of central Spain**

**Flora and Fauna** There are eight national parks in Spain, none of which are in the central area. There are a small number of natural parks, and many areas of great natural beauty. The lack of population density gives the region abundant tracts of unspoilt land.

For general information contact ICONA (Nature Conservation Institute) at Avda Gran Via de San Francisco 35–41, Madrid, Tel: 266 8200.

Nature Reserves:

Monfragüe, Cáceres (Plasencia) 17,852 ha.

Cuenca Alta del Manzanares, Madrid 4,304 h.a

Hayedo de Tejera Negra, Guadalajara 1,304 ha.

(*See* provincial listings for visiting these.)

Particular areas of great beauty are as follows:

**Plasencia:** Monfragüe Parque Natural has some important types of vegetation such as 'Dehesa' (south side) which is found only in the Iberian Perninsular and in north-west Africa, made up of cork and holm oak pasture. North is thick ancient Mediterranean forest. The evergreen shrubs are wild olives, Kermes oak, turpentine trees, strawberry trees and stone pines. Underneath is a layer of cistus, lavender, broom, bladder senna and wild herbs.

This is an important breeding ground for birds of prey. Black vultures and Spanish Imperial eagles (both under threat from extinction) breed here as do goshawks, sparrowhawks, and booted eagles. Griffon and Egyptian vultures are also frequently seen. In addition Golden eagles, Bonelli and Short-Toed eagles, peregrines, kestrals, ravens, and choughs breed here too. The rare black-winged kite is more difficult to see. Black storks and black vultures nest mostly in the plains.

Smaller birds one can expect to see include hoopoes, woodchat shrikes, bee-eaters, golden orioles, and azure-winged magpies. Water birds include great crested grebes, collared Pratincole, cattle egrets, spoonbills and greylag geese.

The rarest animal is the Spanish lynx, it is very seldom sighted. There are also wild cats, fox, badger and Egyptian mongeese. The hunting reserve guards deer and wild boar.

**Madrid** Parque de la Cuenca Alta del Manzanares has two parts divided by the reservoir of Santillana. Both parts are spectacular for their massive granite bolder formations. Iris and narcissi may be found in the lower regions in spring. Various birds of prey fly here, including Griffon vultures.

**Toledo** The Montes de Toledo are covered with holm oak and pine. There is a huge population of roe and fallow deer with many red partridge to be seen.

**Segovia** The Guadarrama Mountains (particularly by Riaza) are huge beech and oak forests. Alpine flowers grow in abundance.

**Duratón Gorge** A deep beautiful gorge cut by the river offering spectacular views and unique microclimates.

**Salamanca** Valle de las Batuecas is a valley by Sierra de Peña de Francia, thickly forested with holm oak and strawberry trees. Within the national hunting reserve are wolves, lynx, roe deer and wild boar. Birds include Imperial eagle and black vultures.

Arribes de Duero an extraordinary deep gorge carved by the Duero which affords spectacular views. The warm flow of air captured within the gorge has created Mediterranean microclimate around the cliff edges.

**Zamora** Parque Natural del Lago de Sanabria is a park ranging in height from 800m (2,409ft) to 2,124m (6,372ft) surrounding a glacial lake. Pyrenean oak, chestnut, holly, yew, hazel all grow here. According to the microclimate and height there is great variety of bulb flora.

Sierra de la Culebra is a national reserve for hunting which has roe and fallow deer, wild boar and large numbers of wolves. The forests are coniferous.

Lagunas de Villafalila are lakes with a large resident population of birds and act as an emigration stopping point for many more. Several species of duck and goose can be seen as well as lapwing, purple heron and flamingo.

**Ávila** the two sides of the Sierra de Gredos are dramatically different. The north side rises slowly with a colder climate and sub-Alpine plants. These include snap-dragons, columbine, star of Bethlehem, lily of the valley, peonies and purple knapweed. The south side rises sheer and abruptly, with a sub-tropical vegetation just above the valley of the Tieter which includes the growing of palm trees, tobacco, citrus trees and peppers. Holm oak forests sit below pine forests above which is bare granite.

The valley bird population includes bee-eaters, golden orioles, azure-winged magpies, stone-curlews and warblers. Several birds of prey may be seen in the central Gredos peaks including black griffon and vultures.

In the national hunting reserve the most prized animal is the *Capra Hispanica* (or Ibex) which may be seen quite frequently.

**Guadalajara** Parque Natural Hayedo de Tejera Negra (partly in the province of Segovia) is thickly forested with beech, yew and oak. The hunting reserve of Sonsaz, lying southwards, guards roe deer and wild boar. The birds of prey here include Golden eagle, red kite and goshawk. Parque del Alto Tajo has deep, forested limestone gorges. The whole region of Guadalajara is filled with superb walks and areas barely touched by cars or visitors.

**Health** For *Servicios de Urgencia* (Emergency Services) dial 091. For immediate help, the Cruz Roja Española (Red Cross) is an excellent national service. *See* province listings for the local numbers (or the local phone book).

**Doctors** The pharmacist (or the police) will be pleased to recommend a nearby doctor. Medicine has a good reputation in Spain. (For English-speaking doctors it is possible to acquire a list from the consulate). A specialist doctor is recommended via a general doctor. Beginning of treatment is swift. The insurance policy (and E11 form for entitlement to medical aid from the Spanish national health scheme) should always be taken on a visit to the doctor to cover payment. For small problems, a doctor expects to be paid in cash immediately.

**Dentists** A pharmacist or the police will recommend a dentist. Bars, restaurants and hotels are useful sources of knowledge about the local medical facilities.

**Hospitals** The most reputed are in Madrid and Salamanca.

**Telephone Exchanges**

| | |
|---|---|
| Madrid 91 | Segovia 911 |
| Ávila 918 | Toledo 925 |
| Cáceres (Plasencia) 927 | Valladoloid 983 |
| Guadalajara 911 | Zamora 988 |
| Salamanca 923 | |

**Embassies** British Embassy, Calle Fernando el Santo 16, Madrid Tel: 419 1528/0208.

American Embassy, Calle de Serrano 75, Madrid Tel: 577 4000.
American Express, Plaza de las Cortes 2, Madrid Tel: 429 7943.
Australian Embassy, Paseo de Colon 143, Tel: 279 8501.
Irish Embassy, Calle de Claudio Coello 73 Tel: 276 3500.
Canadian Embassy, Calle Nuñez de Bilboa 35 Tel: 431 4300.

## Tourist offices:

| | |
|---|---|
| Madrid: | Calle de la Princesa 1, (Plaza de España) Edif Torre de Madrid, Tel: 241 2325. |
| | Aeropuerto De Barajas, Tel: 205 8656. |
| | Calle Duque de Medinaceli 2, Tel: 429 4951. |
| | Estación de Chamartín, Tel: 315 9979. |
| | Plaza Mayor 3, Tel: 266 5477. |
| | Calle Senores de Luzón 10, Tel: 242 5512. |
| Aranjuez: | Plaza de Santiago Rusiñol, Tel: 891 0427. |
| | San Lorenzo de el Escorial, Floridablanca Tel: 890 1554. |
| Ávila: | Plaza de la Catedral 4, Tel: 211387. |
| Guadalajara: | Travesía de Beladiez 1, Tel: 220698. |
| Sigüenza: | Calle Obispo Don Bernardo, Tel: 390850. |
| Plasencia: | Calle Trujillo, 17, Tel: 412766. |
| Salamanca: | Gran Via 41, Tel: 243730, and Plaza Mayor Béjar, Pasco de Cervantes 6, Tel: 403005. |
| Ciudad Rodrigo: | Calle Arco de Amayuelos 6, Tel: 460561. |
| Segovia: | Plaza Mayor 10, Tel: 430328. |
| Toledo: | Puerta de Bisagra, Tel: 220843. |
| | Talavera de la Reina, Plaza de Parque del Prado. |
| Valladolid: | Plaza de Zorrilla 3, Tel: 351801. |
| Tordesillas: | Plaza Mayor 1, Tel: 770061. |
| Zamora: | Calle Clara 20, Tel: 511845. |
| Toro: | Ayuntamiento, Plaza España. |

The Spanish Tourist Office in the UK is at 57–58 St James Street, London SW1A 1LD, Tel: 071 499 1169.

# Madrid and Castile Index

## Note

Page references in *Italics* indicate illustrations.
Page references followed by m indicate maps.